THE BROTHERS BEQUEST

GERMANS IN CHARLESTON, SOUTH CAROLINA

Robert Alston Jones

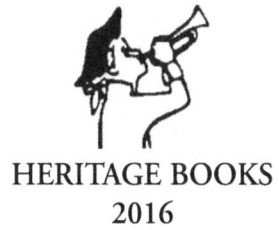

HERITAGE BOOKS
2016

HERITAGE BOOKS
AN IMPRINT OF HERITAGE BOOKS, INC.

Books, CDs, and more—Worldwide

For our listing of thousands of titles see our website
at
www.HeritageBooks.com

Published 2016 by
HERITAGE BOOKS, INC.
Publishing Division
5810 Ruatan Street
Berwyn Heights, Md. 20740

Copyright © 2016 Robert Alston Jones

The cover map shows the area around Bremerhaven along the coast of northwestern Germany. From the American Geographical Society Library, University of Wisconsin-Milwaukee Libraries.

All rights reserved. No part of this book may be reproduced or transmitted in any form or by any means, electronic or mechanical, including photocopying, recording or by any information storage and retrieval system without written permission from the author, except for the inclusion of brief quotations in a review.

International Standard Book Numbers
Paperbound: 978-0-7884-5708-1
Clothbound: 978-0-7884-6417-1

For Bernhard Heinrich, who deserved to have his story told

CONTENTS

PREFACE vii

CHAPTER 1: EUROPE IN THE BACKGROUND 1

CHAPTER 2: GERMANS IN ANTEBELLUM
CHARLESTON—AN HISTORICAL PERSPECTIVE 9

CHAPTER 3: THE ADVENTURES OF BERNHARD
BEQUEST 43

CHAPTER 4: RECONSTRUCTED LIVES 55

CHAPTER 5: DIFFERENT PATHS FOR THE YOUNGER
TWO 109

CHAPTER 6: THE MAYOR OF MOUNT
PLEASANT 133

CHAPTER 7: THE QUIET SEAMAN 179

CHAPTER 8: THE RISE AND DOWNFALL OF
AUGUST 193

AFTERWORD 263

WORKS CITED 267

INDEX 273

PREFACE

The "N.Y./Region" section of the August 25, 2014, edition of *The New York Times* carried the headline "350 Years Ago, New Amsterdam Became New York. Don't Expect a Party." Sam Roberts' article explained how, on August 26, 1664, "the largely defenseless [Dutch] settlement tolerated a swift and bloodless regime change" that subsequently enabled New York to "evolve into a jewel of the British Empire, endowed with a collective legacy—its roots indelibly Dutch—that distinguished it from every other American colony." The rather sardonic second phrase of the headline, "Don't expect a party," was ascribed to present-day New Yorkers' "unanimous indifference" to this anniversary based on "an ambivalence toward the British and a dispassion for the past." Sure enough, the anniversary passed unheralded by New Yorkers and the rest of the nation, despite the significance of the Dutch sensibilities that fashioned the character of the New World's number one city.

Within the next couple of years, a similar historic dispassion is likely to be in evidence some 1000 miles to the south in Charleston, South Carolina. There, a number of anniversaries could appropriately celebrate the role German immigrants played in fashioning the character of one of America's most historic cities: November 2015 marked the 172nd anniversary of the arrival of Captain Heinrich Wieting's first ship, the *Johann Friedrich*, bringing North German immigrants on a regular basis for twenty-five years to Charleston; December 2015 marked the 175th anniversary of St. Matthew's Lutheran Church—the city's "German Lutheran Church"; during the year 2016, the German Friendly Society—still meeting weekly on Wednesday evenings—will sponsor events to celebrate the Society's founding 250 years ago. But in Charleston, as in New York, it is likely that very few in the present community will notice, and doubtful that the city will feel obligated to throw anything like a commemorative party for its twenty-first-century local citizens. The "dispassion for the past" that allowed the New York anniversary to be ignored and, similarly, those in Charleston, suggests that present-day populations in both cities are readily inclined to leave civic history in the past rather than enthusiastically celebrate anniversaries that are significant markers of historical evolution.

*

The chapters that follow are an effort to bring to light an aspect of the fascinating history of Charleston, South Carolina. My efforts would surely qualify as a labor of love by one of Charleston's native-born—an attempt to explicate the historic city's relationship with its nineteenth-century German immigrants. It is all too easy to overlook the nature and character of the nineteenth-century immigrant community in Charleston. While Charleston was of major importance during colonial and post-colonial times, it declined in importance as other cities expanded and as the original East Coast territory moved westward. Aside from the Civil War, the nineteenth century is a less well-known period in Charleston's history: between its colonial past and its current vitality lie decades of civic and cultural evolution that have been less than inspiring—locally and beyond. In this twenty-first century, except for knowledgeable old-timers, many would be surprised to know that there had even been an immigrant community that transformed the city's character. For the most part, little attention is paid to the interval between when "George Washington slept here" and that fateful 1860 December when the state decided that its people should no longer belong to the Union. It was the subsequent Civil War and its aftermath that brought the nineteenth century to a close and which remains a focus of the general public's and scholars' interest and historical consciousness.

Charleston's diverse immigrant populations—the English, the Irish, the Germans, the Jews—have been featured in a number of scholarly articles and monographs investigating the separate ethnic groups, but none have captured the popular imagination or enjoyed an extensive readership.[1] Within the rather epic phenomenon of nineteenth-century migration, emigration, and immigration—in particular that from Europe to the young United States of America—those who came and lived in Charleston were not part of the mainstream. Indeed, they were only noticeable to those native-born who accepted their presence, sometimes graciously, oftentimes with suppressed prejudice.

The focus here is on what legitimately might be termed "German Charleston." While one can find numerous studies of ethnic immigrant communities in cities to the north and west—the Irish and Italians in the northeastern cities, the Germans in Missouri, Texas, and Wisconsin, the Scandinavians in the Upper Midwest, the German immigrants who came to Charleston in the nineteenth century were hardly on anyone's radar—even in Charleston itself. They were, in several unique ways, a significant percentage of the population[2], and as Charleston evolved beyond

---

1. A recent work by Andrea Mehrländer, *The Germans of Charleston, Richmond, and New Orleans during the Civil War Period* (Berlin/New York: DeGruyter, 2011) cites a number of articles and monographs on the German immigrants in Charleston, but there are only eight items in her list, including one dissertation. Her study acknowledges that the relatively small percentage of immigrants who chose the states of what would become the Confederacy, compared to those who migrated to the northern states, represents in general a neglected ethnic population. A number of studies look at the Irish as immigrants, but none suggest that those in Charleston were in any way unique. Dale and Ted Rosengarten's *A Portion of the People* (University of South Carolina Press, 2002) explicates the long history of the Jewish community in Charleston but does not concentrate on the character of the immigrant community itself.

2. Ira Berlin and Herbert Gutman state that "the peculiar pattern of European migration and settlement in the slave states gave immigrants importance far beyond their numbers and projected foreign-born workers into a place in the Southern working class that rivaled the role played by immigrants in the North. Although a comparatively small number of Europeans migrated to the South during the nineteenth century, those who did generally settled in cities. South Carolina, Georgia, and Alabama had few immigrants, but Charleston, Savannah, and Mobile had many. At mid-century, the foreign-born population of

its colonial zenith to become the Lowcountry's charming and impressively preserved tourist attraction, it was its immigrant—primarily German—community that grew and established a solid middle class that based itself on its European roots and values, and which was instrumental in modifying the character of the older city into what we know today.

The main stories in this volume about *The Brothers Bequest* take place after the Civil War ended. The stage is set, however, by showing how the brothers' relatively late arrival in Charleston was the logical outcome and culmination of developments that had begun much earlier in the century. By the time the Bequest brothers appear on the scene, the German ethnic community had already set down deep roots and was proceeding to become more Charlestonian than German. The story of these three immigrant German brothers, together with their predecessors, is not intended to demonstrate the "contributions" that German immigrants made to the development of the civic character of Charleston, nor to eulogize the individuals who are the main characters. Rather the brothers' stories are set forth as examples—admittedly on a personal and individual level—of the kind of journeys that members of a dominant minority ethnic community undertook in transforming themselves, or letting themselves be transformed, into citizens of a unique Southern city.

I have reconstructed the lives of these three brothers with the building blocks of what I have gleaned from the local newspapers, whose editors, to my advantage, seemed as interested in reporting on the activities and whereabouts of ordinary citizens as on the city's luminaries. The brothers themselves left virtually no written documentation of their existence: no letters, no diaries, no personal recollections, no oral histories passed down through their descendants. It is clear that they were otherwise preoccupied

---

these states reached 3 percent only in the case of South Carolina. But more than a fifth of Charleston's residents, more than a quarter of Savannah's, and almost a third of Mobile's had been born outside the United States" ("Natives and Immigrants, Free Men and Slaves: Urban Workingmen in the Antebellum South," *American Historical Review*, 88, 1983, 1177-78).

and not vain enough to think that what they were engaged in was of any importance to anyone other than perhaps their own family. Ever mindful of their past and what they had come from, their focus was quite obviously on the present, knowing that it would determine their future—whatever that would turn out to be. Their stories contextualize what it was like to pick up life in war-torn, defeated Charleston as the last links in the chain of predecessors who had established a German "presence" in the city. How they fared ran parallel to how Charleston fared as it moved toward the twentieth century, with ups and downs, successes and failures. If as individuals these three German brothers might not warrant consideration as exemplary German-Charlestonians, the stories of their lives speak volumes.

      I am indebted to a number of friends and colleagues who along the way helped immeasurably in getting me to the *Afterword*. It was Dot Glover, one of the librarians in the South Carolina Room at the Charleston County Public Library, who initially suggested that the individual lives examined here were worthy of a detailed analysis. She and her colleagues in the South Carolina Room were my helpful long-distance assistants, willing to perform research I could not undertake in person. At my home base in Milwaukee, many of the staff of the Golda Meir Library at the University of Wisconsin-Milwaukee facilitated my work: I owe them special thanks. I am indebted to Therese Bohn (UW-Milwaukee) for instructing and mentoring me in creating a database to manage the plethora of records at my disposal. She also spent hours conquering word processing matters beyond my abilities. Three UW-Milwaukee colleagues lent invaluable advice: Professor Garry Davis deciphered a number of documents handwritten in the old *Sütterlinschrift*: his trained eye revealed what lay undisclosed despite my efforts to decipher the challenging orthography; Professor Emeritus John Buntin patiently and with great thoroughness read each chapter as I turned it over to him, willingly taking on this task only because he, too, has a "Charleston connection"; Beth Weckmueller willingly proofed my semi-final draft, laundering the fabric of my text into a much cleaner cloth. Finally, Diana Perpich (University of Michigan) was a most patient and forbearing assistant to her often computer-challenged father-in-law.

While none of them bear any responsibility for what I have constructed here, *The Brothers Bequest* project would not have come to fruition without their collective assistance. I am grateful to them all.

CHAPTER 1: EUROPE IN THE BACKGROUND

The remarkable thing about the German immigrants who settled in Charleston during the nineteenth century is that so many of them were all from a small area of what is now northwestern Germany. If one walks through the oldest sections of Bethany Cemetery in Charleston—one of the city's three largest cemeteries—one cannot help but notice that the headstones seem to take special note of the individual's birthplace, and there are relatively few that do not specify a town within the area surrounding Bremen. Many are indeed from the small town of Geestendorf (usually spelled Gestendorf) or from its immediate neighbor, Lehe. This northwest corner of the present-day German state of Lower Saxony bordering on the North Sea anchored one end of what developed as a chain of migration, the other, Charleston. It is true that a number of other German settlements in the United States enjoyed a similar kind of cohesion within their respective ethnic communities, but none other than the one in Charleston stemmed so exclusively from this particular area of Germany. Regional differences invariably manifest themselves in individuals, and in the case of those immigrants who settled in Charleston a close look at the history and nature of their origins gives some sense of who they were and what they were about.

Along the northwestern edge of Lower Saxony, the approximately eighteen-mile-long coastal strip of land known formerly as "Land Wursten" gets its name from the Low-German *Wursaten* or *Wursasses*—terms descriptive of "people sitting on dwelling mounds." As far back as the Stone Age these dwelling mounds were used by the inhabitants of the area to provide living space above the ever-changing sea level. The land to the east of the shoreline is predominantly marshland that has been changed over the years into arable land protected by dikes and shoreline management. By the time the self-governing area became part of Bremen in the sixteenth century (1525), it was primarily farmland of somewhat limited quality.

The majority of the inhabitants of this entire northern area of German lands were of Saxon heritage[1], with an infusion of Friesian the closer to the neighboring and related tribe to the west. They lived in small villages[2] in a sparsely—by today's standards—settled rural setting, with customs and traditions bearing heavily on the individual. The population was not all that indigenous, but rather transient, as individuals moved within a restricted area in search of a sustainable existence. Many operated as seasonal workers or tenant farmers, so that there was little to hold them in place. Few families could trace a lineage back for a hundred years in one place. Marriages were usually with someone from a neighboring village—one could travel only so far—and the small number of inhabitants of one's own village limited the selection at any given point in time. One's class, moreover, determined the marriage prospects: there was little chance of moving out of one's *Stand*, not likely *up*—for man or woman—and all too possibly *down* if one did not own property. Until more modern times, lives were short: in the period between 1700 and

---

1. There may be some dispute about claiming tribal heritage, but there is little doubt that these northern peoples evolved into inhabitants whose characteristics can be differentiated from those whose lineage derives from other regional sources.

2. A village could support only about 250-300 inhabitants. According to one study of Flögeln, a typical 18th century *Geestdorf*, in 1677 there were 36 occupied farms, 8 unoccupied; in 1735 the number had grown to 54, and remained constant until 1825. The increase was due largely to allowing a type of farmer (*Brinksitzer*) at the lower level of society to be counted among the village's legitimate citizenry. (August F. Pech, "Bevölkerungsentwicklung und Sozialstruktur eines nordniedersächsischen Geestdorfes im 18. Jahrhundert, aufgezeigt an dem Dorf Flögeln im Landkreis Cuxhaven," *Jahrbuch der Männer vom Morgenstern*, 1981, 51-53).

1819 the life expectancy for men was 33.5 years, for women, 33.6. Death occurred according to the conditions of the times. Although most church records indicate the cause of death only from about 1780 on, it was usually smallpox, dysentery, scarlet fever, measles, tuberculosis, pneumonia, or the endemic "marsh fever" that took most lives.[3] The infant mortality rate was high, and many women died in childbirth. As a consequence, second and third marriages were common—a widowed parent could almost never maintain a family and an occupation alone.

The social structure of these North German villages was regimented and resistant to change. All individuals owed taxes of time (labor) and harvest—of whatever size—to the entity above them, so that in each instance they were indentured—distinctly not "free."[4] At the very top of the pyramid were royalty and "government" in its several classifications—both of which lived off such peasant communities within their jurisdictions.

The inhabitants of Land Wursten had been building dikes since the eleventh and twelfth centuries—primarily to increase the yield of the marshland that surrounded them and to enable them to plant winter grains. What developed was a closed agrarian society that existed virtually unchanged after the Middle Ages. Except for the heir, most young men left at age fourteen to work in the marshes. The farming system was dependent on the number of animals that could provide manure; these in turn depended on the amount of grazing land or land that could be cultivated for animal fodder. Any increase in population required more land to raise more animals to feed on more fodder. Overgrazing led to deterioration of the land, less nourishment for animals, and thus for the population, decline. Bad harvests and other disturbances, to say nothing of seemingly endless wars and recurrent pestilence, signaled a very precarious existence.

3..Willy Klenck, *Das Dorfbuch von Mulsum im Lande Wursten, Kreis Wesermünde in Niedersachsen* (Frankfurt am Main, 1959), 82.

4. Ibid., 82.

Life in Geestendorf—the small village home of the Bequests, situated just to the south of Land Wursten—would have been similarly tenuous. The original village, the "Dorf" by the River Geeste with fewer than seventy-five inhabitants and probably less than one-third that number of houses, would be merged in the nineteenth century with other small communities to become Geestemünde, ultimately to form part of the major port city of Bremerhaven. The entire area at one point was ruled by Sweden, then Denmark, and in 1715 sold to the Duchy of Braunschweig-Lüneburg. It was not until the mid-nineteenth century that it was destined to become a place on the map that anyone considered of any importance.

The Bequest brothers who immigrated to Charleston belonged to a family can be traced back to the early eighteenth century. The Bequest record begins after the French Revolution at a time when this area was occupied by Napoleonic France. What life was like in Geestendorf during this period is revealed in the occupations of the Bequest family members. The record shows them working as: ferryman; inn keeper; seaman; cottager; laborer; boatman; ship's pilot; skipper; apprentice pilot; sailor; caretaker; smith; blacksmith; master smith; church legal spokesman; highway toll collector.[5]

With almost every Bequest family member working in multiple capacities, it is clear that many of them—like other inhabitants of Geestendorf—worked at jobs supporting a maritime culture. Three Bequests, in fact, died at such jobs, drowning by virtue of storms or accidents at sea. While most families farmed small land holdings, Geestendorf offered some diversity in ancillary work, some of it seasonal, some a steady aspect of the agrarian-based community life. The specification of a master smith and an apprentice ship pilot suggests that the guild system was to some extent still in effect. It can be noted that inheritance also played a role: in several instances, the son carried on the same

---

5. Erika and Klaus Friedrichs, *Das Familienbuch des Kirchspiels Geestendorf (heute Bremerhaven-Geestemünde) 1689 bis 1874* (Bremerhaven, 2003).

occupation of the father. Bohl Nohrden worked as smith or master smith in 1815; his son functioned similarly in 1870. Michael Böse took over as inn-keeper from his father-in-law. Johann Graefer's father was a ship pilot, he, an apprentice pilot in 1845 and pilot by 1852. There were not all than many options, and if one could step into already-filled shoes, there was continuity in the family and in the community. As for inheriting real property, this area of North Germany still operated according to the tradition of undivided property passing to the heir, while in areas to the south and southwest, land partibility led to smaller and smaller holdings passing to subsequent generations with the result that the inherited property was often too meager to sustain an individual family. These traditions affected the migration patterns of the various areas within Germany, and ultimately played an important role in the trends of emigration that swelled in the nineteenth century to unparalleled levels.

By the end of the eighteenth century, the march of history would have affected the inhabitants of the area around Geestendorf. Land Wursten was then part of the Kingdom of Hanover, and in 1803 when Napoleon resumed hostilities with England, he ordered the occupation of that Kingdom that at the time belonged to the English crown: "Hanover's army was dismantled, its arms and revenues were transferred to France, and it was forced to maintain a French occupation army and close its borders to English commerce."[6] Then in the aftermath of Napoleon, the Congress of Vienna in 1815 had the task of putting a fractured Europe back together, realigning its composite parts once again, some states gaining territory, some losing, and some remaining as they had been, but all confronting new challenges that new times had brought into play. In general, it was a period of transition from the traditional political and social order to more

---

6. Alexander Grob, *Napoleon and the Transformation of Europe* (New York: MacMillan, 2003), 89. This is precisely what would bring a certain Frenchman to Geestendorf who would change his name and become the first Bequest.

modern ways, transforming the old into the preconditions for a "capitalist, legally equal, religiously tolerant and rationally governed bourgeois society."[7]

This essentially marginal area of Europe would have maintained a conservative view of changing political and social conditions. But anyone alive at the time would have sensed in the air the tensions between the classes as early revolutionary ideas buzzed throughout the realm in one form or another. There would have been a sense of relief following the cessation of successive hostilities. Individuals would have been sensitive to any impositions on religious practices, whether by a governing authority or by believers of a different creed. And everyone would have known that the revolution in France had upset pretty much everything; no one would have been surprised that again there were foreign troops occupying the region. There would have been rumors suggesting that things were more prosperous elsewhere, that mercantilism and industrialization were changing things, sometimes for the better, sometimes for the worse, but changing nonetheless. And by the first decades of the nineteenth century, everyone would have known that the population itself was growing and that their communities were facing economic and social issues they had not faced in the past.[8]

---

7. Grob, 111.

8. In *German History 1770-1866* (Oxford: Clarendon, 1989), James Sheehan writes: "In the second half of the eighteenth century, the fear of homelessness increased, largely because the most immediate and manifest impact of the vital revolution was to swell the ranks of those on the fringes of the social order. From the middle of the eighteenth century until the middle of the nineteenth—an era of unparalleled social turmoil almost everywhere in Europe—the population grew faster than the economy. . . .As populations expanded, local communities found it more difficult to control their members. This weakening of social controls is apparently behind the dramatic increase in illegitimacy, another mysterious demographic phenomenon that occurred throughout Europe. Rare in traditional society, illegitimacy became more and more common after 1750" (88-89). The Bequest lineage was not immune to this issue.

CHAPTER 1: EUROPE IN THE BACKGROUND

The unparalleled growth in population functioned to instigate the wide-spread movement of people in Europe that culminated in unprecedented rates of emigration—mostly to the United States—during the nineteenth century. Already in 1803 the state of Baden had recognized the right of its citizens to move freely. Other states followed suit. The Charter of the German Confederation of 1815 established freedom of emigration for its member states, and it took no time for individuals under the stress of economic, social, and political pressures to exercise their options. By 1816 there was significant emigration from southwest Germany as the result of crop failures and hunger.[9] The first wave of immigration ("old immigration," predominantly by populations from Germany, Scandinavia, Ireland and Great Britain) would last roughly until just after the American Civil War, during which there was a kind of hiatus before a second wave ("new immigration," by populations from southern and eastern Europe) would begin about 1865 and last until the end of the century. Between the colonial period and the end of the century, almost seven million Germans constituted the "largest single source of immigrants to the United States after that from the British Isles."[10]

A miniscule percentage—but nonetheless a goodly number—of those German immigrants would leave their North German homeland bound for Charleston.

---

9. Despite what appeared to be a liberal approach to emigration, it was not until 1867 that the requirement for official permission to emigrate was abolished, and not until 1870 that one no longer had to prove fulfillment of military service in order to leave. Until these later dates, those inspired for one reason or another to seek relief by emigrating were met with a "semi-official" negative attitude toward emigration, as governments in the various states sought to exercise some control over concerns, on the one hand, with overpopulation and unemployment, and on the other, with inadequate labor pools and faltering economies.

10. Michael C. LeMay, *From Open Door to Dutch Door: An Analysis of U.S. Immigration Policy Since 1820*, (New York: Praeger, 1987), 21-23.

CHAPTER 2: GERMANS IN ANTEBELLUM CHARLESTON—AN HISTORICAL PERSPECTIVE

German immigrants were in Charleston in substantial numbers by the middle of the eighteenth century. The history of St. John's Lutheran Church can be traced back to 1733, possibly earlier. By 1766 those early immigrants had founded the German Friendly Society in support of German interests in the city. They had never congregated in a separate ethnic community, and by the end of the eighteenth century they would have considered themselves Charlestonians rather than German expats. The immigrants arriving during the middle years of the nineteenth century, in contrast, would have to find their way in a southern city of a particular character, not a little Germany into which they might transplant themselves. There was little continuity between the earlier and the later groups, and the experiences of the former had little to do with those of the latter. The earlier immigrants had come from a number of other German-speaking areas and were for the most part seeking religious freedom; those immigrating to Charleston during the nineteenth century came predominantly from the *Plattdeutsch*-speaking North and were driven by other factors. Beyond that, there was little if any concept of a common German ethnicity through which either group might identify with the other. The German Friendly Society's acculturated members were in fact not immediately open to receiving the newcomers landing on their doorstep. Insofar as the older group had been engaged in becoming more like the host society, newcomers likely were looked down upon for bringing to the forefront the differences between the ethnic "foreigners" and the native-born.[1]

The stream of immigrants to Charleston in the nineteenth century must of course be viewed against the background of the European population explosion and the resulting waves of emigration. That it was a predominantly rural population moving because of a general decline in the standard of living is indisputably a factor of the chain migration that brought so many from the German Kingdom of Hanover to Charleston. Not to be discounted as well was the "leaven of democracy" that was in evidence in every part of Western Europe, awakening hopes in the general population for personal freedoms that could only be imagined in a different society. In *The Immigrant in American History,* Marcus Hansen writes:

> What poor people wanted was freedom from laws and customs that curbed individual economic enterprise. In the cities they wished to escape the regulations of guilds and trade unions; in the country they sought exemption from traditional restrictions upon the transfer of land, the working at a trade, or the conduct of agriculture. In other words, they wanted the freedom to buy, sell and bargain, to work or loaf, to become rich or poor.... To enjoy the opportunities of free enterprise and to preserve the fruits thereof—this was the aspiration of the rank and file of immigrants. Republicanism and monarchism were only shadowy backgrounds to something more personal and vital.[2]

---

1. In his *My Father's People: a Family of Southern Jews* (Baton Rouge: Louisiana State University Press, 2002), Louis Rubin makes the same point with regard to the disputes between Charleston's older and newer Jewish congregations.

2. (New York: Harper & Row, 1940), 81-82.

CHAPTER 2: GERMANS IN ANTEBELLUM CHARLESTON—AN HISTORICAL PERSPECTIVE

Such generalities aside, it has been suggested that in many ways Charleston was not the usual city to accept an immigrant population. Despite the fact that the city had once been among the five largest in young America, it was not quite what it had been earlier by the time immigrants began to arrive in the early decades of the nineteenth century. It was nonetheless a city with a unique history and one that was distinctly unlike any other southern city. Although it was no longer the capital, Charleston had enjoyed prosperity during the plantation-dominated economy of the post-Revolutionary years. The invention of the cotton gin had enabled the production of this crop to the point that it had become the state's number one export. Cotton production depended on slave labor, and Charleston, like no other, was a racially divided city: in 1761 there had been 4,000 white persons and 4,000 Negro slaves in the city; in 1790 there were 8,089 whites, 7,684 slaves, and 568 free Negroes—a total of 16,341; in 1820 there were 11,229 whites, 12,652 slaves, and 1,475 free Negroes—a total of 25,356; and by 1850 there were 20,012 whites, 19,532 slaves, and 3,441 free Negroes for a population total of 42,985.[3]

Although German immigrants also populated other cities in the South, e.g. New Orleans, Savannah, Mobile, or Richmond—to be sure in fewer numbers than in northern cities[4]—those who went to Charleston stepped into a patriarchal planter society that ruled over an economy based to a unique degree on an enormous slave population. It was a financially top-heavy society with a

---

3. George C. Rogers, Jr., *Charleston in the Age of the Pinckneys*. (Norman: University of Oklahoma Press, 1969), 141.

4. "At mid-century, when fully one Northerner in seven had been born outside the United States, only 5 percent of the Southern free population was foreign born, and a disproportionate number of these resided in the border states. Ten years later, the margin had widened as European migrants surged into the North, while they continued to dribble into the South. On the eve of the Civil War, when fewer than one free Southerner in fifteen had been born outside the United States, immigrants composed nearly a fifth of the population of the free states." (Ira Berlin and Herbert G. Gutman, "Natives and Immigrants, Free Men and Slaves: Urban Workingmen in the Antebellum South," *American Historical Review*, 88, no. 5 [December, 1983], 1176).

broad base of the poor and enslaved supporting an aristocracy of the wealthy. According to historian Michael Johnson,

> [t]he strength of the patriarchy rested ultimately not just on the quantity but on the nature of the estate: land and slaves. The Charleston planters were among the nation's largest landowners; their mean real estate value of $27,300 easily put them among the top 1 percent of landowners in the nation. Even the planters' $13,000 median real estate value was more than that owned by the top 2 percent of American men. In fact, a full 60 percent of the Charleston planters owned more real estate [in dollar value] than 97 percent of their countrymen. Slightly less than 7 percent of the planters were grandees with more than $100,000 worth of real property, a level attained by just under five American men in ten thousand—a disproportion in favor of the Charleston planters by a factor of 137.[5]

Beyond this chasm between the wealthy and the less affluent, Charleston early on was a nervous city. In the social environment of a majority ruled by a minority, the Denmark Vesey slave "insurrection" in 1822 transformed the city into something like a police state:

> The white community viewed the slave conspiracy of 1822 . . . as a direct threat to its existence. The immediate repercussions were trials, mass public hangings, meetings of outraged citizens and ensuing legislation, but the conspiracy also marked the beginning of a new and extended era of repression. The city . . . never again relaxed the outward forms of vigilance. To

---

5. "Planters and Patriarchy: Charleston, 1800-1860," *The Journal of Southern History* 46, no.1 (February 1980), 53.

CHAPTER 2: GERMANS IN ANTEBELLUM CHARLESTON—AN HISTORICAL PERSPECTIVE

supplement its sizeable police force the city... established a town guard, a force of 100 men. They were uniformed, trained and heavily armed, being issued with muskets and bayonets as well as alarming devices such a rattles. Whites as well as blacks were dealt with at the guardhouse, but the list of offenses for which blacks could be held liable was much larger.[6]

For the immigrant, then, Charleston presented particular challenges—social, economic, and personal. Despite those challenges, the immigrant could envision opportunity. If within Charleston's social pyramid[7] there was somehow space between the high and the low to accommodate those vying to create a middle—that would be the role for the immigrant. The Germans managed to find their niche better than most.

Some nine months before South Carolina's John C. Calhoun was sworn in as Vice President of the United States, young Johann Rosenbohm took leave of his North German village and embarked on a sailing vessel bound for the United States. He was a 19-year-old passenger on the *Constitution* that arrived in

---

6. John P. Radford, "Race, Residence and Ideology: Charleston, South Carolina in the Mid-Nineteenth Century," *Journal of Historical Geography*, 2, no. 4 (1976), 331.

7. "Socially Charleston was intricately layered. The old planter families, mainly Episcopalian and Presbyterian, whose domain lay south of Broad Street, were at the top, and thereafter came Methodists, Lutherans, Baptists, Roman Catholics, Jews, and various denominations of blacks. As often happens in communities with marked social gradations, the ordering replicated itself among the various ethnic groups. Thus the old Roman Catholic families of French ancestry considered themselves superior to the Catholic newcomers from Ireland and Germany, who in turn looked down on the Italians. The African Americans were arrayed in a hierarchy that ranged from the light-skinned antebellum free men of color—many of whom were artisans, barbers, and merchants—and their families downward to the vast majority of blacks, who had been plantation laborers in slavery days." (Louis D. Rubin, *My Father's People: a Family of Southern Jews*, [Baton Rouge: Louisiana State University Press, 2002], 9).

New York from Bremen on June 21, 1824. Exactly when he made his way south to Charleston is not known, but he was naturalized as a U.S. citizen in Charleston in October of 1830. His story is relevant here because he was the first link in the chain of migration between Charleston and Geestendorf/Geestemünde of an extended family to which the three Bequest brothers belonged. That they could acknowledge Johann Rosenbohm only as a distant relative by marriage is an indication of how strongly the chain pulled once it was in place.

The *Constitution*'s passenger manifest lists young Rosenbohm's occupation as confectioner. Once in Charleston, he established himself as a merchant and after his naturalization was financially stable enough to purchase and sell a house on Charleston's St. Philip Street. He was granted a U.S. passport in 1836 and returned to Germany that same year to marry Caroline Huhn. Back in Charleston, the couple settled into a larger house on the corner of Church Street and Stoll's Alley which Johann purchased for $3,000 dollars.

By 1839, however, the German-American Rosenbohm decided to leave Charleston. He left his store and its stock worth $2,849.35 to be disposed of by a legal representative. Rosenbohm went to New York, taking his wife and children. The family must have had sufficient means to make a return visit to Germany in 1841: four Rosenbohms arrived in New York from Bremen on the *Charlotte* on June 1, 1841: Johann (now "John Henry"), 37; Caroline Louise, 22; Catherine, 2 1/2; and Auguste, a 1-year-old infant. They were cabin passengers—not in steerage—and arrived with "seven boxes and beds." The same ship would return the following November to bring Johann's widowed father, Caspar Rosenbohm, to America. The father did not stay with his son in New York, but came instead to Charleston and took up residence in his son's house on Church Street. Johann Rosenbohm died in New York in May of 1843. The house in Charleston was put up for auction in 1845 to satisfy a debt owed to his executor and was purchased by Johann's brother-in-law, Herman Knee. Caspar Rosenbohm lived in the house on Church Street until his death in 1852.

CHAPTER 2: GERMANS IN ANTEBELLUM CHARLESTON—AN HISTORICAL PERSPECTIVE

That Johann Heinrich/John Henry Rosenbohm undertook to make his fortune as a merchant is indicative of a pattern that would become typical of German immigrants to Charleston—a city characterized by a wealthy planter/plantation elite with an aversion to manual labor, a black majority/slave laboring class which served the white population in almost every capacity, and a small class of free laborers and artisans who practiced the service functions that the composite society relied on. The immigrant was challenged to find the niche where he could operate without displacing and antagonizing what was already in place. Rosenbohm's effort was to establish a business—whatever its exact nature—that he could expect to be patronized by his fellow immigrants and one that would serve an existing neighborhood of both native and foreign-born without suggesting any hint of competitive arrogance. It was the case that, as a group, "immigrants entered Southern society at the bottom of the free social hierarchy and made up a large part of the lower ranks of urban society." In the thirty years after J. H. Rosenbohm became a merchant, "native-born white men composed better than two-thirds of the male merchants, political officials, and professionals in Mobile, Charleston, and other Southern cities, while foreign-born men equaled a similar proportion of petty proprietors—grocers, restauranteurs, stable keepers, and the like."[8] By mid-century, German immigrants to Charleston worked in trade or craft occupations that did not infringe upon the labor territories of free blacks or hired-out slaves. The number of grocers in Charleston seemed to grow exponentially: by 1870, 80 percent of all Charleston's groceries were owned by Germans.[9]

It is somewhat surprising that young Rosenbohm would abruptly leave Charleston in 1839, abandoning his store to have it

---

8. Ira Berlin and Herbert Gutman, "Natives and Immigrants, Free Men and Slaves: Urban Workingmen in the Antebellum South," *American Historical Review* 88, no. 5 (December 1983), 1178.

9. Andrea Mehrländer, *The Germans of Charleston, Richmond and New Orleans during the Civil War Period, 1850-1870* (Berlin/New York: DeGruyter, 2011), 40.

liquidated by someone else, rather than carefully settling his affairs and deliberately planning a change of course. In the absence of any personal record, we might speculate that it was the overwhelming political turmoil of the time that led to his seeming haste to leave Charleston. Within four years of his arrival in New York, Johann would have seen Andrew Jackson elected President of the United States in 1828, and by 1832, the German immigrant's adopted South Carolina would become politically and economically embroiled in the nullification crisis[10] which the state created with its 1832 Ordinance of Nullification. This crisis dominated South Carolina and Charleston politics, ultimately put South Carolina as a state in a category by itself, brought forth the volatile career of John C. Calhoun, and was ultimately precedent to the secession of the state from the Union less than thirty years later. The state's and city's population was almost evenly divided on the nullification issue, and it is easy to imagine how disconcerting it would have been to be a foreigner in this context, to know which side to take, to know what it all presaged for one's

---

10. The "crisis" was caused by the dispute between President Andrew Jackson and John C. Calhoun over federally imposed tariffs. Charleston was torn between "Unionists" and "Nullifiers." In the 1832 legislative race, "[t]he Nullifiers swept to victory in Charleston and across the state and the new legislature convened in Columbia in November and issued an ordinance that declared the tariff acts of 1828 and 1832 null and void. On December 10 President Jackson condemned he Act of Nullification as treason and warned that he would use force to prevent it. The legislature first promised to meet force with force, but on January 21, 1833, a convention of Nullifiers assembled in Charleston to postpone the date on which nullification was to go into effect, February 1, 1833. By this time other Southern states were condemning South Carolina's course as 'alarming' and 'reckless.' Seeking compromise, President Jackson on March 2 signed a lower tariff bill and the Force Act to compel South Carolina's compliance with the law. Sixteen days later the South Carolina legislature repealed the Ordinance of Nullification, but nullified the Force Act. A compromise had been reached temporarily, but the principle of nullification was still very much alive in South Carolina. For a few short years tensions between Nullifiers and Unionists persisted on Charleston's City Council until both factions subordinated their feud for the sake of harmony and unity." (Walter Fraser, *Charleston! Charleston!* [Columbia: University of South Carolina Press, 1989], 210).

CHAPTER 2: GERMANS IN ANTEBELLUM CHARLESTON—AN HISTORICAL PERSPECTIVE

future—a future that had been projected to be free of the political discord and instability rampant in Europe: the old life in Europe supposedly had been exchanged for a new one, a more peaceful and stable existence in a place that had put its revolution to rest. For the German immigrant, the adamant defense of states' rights against the passage of laws designed for the good of a united country might have seemed threatening and a cover-up for an increasingly divisive sectionalism defending the "peculiar institution" of slavery on which the South depended. Rather than fall in with the nullifiers and risk offending the other half of the community over a policy which he could hardly have fully understood, both discretion and uncertainty might have helped Johann Rosenbohm decide to abandon his efforts in Charleston and seek refuge in the North.

On the other hand, it might have been an appreciation of the fact that life and property in Charleston at the time were in fact not all that secure. For the immigrant from rural, maritime, coastal North Germany, the sequence of destructive fires that ravaged large sections of the urban neighborhood would have been unsettling. Even though his store on the corner of Queen and Meeting Street was spared, the neighboring St. Philip's Church was destroyed by fire in 1835, and the great fire of 1838 took away a large section of the lower city not far from his residence on Church Street.

These conjectures only suggest that the Charleston framework that the early nineteenth-century German immigrant met prior to the 1840s was one that had few guarantees, required a determination to accommodate countless new and unexpected factors for which one was inadequately prepared, challenged by political and moral positions unshared with the native-born hosts barely receptive to one's "different" status.

The chain that Johann Rosenbohm initiated, possibly not inadvertently, grew by successive links. Each of his three sisters, ended up in Charleston: his sister Adelheid had married a Bequest in Geestendorf. She came to Charleston as a widow with her daughter Adeline, who would subsequently marry Frederick Schroeder at St. Matthew's German Lutheran Church. Another sister, Anna Maria, and her husband from the Black Forest, Nicholas Fehrenbach, emigrated shortly after their first child was born (1831) in Geestendorf. Their second son, Nicholas Jr., was born in Charleston in 1833, and six of their other children were Charleston natives. Johann's third sister, Catharina, was the wife of Hermann Knee, a prominent figure in the developing ethnic community who was instrumental in the establishment of the Lutheran community in Walhalla, SC. It was Adelheid Bequest's husband's nephews, Bernhard Heinrich, Carsten August, and Johann Ludwig—the Brothers Bequest—who would immigrate to Charleston after the Civil War and whose stories constitute the following chapters.

For the German immigrant, the numerous advertisements—many of them idealized or founded on misinformation—about the freedoms that America offered, such as the unlimited opportunities that could be had in the cities or the countryside, or the chance to farm one's own land or pioneer new territory unencumbered by laws and rules, were likely trumped by the pull of the unique connections that Charleston had with the North German communities in the vicinity of Bremen. Charleston had long enjoyed a significant trade relationship with Bremen, with ships crossing the Atlantic taking Charleston exports, predominantly cotton and tobacco, to northern Europe through one of its major ports, among them Bremen.[11] That German port had developed in competition with neighboring Hamburg and other European trading centers, and by the early decades of the nineteenth century had undertaken to enlarge its role and to secure its existence as a port. By 1827 the Hanseatic city had secured a treaty with the government in Hanover to purchase land on the Weser estuary to develop a more navigable harbor. The acquisition of an area of land between the Geeste and the estuary of the Weser in the district of Lehe led to the creation of the city of

---

11. The city's dynamic commercial link with northern Europe was undercut somewhat in 1793 when Baltimore assumed priority in trade with Bremen.

CHAPTER 2: GERMANS IN ANTEBELLUM CHARLESTON—AN HISTORICAL PERSPECTIVE

Bremerhaven. The founding of Bremerhaven coincided with the significant increase in the rates of emigration during the late 1820s and early 1830s, and the Bremen authorities sought out the emigrant trade in support of the city's new port capacities. The emigrant became a commodity to be exchanged for goods: "Inland freighters, on water or land, brought emigrants to Bremerhaven, where they picked up merchandise for their return to the interior. Steamships appeared on the Weser in 1843; then railroads became significant, and eventually special emigrant trains arrived regularly at Bremerhaven, on the first and fifteenth of the month during the season, from marshaling points inside Germany."[12] The city of Bremen and its port of Bremerhaven, encompassing the earlier communities of both Geestendorf and Geestemünde, almost immediately passed legislation aimed at protection of the emigrants who waited there to board ships to take them to their U.S. destinations. In 1832 and 1834 laws were passed that regulated inns and other accommodations providing temporary shelter, and requiring ships leaving port to provide adequate space for passengers and to carry sufficient food supplies for a crossing that could take up to three months. Shipping companies were required to carry insurance in the event of shipwreck on European shores. In the mid-forties, the authorities in Bremen undertook to comply with new American regulations stipulating an increase in the amount of space per passenger and "forbidding the embarkation of a criminal or a deserter on pain of a hundred-thaler fine imposed upon the captain." By 1849 an emigrant hostel, the *Auswanderungshaus*, had been built, a facility able to feed 3,500 emigrants and to sleep 2,000 at a time. While Bremerhaven became the most popular embarkation point for the majority of nineteenth-century emigrants from northern and central Europe, it was literally on the doorstep for the emigrant families living in this northwest corner of Hanover, in Geestendorf or Geestemünde itself, or in Land Wursten just to the north.

---

12. Mack Walker, *Germany and the Emigration 1816-1885* (Cambridge, MA: Harvard University Press, 1964), 88.

Another factor that heavily influenced the link between Bremerhaven and Charleston and that effectively anchored the chain at both ends was the career of Captain Heinrich Wieting. In the employ of the Bremen shipping company of N. Gloystein Söhne, Wieting commanded three ships, the *Johann Friedrich*, the *Gauss*, and the *Copernicus* from the 1840s to the late 1860s, usually bringing twice a year on average some 200 emigrants to Charleston each trip.[13] The record of Wieting's departures from Bremerhaven and arrivals in Charleston and New York is set forth in the table following:[14]

An analysis of the record provides a good sense of the traffic across the Atlantic during those years, and particularly the role that Charleston played on the receiving end. While Wieting sailed on occasion to other ports, his transatlantic passages carrying immigrants and goods were only between New York or Charleston and Bremerhaven. Some of the passengers were undoubtedly immigrants returning from visits back home: the majority disembarking in New York or Charleston, however, would have been immigrants, not travelers, following the trail of those relatives or friends who had preceded them. Wieting's eight crossings to New York carried a total of 1,465 passengers, while the twenty-five trips to Charleston brought 3,350 individuals to their southern destination. The average length of the trip on these sailing ships was more than a month, sometimes almost two months, under conditions that were trying in spite of everything Wieting and the Bremen authorities had done to make the passage tolerable.

---

13. The record of Wieting's correspondence with his employer is the subject of a recent volume, *"Was fernern vorkömmt werde ich prompt berichten": Der Auswanderer-Kapitän Heinrich Wieting Briefe 1847 bis 1856* ("Whatever happens next, I will report": The letters of the Immigrant-Captain Heinrich Wieting), Jörn Bullerdiek and Daniel Tilgner eds. (Bremen: Temmen, 2008).

14. Bullerdiek and Tilgner, 285.

CHAPTER 2: GERMANS IN ANTEBELLUM CHARLESTON—AN HISTORICAL PERSPECTIVE

SHIP	DEPARTED	DESTINATION	ARRIVED	#PASS	#DAYS
J Friedrich	4 Nov 1843	Charleston	--		
J Friedrich	29 Apr 1844	Charleston	14 Jun 1844	23	46
J Friedrich	6 May 1845	New York	19 Jun 1845	140	44
J Friedrich	7 Oct 1845	Charleston	25 Nov 1845	131	49
J Friedrich	5 Oct 1846	Charleston	--	116	-
J Friedrich	19 Mar 1847	New York	1 May 1847	140	43
J Friedrich	8 Oct 1847	Charleston	15 Nov 1847	135	38
J Friedrich	19 Mar 1848	New York	30 Apr 1848	126	42
J Friedrich	10 Nov 1848	Charleston	--	122	-
J Friedrich	19 Apr 1850	New York	16 May 1850	126	27
J F/Leontine	20 Oct 1850	Charleston	--	125	-
Copernicus	6 May 1851	New York	19 Jun 1851	217	44
Copernicus	7 Nov 1851	Charleston	--	135	-
Copernicus	6 May 1852	New York	10 Jun 1852	249	35
Copernicus	12 Oct 1852	Charleston	28 Nov 1852	190	47
Copernicus	21 Apr 1853	New York	30 May 1853	229	39
Copernicus	6 Oct 1853	Charleston	21 Nov 1853	242	46
Copernicus	5 Apr 1854	New York	18 May 1854	238	43
Copernicus	8 Oct 1854	Charleston	24 Nov 1854	258	47
Copernicus	9 Oct 1855	Charleston	--	176	-
Copernicus	6 Mar 1856	Charleston	27 Apr 1856	14	52
Copernicus	7 Oct 1856	Charleston	24 Nov 1856	223	48
Gauss	12 Oct 1857	Charleston	23 Nov 1857	233	42
Gauss	9 Apr 1858	Charleston	16 May 1858	36	37
Gauss	10 Oct 1858	Charleston	18 Nov 1858	197	39
Gauss	7 Mar 1859	Charleston	4 May 1859	18	56
Gauss	8 Oct 1859	Charleston	19 Nov 1859	161	42
Gauss	11 Feb 1860	Charleston	20 Mar 1860	7	37
Gauss	14 Oct 1860	Charleston	4 Dec 1860	227	51
Gauss	14 Mar 1861	Charleston	--	11	-
Gauss	6 Oct 1867	Charleston	--	158	-
Gauss	6 Oct 1868	Charleston	29 Nov 1868	78	4

Looking at the list, one cannot help but notice the hiatus in the Bremerhaven-Charleston traffic after the departure from Bremerhaven of the *Gauss* on March 14, 1861. The Civil War would begin in Charleston a month later, and the eleven intrepid souls who set off in March would arrive just after the first shots had been fired at Fort Sumter. The political situation in the U.S. was a hot topic in Europe, and the more timorous would have had second thoughts about emigrating at that point—to Charleston for sure—since the outcome of South Carolina's secession the previous December would shortly precipitate military action there between the southern Confederacy and rest of the Union.[15]

The list's entry for 20 October 1850 indicates a joint crossing by the *Johann Friedrich* and the *Leontine*: behind that lies the traumatic tale of the shipwreck of the *Johann Friedrich* on a sandbar off the coast of England at Harwich. The passengers were rescued and returned to Bremerhaven, then safely delivered to Charleston by Captain Thormann of the *Leontine*. On the following January 26, 1851, an address expressing the public's gratitude was given by Pastor Müller of St. Matthew's German Lutheran Church, and on the twenty-eighth the Charleston German newspaper, *Der Teutone*, published a notice of thanks to both captains and Wieting's Gloystein Söhne for saving the lives of the 125 passengers on board. It was signed by sixteen passengers in the name of all the others. The same notice was subsequently published in the *Weser-Zeitung* on February 22, as was Pastor Müller's sermon. Both the German and the American readers obviously felt the close personal connections that existed between the two communities. The *Johann Friedrich* shipwreck episode is further detailed in a small diary held in the manuscript collection of the University of South Carolina: it is the diary of Alexander

---

15. By the time the war was over, steamships had begun to overtake transatlantic routes and offered shorter and safer passage: in 1868 sixty-four steamships brought 36,279 passengers from Bremerhaven to New York, while sixty-two sailing ships carried 15,451 on the same route (Bullerdiek and Tilgner, 270).

CHAPTER 2: GERMANS IN ANTEBELLUM CHARLESTON—AN HISTORICAL PERSPECTIVE

Melchers, one of the passengers on the fated *Johann Friedrich*. He was the younger brother of Franz Adolph Melchers, who had established himself in Charleston as the editor of the *Deutsche Zeitung* and who, together with Wieting and another immigrant, would become part of a triumvirate of influential men giving direction to the community of German immigrants gathering in Charleston.[16]

Although other ships traveled regularly between Charleston and Bremerhaven, it was Wieting's caring and personalized concern for the well-being of his passengers, as well as his regular schedule, that buttressed the chain of migration between Bremerhaven and Charleston. Those whom he had brought were a magnet for those friends and relatives in the communities close to Bremen still contemplating emigration. Besides, Wieting was a local: born 1815 in the village of Rönnebeck, not far from Bremen, he himself was resident in Geestemünde, and his name would have been a household word in the surrounding communities. When waiting in Charleston for his ship to be readied for departure, he participated in the life of the German community like a local citizen. His veneration by the Germans he had been instrumental in bringing to the city was known on both sides of the Atlantic, and his death in Charleston in 1868 was a heartfelt loss to the Charleston community. He is buried in Bethany Cemetery in Charleston. One side of his monument's base in English names the three ships that brought the immigrants to Charleston; the opposite side in German indicates his birth in Rönnebeck and his death in Charleston.

That Wieting's sailings would serve to encourage so many emigrants from the area is evidenced in the lists of passengers who traveled with him. The list of passengers embarking in Bremerhaven was usually published in the German newspaper in Charleston approximately two weeks before the expected arrival

---

16. Alexander Melchers would also become a leader in the Charleston German community: he was a captain in the Palmetto Riflemen, was president of the German Rifle Club (1868-1873), and president of the German Friendly Society from 1874 to 1875.

date, furnishing the names of the passengers as well as the towns they came from. While in any given list there are many citations of localities in other German states, the majority of the names and places of origin consistently indicate that Wieting's passengers were from towns and villages close to Bremen and Bremerhaven. Michael Bell goes so far as to say that Wieting was something of a gate-keeper of Charleston's German community:

> Wieting certainly knew what type of immigrant would "fit-in" with Charleston's German-America, and he had his own reputation to protect as well. . . . He certainly would not knowingly have transported persons likely to cause political dissension, social difficulties, or those without the ability to sustain themselves financially. Had a known German radical or socialist sought passage with Wieting to Charleston, one wonders if Wieting would have carried him to the city, or suggested that he disembark a New York.[17]

Another local—the third member of the triumvirate mentioned above—was Johann Andreas Wagener. Born in 1816 in Sievern, a town of about 500 located north of Bremerhaven in Land Wursten, Wagener came to Charleston in 1833 or 1834 after first landing in New York. He was one of twelve children; eight of his siblings followed him to take up residence in Charleston.

The 33-year-old Johann Andreas moved with alacrity as soon as he came to Charleston to become perhaps the main culture broker of the German immigrant community. Within twenty-five years, Gertha Reinert writes, Wagener had

> founded the German Fire Company (1836), St. Matthew's Lutheran Church (1840)...the German newspaper *Der Teutone* (1844), the German

---

17. Michael Everette Bell, "Regional identity in the antebellum South: how German immigrants became 'Good' Charlestonians," *The South Carolina Historical Magazine* 100, no. 1 (January 1999), 17-18.

CHAPTER 2: GERMANS IN ANTEBELLUM CHARLESTON—AN HISTORICAL PERSPECTIVE

colony of Walhalla, Pickens District (1848), and a number of beneficial clubs and societies for mutual support and interaction. . . . [He] became a respected, successful officer in the Civil War. In 1861 he commanded the German artillery in the bombardment of Fort Sumter. During the same year he equipped a company commanded by Captain Bachmann and composed entirely of Germans for the Virginia campaign. Also in 1861 his regiment built and defended Fort Walker on Hilton Head Island at the battle of Port Royal. In 1863-64 he commanded the militia forces in the defense of Charleston. In 1866 Governor Orr commissioned him a brigadier general of South Carolina militia. After the Civil War [he] began to participate in South Carolina politics. . . . In 1865 he was a member of the constitutional convention and the first legislature after the adoption of the new constitution. In 1871 he was elected mayor of Charleston, and in 1876 he was a delegate to the Democratic convention in St. Louis and chosen elector-at-large from South Carolina.[18]

After his sudden death in August of 1876 in Walhalla, the community of Lutherans in up-state South Carolina he had been instrumental in founding, his body was brought back to Charleston with great ceremony to be interred in Bethany Cemetery.

By the middle of the century, then, the German community in Charleston would already have several movers and shakers working on its behalf. They would function in leadership positions and their work would resonate positively with the

---

18. "Turning my Joy into Bitterness": A Letter from John A. Wagener," *The South Carolina Historical Magazine* 100, no.1 (January 1999), 51.

Charleston native population.[19] Those who had come earlier would be followed by what would become a growing tide of newcomers starting already in the 1830s. A number of them who would be instrumental in the evolution of the community were there by 1835, and when Captain Wieting began his regular transatlantic deliveries there would be a continuing infusion of new German blood. By mid-century the German ethnic community had become a recognized entity on the city's social, political, and cultural stages.

Collectively, the immigrant Germans were a transformative force in Charleston's evolution:

> [N]ext to the English the German people have unquestionably had the greatest influence in determining the character of the city. Since the second quarter of the eighteenth century they have constituted numerically a large portion of the population. In commerce, in civic affairs, in religion, and in music their part has been particularly significant. German is the only

---

19. In his *New Men, New Cities, New South: Atlanta, Nashville, Charleston, Mobile, 1860-1910* (Chapel Hill: University of North Carolina Press, 1990), Don H. Doyle cites the success of John C. H. Claussen as another success model among "Charleston's 'industrious' and 'pushing' German entrepreneurs" (127-28). Claussen had established a flour mill on Anson Street in early 1860, and according to Doyle, supplied bread to the Confederate troops during the war. He was such a pillar of the German community that there was a grand civic celebration of his and his wife's 50th wedding anniversary in 1898. The event was written up and published in book form by F. Münch. *Das fünfzigjährige Hochzeits-Jubiläum des Gold-Jubelpaares J.C.H. Claussen und seiner Gattin Dorothea, geb Fincken: feierlich begangen als Familienfest, Sonntag, den 25. April 1897, als Volksfest, Montag, den 26. April 1897, als Nachfest, Montag, den 3. Mai, 1897* (Charleston, 1898). With his financial resources Claussen supported the interests of numerous North German immigrants; in 1859 he adopted several boys from the Charleston Orphan House and employed them in his bakery. Claussen was also later instrumental in recruiting Germans to Charleston after the war. Claussen's bakery was supplying bread to Charleston citizens into the 1950s.

CHAPTER 2: GERMANS IN ANTEBELLUM CHARLESTON—AN HISTORICAL PERSPECTIVE

language other than English which has ever had a wide usage in Charleston.[20]

On an individual level, nonetheless, each had to make his or her own way, and while the leaders demonstrated remarkable success, not every immigrant would have judged life in Charleston to be the proverbial bed of roses.

The life story of Adeline Bequest[21] and her husband Frederick Eduard Schroeder, for example, is unremarkable, yet poignantly representative. Married in 1852 in Charleston at St. Matthew's German Lutheran Church, the young couple had five children in the decade between 1853 and 1863, with only one—their son Julius, born in the first year of the Civil War—surviving to adulthood. Frederick was a merchant and operated a cigar store. Their children were born during the turbulent decade leading up to the Civil War when Charleston was a hotbed of political unrest. The circumstances they faced would not have been what they had anticipated in coming to America. Many native-born Charlestonians looked down on working-class immigrants as "a worthless, unprincipled class . . . enemies to our peculiar institution [slavery] . . . and ever ready to form combinations against...the peace of the commonwealth."[22] In the face of an endemic prejudice—no matter how superficially indulgent the host society might appear—the immigrant had to tread lightly so as to avoid overt competition with the enslaved labor class who were hirable, capable, and well attuned to taking care of the needs of their owners. As the owner of a cigar store,

---

20. J. H. Easterby in his introduction to *The History of the German Friendly Society of Charleston South Carolina, 1766-1916. Compiled from original sources by George J. Gongaware* (Richmond: Garrett & Massie, 1935), xv.

21. Adeline Bequest was Johann Rosenbohm's niece. She may also be considered the closest connecting link to her first cousins, the Bequest brothers, who came to Charleston after she had died.

22. Walter J. Fraser, Jr., *Charleston! Charleston! The History of a Southern City* (Columbia: University of South Carolina Press, 1991), 227.

Frederick Schroeder, like his wife's uncle, purposefully sought to establish himself in an unoccupied corner of a uniquely constrained labor market.

It was not only the choice of a line of work, but also the social and cultural context that would challenge the immigrant. In 1846, the U.S. declared war on Mexico, and the ensuing arguments about permitting or banning slavery in the territories acquired during the war swept the matter of slavery from under the rug into the vociferous political arena. When in 1849, thirty-six black inmates escaped from the Charleston workhouse, a kind of hysteria broke the surface, reminded white citizens of the 1822 Denmark Vesey "affair," and confirmed the ever-present threat to a repressive society.

After the mid-1850s, just when the Schroeder couple was beginning married life as immigrant residents, Charleston began to suffer an economic downturn:

> The economic downturn coupled with the steady stream of immigrants, sailors, and vagrants who straggled into the city seeking work caused growing unemployment. By the mid-1850s approximately 40 percent of the white population of nearly 9,000 were recent Irish or German immigrants. From 1850 to 1856 the number of inmates in the city's Poor House rose from 691 to 1,363 and the ratio of foreign-born to native reached seven to one. Class divisions became as obvious as racial divisions. Economically most whites living in the city had more in common with blacks than with the white elite.[23]

By the late 1850s, Charleston's leaders made a concerted effort to improve conditions in the city, and, indeed, a significant amount of money was spent in beautifying certain sections,

---

23. Fraser, *Charleston! Charleston!*, 235.

CHAPTER 2: GERMANS IN ANTEBELLUM CHARLESTON—AN HISTORICAL PERSPECTIVE

although nothing seemed to cure the city of the yellow fever pestilence. In 1860, Frederick Law Olmstead claimed that Charleston had "the worst climate for unacculturated whites of any town in the United States." And by the time the war was imminent, Charleston had come to resemble a military garrison:

> With a population of 40,522 in 1859—it had declined about 2,500 since the beginning of the decade—the city of Charleston ranked twenty-second in the nation, although in manufacturing it ranked only eighty-fifth. The most populous of the South Atlantic ports and the major distribution center for the state, Charleston more closely resembled a modern police state than any other city in the nation. Frederick Law Olmstead observed that "the cannon in position on the parade ground, the citadel, . . . with its martial ceremonies, the frequent parades of militia . . . the numerous armed police, might lead one to imagine that the town was in a state of siege or revolution."[24]

It was, of course, during these times that Captain Wieting, quite literally, was unloading boatloads of German immigrants onto the wharves in Charleston, the large numbers of newcomers doubtless causing tension with the native whites and their slave labor force. For the most part, however, the Schroeders and their fellow German neighbors living in the unsettled and ever-changing Charleston scene, kept their heads down and minded their business. They might well have thought they would have experienced fewer traumas—natural and political—had they stayed in their Hanoverian homeland.

Frederick and Adeline Schroeder would witness the first action in the Civil War—the bombardment of Fort Sumter in the Charleston harbor—although that famous first shot would likely

---

24. Fraser, *Charleston! Charleston!*, 241.

have been more worrisome for the immigrant than celebratory, as it was for the native-born. The couple had buried three children by 1860, and Adeline was pregnant with their fourth child during the critical months leading up to the action in April of 1861. Julius Nicholas was born just two months later, and Adeline herself would die in 1864 before the war was over. The family belonged to the St. Matthew's congregation, and Frederick served early on as financial secretary to the Church. He was among the original pew holders (No. 107) when the newly built church's pews were sold to members of the congregation in 1872. The 1900 Census shows him heading a household with his son Julius (also a "cigar dealer") and wife, and four grandchildren between the ages 5 and 10. He had lived in Charleston for fifty-one years. When he died a widower in 1901, he was living at the same address—111 Wentworth Street—where he had lived with his mother-in-law (Adelheid) and where she had died six years previously. The entire family is buried in Bethany Cemetery in a plot close to the cemetery's entrance gate. A laurel crown sits atop a broken obelisk marking the grave of Adeline.

In all their ordinariness, the Schroeders represented a kind of middle-of-the-road German immigrant experience. Many of their compatriots, even if they fell short of becoming one among the ethnic community's leading figures, could claim to have climbed higher on the ladder of success, acquired more wealth, touched and influenced a wider circle of acquaintances. Others, either relatives, friends, or acquaintances, failed miserably, eked out but a mere existence, resorted to putting their children in the orphanage, failed to rise above the competition, took to drink, abandoned their families, moved on, or died trying. The Schroeder story is but one variation of the immigrant experience in Charleston prior to the historical caesura marked by the Civil War.

As was suggested earlier, the German immigrants to Charleston—whatever their individual trajectory—had to find a way to accommodate the "peculiar institution" that dominated the social structure throughout the southern states. No matter its contemporary acceptability and historic footing in the South, slavery presented the immigrant community that had chosen

CHAPTER 2: GERMANS IN ANTEBELLUM CHARLESTON—AN HISTORICAL PERSPECTIVE

Charleston for home with unique circumstances that few other migrants had to face. Slavery presented an inherent predicament for the immigrant who wanted to become a useful member of a society that advocated human bondage and that defended its morality with unadulterated conviction.

Slavery was the foundation on which almost everything was built. It was a given long before it was questioned and a way of life that few natives imagined could ever be changed. When the matter of slavery began to roil the surface of life after the 1830s, the complex issues involved in a culture based on it would have gnawed at the newly arrived immigrant and likely caused headaches and heartaches that no amount of equivocation could resolve. Already by the time Johann Rosenbohm was resident in Charleston, the politics of nullification clouded the air. How would the intrepid, even bold, young immigrant—no matter how reactionary against the conditions at home in a volatile Europe—respond knowledgeably to the arguments of states' rights versus those of the newly fashioned nation? Could he appreciate, as one historian put it,[25] that "[n]ullification was the hand against the nation . . . [t]he purpose [of which] was to force each man to make a personal choice for the state or against it"? With feet barely on South Carolina soil, the immigrant was hardly in a position to make such a choice nor understand why he should have to.

While slavery was endemic throughout the South, the case can be made that its character in Charleston and South Carolina was different from everywhere else. By the middle of the nineteenth century, South Carolina was a slave state in its entirety, and by 1860, before it seceded from the rest of the country, "the lack of immigration to South Carolina had produced a white population that was 96.6 percent South Carolina born. Hence, the state and its governing class were little influenced by outsiders from other states or abroad. In 1850 and 1860 respectively, 91.8 and 93.0 percent of the Palmetto State's legislators had been born

---

25. George C. Rogers, *Charleston in the Age of the Pinckneys* (Norman: University of Oklahoma Press, 1969), 162.

in South Carolina. These percentages were by far the highest in the Lower South."[26] Numerically, the governing class operated in the context of a population in which they were a minority. If in 1850 the 19,532 slaves and 3,441 free Negroes outnumbered the city's whites by almost 3,000,[27] that was the reality that met the immigrant head-on, a kind of social and political wall against which there could be little resistance if one had any questions on the matter. In reality the immigrant was in no position to question anything about the order of the society into which he had moved.

From the perspective of the typical immigrant, anyone with wealth owned slaves; the poor did not. More than likely, the immigrant would find him/herself in the economic category of the poor, eligible to be counted among the three-fourths of the city's population that did not own slaves. The relationship between wealth and slave ownership confirmed the ordinary immigrant's position at the bottom of the ladder: "Nine out of ten people who had less than $5,000 were slaveless. Of those who owned $5,000 or more, over three quarters were slaveholders. The mean wealth of slaveholders was $21,264, twelve times greater than that of nonslaveholders. Altogether, slaveholders owned 82 percent of all the wealth in the city." And if not already obvious, it was this distinction between slaveholders and nonslaveholders that "focused and reinforced the differences between Charleston's working class and the planters, merchants, and professionals who composed the city's economic elite."[28]

Aside from the great divide between the wealthy elite and the struggling underclasses, the immigrants would always constitute a minority within the overall social structure. While their numbers seem especially modest when measured against a

---

26. John Barnwell, *Love of Order: South Carolina's First Secession Crisis* (Chapel Hill: University of North Carolina Press, 1982), 8.

27. Rogers, 1969, 141.

28. Michael P. Johnson, "Planters and Patriarchy: Charleston, 1800-1860," *The Journal of Southern History*, 46, no. 1 (February 1980), 73-74.

CHAPTER 2: GERMANS IN ANTEBELLUM CHARLESTON—AN HISTORICAL PERSPECTIVE

total native-born population that includes both black and white—10.8% in 1850, 15.55% in 1860—the foreign-born comprised only about a quarter of Charleston's white-only population in 1860.[29] In this minority status, the immigrant was playing on an uneven field, forced to accommodate a majority to which he was unequal in more ways than one. For the immigrants swept ashore by the transatlantic migration current and planting themselves in the South from the 1830s on, the political and cultural forces at work there would have been almost unfathomable—if they were understandable even to the native-born. The overwhelming complexity of the issues that were being argued must have left the uninitiated immigrant bewildered and torn if he attempted to justify his own position in the scheme of things, or if he had to make a decision as to which side he could/would/should support. The principles of the proslavery arguments, the matter of the expansion of slavery into newly acquired territory, the instigation of southern nationalism, partisan and sectional rivalries, and the possibility and justification of secession were additional agents of stress burdening the immigrant trying to establish a new life in Charleston.

The few historians who have written on the German immigrants to Charleston suggest that the newcomers approved of slavery and were enthusiastic supporters of secession and the war effort in the Confederacy. Andrea Mehrländer writes: "The Germans of Charleston approved and supported the institution of slavery and swore absolute loyalty to their adopted home." She cites the fact that although by 1860 the number of slaveholders in the city had declined, 8.9% of the Germans in the city owned a total of 325 slaves, and that "in the case of secession, this clearly meant a decision in favor of leaving the Union."[30] Michael Bell

---

29. Christopher Silver, "Immigration and the Antebellum Southern City." (master's thesis, University of North Carolina, 1975), 10-11.

30. "'With more Freedom and Independence than the Yankees': The Germans of Richmond, Charleston, and New Orleans during the American Civil War", in Suzannah J. Ural, ed., *Civil War Citizens: Race, Ethnicity, and Identity*

sees "acceptance of the practice" in the fact that while "fewer of Charleston's German heads of household than Richmond's owned slaves (about 5 percent in 1860) they owned more of them (an average of 4.75 each)."[31] Such statistics, however, are rather sweeping generalizations, and other historians take a more cautious stance: "[W]hite southerners fought the Civil War to preserve slavery. The German Charlestonians' response to the Civil War was mixed, and most of the Germans who fought for the Confederate Army were not committed to a slave society."[32] Forced, as it were, to accommodate themselves to the overweening racial prejudice of a society that sanctified bondage, immigrants invariably would have had to suppress their own moral sense and align their personal quest—one that had its basis in the *freedom* of the individual—with its antithesis. "[I]f free workers were pulled in all directions, their allegiance to the slave regime was never firm. Men and women who had fled the landlord-dominated societies of Western Europe were hardly predisposed to sympathize with the planter class. Slavery remained the linchpin of the southern order, and the relationship of free workers to that institution continued to be ambiguous at best. Many were too newly arrived to understand it, and some found good reason to oppose it."[33]

Andrea Mehrländer's study of the German communities in Charleston, Richmond and New Orleans between 1850 and 1870 demonstrated that immigrants in these three southern cities

---

in America's Bloodiest Conflict (New York: New York University Press, 2010), 66.

31. "Regional Identity in the Antebellum South. How German Immigrants became 'Good' Charlestonians," *The South Carolina Historical Magazine*, 100, no. 1 (January 1999), 16.

32. Jeffrey G. Strickland, "How the Germans Became White Southerners: German Immigrants and African Americans in Charleston, South Carolina during Reconstruction," *Journal of American Ethnic History* 28, no.1 (2008), 61.

33. Berlin and Gutman, 1983, 1197.

exhibited different behaviors, and that the different metropolitan areas had only in common their location in the South. While much of the difference stemmed from the geographical location, economy, and character of the host city, just as much stemmed from the nature of the ethnic communities that settled in the respective locations. All of those factors impacted the Germans in Charleston and qualified their behavior.

As suggested earlier, the immigrants who arrived in Charleston in the 1830s and 1840s found an already-established and acculturated German community that welcomed them less as fellow countrymen—at the time there was, in fact, no *country* common to them all—than as newcomers of a somewhat lesser sort. When the earlier ones had come, slavery was a part of the culture that had not been questioned and that since had been accepted as a matter of course in the process of acculturation. These were the founders of the German Friendly Society—men such as Michael Kalteisen from Württemberg, Jacob Sass from Hesse, John Siegling from Erfurt—an immigrant group described as "efficient, tidy, and educated."[34] The *Neudeutschen*, in contrast, entered a society that was on edge, that felt threatened by an enslaved population that was difficult to control, that was accosted by political issues such as nullification, states' rights, political-party squabbles more and more oriented to regional differences, and that, before long, felt hemmed in by a developing and increasingly viral abolitionist movement that interfered with the status quo. These new Germans, nonetheless, let themselves in, settled throughout the city, and set about to quietly find their place in their newly adopted home.

As this relatively insignificant minority group of Lutheran Germans from the Kingdom of Hanover and the neighboring Duchy of Oldenburg arrived in increasing numbers, they coalesced into a recognizable ethnic group, and it seems not to have taken too long before they—by virtue of their agreeable habits—won acceptance by the city's native-born as well as by their esteemed

---

34. Rogers, 1969, 146.

and now-acculturated compatriots who had preceded them. As mentioned earlier, a number of leaders—the triumvirate of John Andreas Wagener, Franz Adolph Melchers, and Heinrich Wieting—emerged from among them to become acknowledged representatives of the larger group—leaders and culture brokers who tried to effectively manage the rank and file among the immigrants, as well as the immigrant image within the Charleston community. Michael Bell suggests that for a substantial number of immigrants, it was the case that Wieting brought them to Charleston where they then benefitted from the financial and social infrastructure that Wagener had helped to create, all the while being tutored by the newspaper editor Franz Melchers, as he "translated Charleston and America to the new immigrants, interpreting the city's institutions in the immigrants' own language." 35

Mehrländer portrays the Charleston German community as unconditionally loyal to the South. She emphasizes the fact that during the years leading up to secession and the subsequent war, Charleston's Germans rallied to the cause by fielding numerous militia companies. It was a fact that by 1860 "Charleston's German minority not only had the oldest German militia unit in the United States—the Charleston German Fusiliers of 1775—but also could support six active militia companies of which five were formed between 1842 and 1859, including the only ethnic German cavalry militia of the South." She argues that the founding of these militias indicated the strong desire of the ethnic community to participate in the military and political culture of the adopted country. The members of these militias, she suggests, held considerable sway over the community at large: the community's social life

> was almost completely in the hands of . . . twenty-four militia officers who, through a complex

---

35. Michael E. Bell, "'Hurrah für dies süsse, dies sonnige Leben': The Anomaly of Charleston, South Carolina's Antebellum German-America." (PhD diss., University of South Carolina, 1996), 254.

network of clubs, nepotistic connections, and their business contacts as merchants, had created a watertight structure of mutual interests that allowed them to reach nearly every aspect of community life. The German officers of the antebellum militias of Charleston were democratically oriented, loyal adoptive citizens of South Carolina, and more than one-third of them belonged to the group of slaveholders. Because of their publicly declared acceptance of the Southern way of life, there existed a symbiosis based on mutual respect between the natives and the German immigrants.[36]

Mehrländer confirms what Bell had earlier proposed: that Charleston's late antebellum German community was "guided" in such a way as to prevent embarrassing situations from breaking out between the native-born whites and the Germans.

Without disputing the evidence that a symbiosis between the immigrant and native communities existed and that to external appearances the German minority presented a uniform front, a number of factors call into question the solidarity that some commentators find distinctive. It is somewhat specious to judge German immigrants' loyalty to a Southern way of life when the native population, in defense of its system of slavery, was rabidly intolerant of outside interference. Furthermore, to see in the immigrants' social behavior a consensus with a Southern morality that was based on the inferiority of a laboring class serving a propertied elite—the latter whose ranks were essentially closed to the immigrant—is to look no further than outside appearances. No matter how loud the message coming from the *Deutsche Zeitung*, no matter how congenial the brotherhood in any of the numerous associations, the immigrant knew in his heart that he was a guest in this community and that his conduct was under constant scrutiny. With or without instruction, Charleston's Germans

---

36. Mehrländer, 2010, 66-67.

appeared to be so well-behaved because they were so anxious to please. They consistently demonstrated the propriety that would keep them in the good graces of their hosts. The *Neudeutschen* had not only to prove themselves to the *Altdeutschen*, but also to the wealthy planter society in which they would look for a modus vivendi. Better to do the right thing than to cause any trouble. When the corporate society appeared in trouble, it would be advisable to lend support—outward support at least. When in Charleston, it would be politic to do as Charlestonians did and to adopt the ways of those who held the reins. As long as one stayed on the side of the most-of-the-time-comprehensible majority, there were advantages to lying low and getting on with the business at hand—that is, becoming a productive member of the local community and carving out a sustainable existence for oneself and one's family. That they vied for acceptance by the community at large led them to accept many of the ways of that community, for open dissent would carry risk, and any attempt to swim against the current would invoke unnecessary hardship when things were already hard enough.

Understanding this fundamental nature of the German immigrant's experience in Charleston goes a long way in explaining the ethnic conscience as frequently a troubled one. It was not the case, however, that "a German has only to be a German to be utterly opposed to slavery. In feeling, as well as in conviction and principle, they are antislavery," as the abolitionist Frederick Douglas had stated in 1859. Douglas could make such a pronouncement on the basis of his acquaintanceship with those antislavery German-Americans—"radical democrats" who "traced their ideological ancestry back to the European Enlightenment by way of the eighteenth and nineteenth-century Age of Revolution."[37] The fact was that there were not many *radical*

---

37. Bruce Levine, "Against All Slavery, Whether White or Black": German-Americans and the Irrepressible Conflict," in *Crosscurrents: African Americans, Africa, and Germany in the Modern World*, David McBride, Leroy Hopkins, and C. Aisha Blackshire-Belay, eds. (Columbia: Camden House, 1998), 59.

democrats who settled in Charleston to escape the European "Age of Revolution." Hardly any of the Germans in that city would have assumed anything like a radical stance on any issue. If any one of them had harbored or demonstrated radical or ostensibly "enlightened" thoughts regarding the South's peculiar institution, s/he would have sensed the distinct vulnerability of the lone voice in the wilderness. In Charleston the pressure of the culture would keep the ethnic community in line, and it was the sought-after approbation of the larger community that kept the symbiotic relationship healthy and immune to disruption.

For Charlestonians—both native and immigrant—the reality of the relationship between whites and blacks was admittedly different compared to any other southern city, and there was every reason why South Carolina was moved to lead the efforts toward disunion and why it was considered by the nation to be the hotbed of rebellion. For almost a decade South Carolina's leading citizens and its legislators had waved their banner and, unsatisfied with any mediating compromises, had moved inexorably toward independence and resumption of the state's "position among the nations of the world as a separate and independent State; with full power to levy war, conclude peace, contract alliances, establish commerce, and to do all other acts and things which independent States may of right do."[38] As of December 20, 1860, the ordinance signed in Institute Hall on Meeting Street[39] made it official: "We, the People of the State of South Carolina, in Convention assembled, do declare and ordain. . .that the union now subsisting between South Carolina and other States, under the name of 'The United States of America,' is hereby dissolved."

---

38. *Declaration of the Immediate Causes which Induce and Justify the Secession of South Carolina from the Federal Union; and the Ordinance of Secession.* (Charleston, 1860), 10.

39. In the same building that housed the "Teetotaler" restaurant— owned and run by Johann Rosenbohm's nephew, Nicholas Fehrenbach, Jr.

The Charleston immigrant would doubtless have had some second thoughts about what had transpired. Led, pushed and pulled by contending but influential forces, the non-native, antebellum Charleston immigrant surely would have been stressed by the tension between his inherited cultural tenets and those of his hosts. How easily could the immigrant accept the notion that what had been the beckoning, *United-through-revolution*-States—a *unified-by-trial* nation offering new hope, opportunity, freedom, and independence—should be dismissed, broken up, by a host community persistently arguing a separatist and untested ideology? Even if the immigrant mind could comprehend the superficial arguments, to say nothing of the writing between the lines, it was impossible to swim against the current or to resist a populace that had been whipped into a secession frenzy that celebrated separation and condemned anyone who did not dance to the South Carolina tune. Ever since their individual arrivals during earlier years of the century, what might have seemed like white noise that had begun when the concept of nullification was first being discussed and disputed had, by the election of Abraham Lincoln in 1860, been turned up to a deafening decibel level. Indisputably not in control of what was happening, the immigrant might well have felt that the 1860 ordinance was a step that would surely bring darker times. While most South Carolinians had talked themselves into thinking that their defection from the Union would somehow be peacefully accommodated, most European immigrants would have thought it folly not to expect serious repercussions. They would have been sympathetic to the sentiment expressed by the elderly South Carolina statesman, Judge James Petrigru, who declared "South Carolina...too small for a republic, and too large for a lunatic-asylum."[40] Over the months that followed, those who were immigrants would be condemned to sit by and watch the changes that would affect their new world.

---

40. Adam Goodheart, *1861. The Civil War Awakening* (New York: Alfred A. Knopf, 2011), 12.

CHAPTER 2: GERMANS IN ANTEBELLUM CHARLESTON—AN HISTORICAL PERSPECTIVE

The courses of individual immigrant families ran in parallel to the cultural forces that were in play on the municipal, regional, and national stages during the years leading up the Civil War. There was no avoiding the political upheaval that led to secession and the subsequent military engagement between a confederacy of rebellious states and a Federal government defending the constituency of the Union. They would have to accommodate what became the new law of the land, would have to recognize that they were residents of a rebellious State, would have to suffer through Charleston's unprecedented, 567 days-long bombardment—"an instrument of terror to carry out the wanton destruction of private property and the persecution of a civilian population."[41] Before and during the war, did they believe, like John Andreas Wagener, that "the Negro must be ruled by force" and, if necessary, "with the help of the whip"[42], and therefore subscribe openly to the oligarchs' program to separate the State from the Union in order to maintain their "right" to own slaves? Did the German immigrant sense the heavy hand of the newly formed Confederate government when its Banishment Act of August 1861 forced them to declare their loyalty to the Confederacy in order to remain in their new country—the country that overnight had rejected the one to which they had immigrated? What did they all feel when hostilities seemed to be on their very doorstep? How strong was the sense of loyalty to a political and cultural entity that had been cultivated by the native majority and forced on the less acculturated newcomers? Did one question it, or go with the flow? Did the immigrant participate in the black market, encourage and benefit from the blockade running that sustained everyday and mercantile life in a city and country under siege?[43]

---

41. Chris W. Phelps, *The Bombardment of Charleston 1863-1865* (Gretna, LA: Pelican, 2002) 10.

42. Mehrländer, 2010, 74.

43. The answer is "yes." Frederick Schroeder, in defense of his own business interests, was one of the Charleston merchants—many of them

By February of 1865, Charleston was indeed the "mere desolate wreck" General Sherman had described.[44] The lower half of the city was now totally uninhabited, and those who had survived were destitute. Few immigrants took the time to record their impressions of their own survival or the losses they had suffered. Perhaps it was because they had less to start with, and thus less to lose, not as far to fall, as it were, as those who were in society's top echelons. If they had managed to survive, there was little choice but to pick up the pieces and try to move on. By this time they would no longer think of themselves as guests in a host community who had best demonstrate good behavior—they had been through both the thick and the thin and justifiably had little sense of gratitude to those who had swept them along with this tide that had brought no reward and little more than existence itself. The remnant of life in Charleston after Appomattox would be nothing they had expected or wished for. But like their native-born neighbors, the German Lutheran community was similarly determined in defeat to survive and prosper through the remaining years of the century. Like the widower Frederick Schroeder, the majority of the now-settled immigrants of North German origin would become participating and acculturated Charleston citizens as the city resurrected itself to move into the twentieth century.

German—who were invested in the William Bee Importing and Exporting Company, the first of a total of five trading companies that were incorporated in South Carolina in 1862-63 for the purpose of running the blockade. The *Charleston Daily Courier* of January 22, 1862, in fact, bragged about the Schroeder firm's success in bringing goods in through the "inefficient blockade": "Our enterprising friends, the Messrs. Schroder Brothers, who have proved so often successful in running the sham blockade instituted by the Lincoln Government, have just received, by their hitherto successful medium, a very select assortment of the choicest brand of Segars, Cigarettos, etc. Their establishment is in Meeting street, next adjoining the Mills House, where they will be happy to receive their friends and customers at hours set forth in their advertisement in another column of this day's *Courier*, and to which we ask reference." The name of the "successful medium" was purposefully undisclosed.

[44] Fraser, *Charleston! Charleston!*, 268.

CHAPTER 3: THE ADVENTURES OF BERNHARD BEQUEST

The Civil War had just begun, the first shot already fired, when the eldest of the Bequest brothers—a mere seventeen-year-old—arrived in the rebel city. The Federal garrison had been forced to leave Fort Sumter, and President Lincoln had already issued his notice of intent to blockade the ports of the newly formed Confederacy. The temperature of everything was on the rise as the young Bequest's ship slipped into Charleston harbor and the teenager from Geestendorf set foot on South Carolina soil. But before this story gets ahead of itself, some important background is in order.

As was suggested earlier, the Geestendorf Bequest family had its inception in the French Revolution. The historical record attests to the fact that under Napoleon and the three Coalition Wars the map of Europe was completely redrawn: on the German map, the number of German states was reduced from more than 300 to 39. By 1808, the thousand-year-old Holy Roman Empire had been effectively dissolved. Among all the changes in government and allegiances, North German lands—primarily the Kingdom of Hanover and the Hansa cities of Hamburg, Bremen, and Lübeck—together with the Kingdom of Holland and the Grand Duchy of Oldenburg, were annexed to France in 1810 and the territory was considered to be one of the *pays réunis*. At that point in time, the village of Geestendorf lay in occupied territory. When Napoleon tried to isolate Britain—whose king was a German to whom the Kingdom of Hanover belonged—he sought to control the northern coast of Europe by imposing a blockade and sending additional troops and customs officials to major ports. The coastal town of

Geestendorf would have received some attention in this regard, and the presence of French military officers, specifically naval officers, in the North German town/village that was in territory annexed to France was a fact of life that local citizens had no choice but to accept.

The Nohrden family had been farmers in Hanoverian Geestendorf since the seventeenth century and those living at the beginning of the nineteenth century were witness to the presence of French naval officers stationed in the vicinity. In her early twenties, Meina Nohrden, born in 1787, met a French naval officer by the name of Bequet Benoir Olivier and subsequently gave birth to twins on July 13, 1811. The church record indicates that a corporal in the French navy by the name of Bequet Benoit Olivier, born in "St. Benoit du Sonde im Department de Cisle milaine" had acknowledged that he was the father of the twin boys born to Meina at 6 p.m. two days prior in the house of her father, and that the infants had been baptized that very day. One son was named Johaim, the other, Betja-Benedic.[1]

Three months later, on October 24, 1811, Bequet Olivier and Meina Nohrden were married in her home. The groom's military assignment in Germany may have seemed permanent enough for him to take this step; perhaps he already had intentions to stay in the area in spite of his military obligations; possibly he and Meina had determined that their relationship was worthy of being legitimized. Part of the reality was the fact that the French Empire would collapse by 1813: despite wide-spread conscription, desertions were common, as well as self-mutilation and marriages—both of which exempted one from military service. In the case of Bequet and Meina, the corporal did not return to France, and in the years following, the family took its legitimate

---

1. The birthplace of the twins' father is the German pastor's mishearing of *St. Benoit des Ondes*, a village on the coast of Brittany, not far from St. Malo and St. Michel; what appears in the handwritten church record as *Department de Cisle milaine* is again a mishearing of what the corporal would have spoken as *Department d'Ille et Vilaine*, the official designation for that larger geographical region of France in which St. Benoit des Ondes is located; the name *Johaim* is a French form of *Johann*.

CHAPTER 3: THE ADVENTURES OF BERNHARD BEQUEST

place in the community. Over time, the French naval officer became an integrated member of the North German, very Lutheran, community.

On February 11, 1820, Meina gave birth to another set of twins, a daughter Meina, who lived only one day, and a son Ludwig. By 1826, the church record indicates that Bequet had transformed and germanicized his name to become *Bernhard Olivier Bequest*—using his Christian name as his surname, his middle name (Benoit) as his Christian name *Bernhard*, with his original surname converted into his middle name. The addition of the *s* in the transformation of *Bequet* into *Bequest* was probably an attempt to make the French into something more German, although it would still have been awkward to sound for the North German speakers of *Plattdeutsch*.

On December 2, 1832, the church recorded the marriage of the bachelor Bernhard Bequest, son of local resident Benoit Olivier Bequest, to Margarethe Adelheid Rosenbohm, daughter of Caspar Rosenbohm, also a local resident. This young Bernhard who now surfaces in the record is one of the twins born to Meina in 1811. His original Christian name "Betja-Benedic" had been changed to Bernhard by the time he was confirmed in 1827. It turns out that Bernhard's marriage was also a little after-the-fact: the local church recorded the baptism of the couple's first son, born April 12, 1833, also named Bernhard. The young father's name is given as Bernhard Bequest, his occupation is farmer, the same as that of his maternal grandfather, Johann Nohrden. Bernhard and Adelheid's son lived only for a year. Then on January 12, 1835, the couple had a daughter Adeline, and it was she who would later emigrate with her widowed mother and marry Frederick Eduard Schroeder in Charleston.

It was another Bernhard, however, who would immigrate somewhat later to Charleston. This was the son of Ludwig—the surviving twin born to Meina and Bequet in February of 1820. Ludwig Bequest and his wife Tette Hencken were parents to six children: Bernhard Heinrich (b. December 20, 1844), Johann Ludwig (b. February 27, 1847), Minna Henriette Cathrine (b. April 20, 1849), Carsten August (b. August 13, 1851), Dorothea Louise

(b. September 26, 1854), and Therese Rebecka (b. December 20, 1857). The three sisters remained in Geestendorf, while their three brothers would come to Charleston, with Bernhard Heinrich leading the way.

Bernhard Heinrich, the eldest, arrived in Charleston in rather dramatic fashion. According to a rather obscure volume on Confederate military history published in 1899,[2] Bernhard Bequest arrived in Charleston "two weeks after the capture of Fort Sumter," that is, toward the end of April, 1861. Not incidentally, it was reported in the Charleston *Mercury* of May 3 that Captain Wieting's ship, the *Gauss*, had arrived Charleston on the second after a forty-five day crossing from Bremen. According to the paper, twelve named passengers disembarked. These would be the "intrepid" souls mentioned earlier in chapter 2 who were brave enough to depart for Charleston despite reports of the tinderbox conditions there ever since the state's secession the previous December. The list of Wieting's ships bringing immigrants to Charleston and New York cited earlier in chapter 2 does not furnish arrival dates for eight of the thirty-four voyages, but the specified departure of the *Gauss* from Bremerhaven on 14 March fits convincingly with the arrival of that ship in Charleston at the beginning of May after a month-and-a-half-long voyage. Despite the disembarkation of one additional passenger (twelve, rather than eleven as in the Bullerdiek and Tilgner listing), however, there is no one by the name of Bequest among the passengers listed. In view of the military history's date of "two weeks after ... Fort Sumter," the verified early May arrival date, and the fact that the March 14 sailing was the sole crossing of the *Gauss* to Charleston in 1861 and the sole departure of one of Wieting's ships until after the war, it seems more than likely that young Bequest had managed to arrange his passage to Charleston as a member of the *Gauss's* crew.

---

2. Ellison Capers, *South Carolina*. Vol. 5 of Clement A. Evans, ed., *Confederate Military History: a library of Confederate States History*, (Atlanta: Confederate Publishing Co., 1899).

CHAPTER 3: THE ADVENTURES OF BERNHARD BEQUEST

According to the writer of the brief biography, "the Confederate flag was flying, and he [Bequest] promptly declared his allegiance to it." Then, "only a few months later,"

> Bequest hid himself on the little blockade-running steamer, Ruby, and on revealing his presence after the boat was at sea, was put to work as coal-passer during the trip to Nassau. At that port he shipped on the blockade-runner Stonewall Jackson, Captain Black commanding, which on the first trip out was sighted and chased by the United States cruiser Tioga, and compelled to throw overboard part of her cargo and put back to Nassau. This unfortunate vessel at her next attempt to reach Charleston was fired upon and struck as she was crossing the bar, and run ashore, where she was burned with the cargo, young Bequest making his way thence to the city with the mail pouch. His next voyage was from Wilmington, and reaching Nassau he shipped on the Fanny, Captain Moore, with which he made four successful trips. Later he was on the Cyrene, but being taken sick at Nassau, he returned to his home in Germany in June, 1864, and remained until September, when he sailed to Nassau by way of New York, and made a trip into Wilmington on the Rosso Castle. Sailing again on the Watson, they reached the Wilmington bar in time to witness the terrific bombardment of Fort Fisher, upon the fall of which fort blockade-running came practically to an end. Returning to Nassau, he opened a small store and remained there until October, 1865.[3]

---

3. Capers, 455.

Now before looking into the adventures of the young Geestendorfer ostensibly coming to the aid of the young Confederacy, a few caveats are in order. It turns out that the short biographical account cited above, tucked away in a volume of Confederate military history, was written by a Bishop of the Episcopal Convention of South Carolina. Ellison Capers, a South Carolinian born in 1837, was a former Brigadier-General in the Confederate Army who after the war served as Secretary of State for South Carolina. In 1867 he entered the Protestant Episcopal ministry, received his DD degree from the University of South Carolina in 1889, and was elected Bishop by the Convention of South Carolina in 1893.

The fact that Capers found Bernhard Heinrich Bequest worthy of mention among the individuals of significance to South Carolina's military history during the Confederacy suggests that Bequest's adventures had somehow come to the Brigadier-General's attention—either through personal contact, the war-time rumor mill, or via some other means—and, moreover, that they were sufficiently "notable" in the eyes of a military historian to warrant according the young Bequest recognition as an individual who had helped and furthered the Confederate effort. Apparently in the course of his crewing on numerous blockade runners, the young Bernhard Bequest had made a name for himself and become an acknowledged actor in the Confederacy's efforts to sustain itself.

The Capers account that told of young Bernhard Heinrich's blockade-running days seems to have been written in awe of Bequest's youth and daring. Capers called it a "romantic story" and noted that the German native had begun a "seafaring life" at the age of fourteen. The escapades of Bequest as related by Capers are indeed impressive, even if only somewhat cursorily outlined. Each of the ships he is said to have worked on can be accounted for. The *Ruby* was in operation until June 10, 1863, when, under Captain Peat, she "got around on Folly Island. . . . Late the next day the Federals discovered and opened fire upon her. Captain Peat thereupon set her on fire, and then he and his crew took to small boats. Though shot at by cannon and

CHAPTER 3: THE ADVENTURES OF BERNHARD BEQUEST

small arms they escaped."[4] The rescue of the mail pouch by young Bequest after the destruction of the *Stonewall Jackson* under Captain Black was noted in a report of the vessel's capture in the Richmond, VA *Daily Dispatch*, with a "Charleston, April 12" (1863) dateline. Capers' *Rosso Castle* is more accurately the ship *Rothersay Castle*, and his *Cyrene* is the long-serving *Syren*. The *Watson* was indeed still at work in early 1865 when Wilmington's Fort Fisher fell in January. Maritime records show that the *Watson* sailed for Nassau mid-February 1865, possibly taking Bequest back to Nassau where he purportedly stayed until October of that year.

The reality of Bequest's blockade running, of course, was not all that "romantic," and it was not the case that Bequest just took to the sea with the wind behind him, looking for adventure. He came from a family of seafarers in Geestendorf who had for generations lived and worked the North German coast either as sailors of one kind or another and/or as small farmers. His grandfather, a Frenchman, had been in the French navy and described as a "navigator", a ferryman and a sailor; his father worked as a ship's carpenter, a boatman, a skipper, and as a ship pilot. For certain, the sea was in his blood, but when he began his "seafaring life" at age fourteen it was likely because his father Ludwig had died in 1859, aged thirty-nine. As the eldest of six children, he would have been expected to assume his position as the head of the family. But these were not the times for the younger generation to accept the expectations of tradition. After his father's death, opportunity for advancement in his native Geestendorf—which by this time had been incorporated into the free port city of Bremerhaven as the major center for emigration from German lands—would have been overshadowed by the pull of opportunity in the United States, even if that country on the other side of the Atlantic seemed to be headed for fracture into two sections. Bequest had not yet been born when Hanover's union with Britain had been dissolved (1837) and he grew up during a

---

4. Maxwell Clayton Orvin, *In South Carolina Waters*, (Charleston, 1961), 50.

period of revolutionary changes taking hold on the European continent. Though young in years, he likely would have perceived that neighboring Prussia was on the rise in contention with Austria to take control of European lands, although he may not have been prescient enough at age sixteen in 1861 to forecast that it would only be five years into the future that Prussia would press its heavy foot on his native soil to turn the Hanoverian "Kingdom" into a Province of the rising militant, new-European power.

That he should set out across the sea to arrive in Charleston in early 1861 had undoubtedly to do with the fact that he could make the crossing with his fellow Geestendorfer and well-known immigrant mentor, Captain Heinrich Wieting, and the fact that he had family in Charleston where Wieting's ship was headed. Wieting's *Gauss* departed Bremerhaven before the firing on Fort Sumter, and the fact that it arrived after hostilities had begun was not anything that Wieting or the teen-ager could have planned for. If reports of conditions in the United States were to be believed, young Bequest had every reason to think that time was running short for him to seize the day and to take his chances like others had done before him.

In his account of Bequest's arriving when "the Confederate flag was flying", Capers seems anxious to assure his potential readers that "he promptly declared his allegiance to it." This rhetoric can be easily attributed to wishful thinking on the part of the ex-Brigadier-General, but it seems nonetheless somewhat heavy-handed to ascribe such patriotism to a seventeen-year-old who, after all, was not yet a citizen, not even, apparently, a committed immigrant. Bequest's actions, "several months later" when he took up blockade running by stowing away on the *Ruby*, suggest that the young German was more interested in the potential of financial reward and the chance to use his sea legs than in demonstrating an ideological stance in support of the newly formed Confederacy desperate for resources.

Young Bequest, of course, would have known of the other family members already in Charleston. It seems likely that he would have attempted to join up with his aunt Adelheid and his first cousin Adeline and her husband Frederick Schroeder,

CHAPTER 3: THE ADVENTURES OF BERNHARD BEQUEST

although there is no record of any family reunion. One of young Bequest's Charleston connections, however, was another Geestendorfer and near-relative, Nicholas Fehrenbach, Jr. Nicholas—born in Charleston in 1833—was almost twelve years older than Bernhard, but they were of the same generation. Nicholas was a successful businessman when the war started, and a well-known figure in the Charleston German community.[5] As head of his own family, Nicholas had early on engaged his younger brother as his substitute in Confederate service, but had subsequently re-joined the war effort by enlisting as steward on the blockade runner *Margaret and Jessie*. Whether or not Nick Fehrenbach initially influenced the younger Bernhard in getting involved in blockade running, the two would have much to share later on. The *Margaret and Jessie* was originally the British steamer *Douglas* that was anchored in Charleston on Christmas Eve of 1862. It subsequently became a blockade runner commanded by Charleston's Captain Robert W. Lockwood. On the *Margaret and Jessie*'s thirteenth and final voyage to Wilmington, North Carolina in early November of 1863, with a mixed cargo valued at half-a-million dollars and with eight passengers,

> [n]ear the North Carolina coast she was sighted and fired upon by the U.S.S. FULTON. Hit several times Captain Lockwood managed to turn the ship and headed back to sea, followed by the FULTON. During the chase most of the cargo was destroyed. The next day, November 5, after being chased more than fourteen hours Captain Lockwood was forced to surrender. He reported

---

5. It was in his home that Captain Heinrich Wieting died of typhus in December of 1868 (Mehrländer [2011], 37-38), bringing the immigrants' Geestendorf-Charleston connection to its post-war conclusion. That the Bequest brothers' first cousin, Adeline Schroeder, was a first cousin to Nicholas Fehrenbach suggests that they were all "related" in more ways than one.

that he would have taken to his boats and blown up his ship had it not been for the two lady passengers. He and his crew, and the passengers, were sent to New York and placed in the Eldridge Street jail.[6]

The incident made the news in Charleston. Both the *Charleston Courier* and the *Mercury* reported on November 16 that "Northern accounts state that the United States steamer *Fulton* reached New York on the 8th instant, having in tow as a prize the steamship *Margaret and Jessie*, from Nassau for Wilmington, N.C....The *Margaret and Jessie* was the property of the Charleston Importing and Exporting Company of this city."

The fact that the ship was owned by the Charleston Importing and Exporting Company in which Nicholas Fehrenbach

---

6. Orvin, *In South Carolina Waters*, 52-53. The Orvin account conflicts with that found in Angus Konstam's *Confederate Blockade Runner 1861-65* (Oxford: Osprey, 2004), 44: "...She was 211ft long, with a 26-ft beam and a draft of 10ft. Her sidewheel engines gave her a very respectable maximum speed of 15 knots, and when she was first built she was lauded as the fastest steamer in the world. In November 1862, she was purchased for use as blockade runner, and made her first voyage to Charleston, slipping through the Union blockade to enter the port in late January 1863. She was then renamed the *Margaret and Jessie*, and made 18 more voyages between the Confederate seaboard and Nassau, five from Charleston and three from Wilmington. She was finally captured on her 20th return voyage on November 5, 1863, by the USS *Nansemond* while trying to slip into Wilmington. Taken into Union service as the USS *Gettysburg*, she ended the war as part of the North Atlantic Blockading Squadron, stationed as a 'chaser' off Wilmington." While it is often frustrating to know which account of a particular blockade runner is the accurate one, in this instance the fate of the *Margaret and Jessie* as reported in Stephen R. Wise's *Lifeline of the Confederacy: Blockade Running During the Civil War* (Columbia: University of South Carolina Press, 1988), 139, gives both accounts some credence: "At daybreak the blockade runner was sighted by the gunboats *Keystone State* and *Nansemond* and the Army transport *Fulton*. All three joined the pursuit and by 11:30 a.m. the *Nansemond* was within cannon range and began firing on the fleeing vessel. Although rough seas soon forced the *Nansemond* to slow her speed, the larger *Fulton* cut through the waves and forced the *Margaret and Jessie* to surrender. She was taken north, condemned, purchase by the Union Navy, and converted to the gunboat *Gettysburg*."

CHAPTER 3: THE ADVENTURES OF BERNHARD BEQUEST

was invested suggests that it was potential financial reward that would have inspired the businessman-on-the-make to be thus involved in the war effort. The profits made by such trading companies exporting cotton through Nassau to Europe and bringing in arms, munitions, everyday necessities, as well as luxury goods, were enormous; captains and crews were paid rates that made the risks involved seem minimal compared to the rewards. The risks involved would have been even fewer for the younger seafarer looking for opportunity for quick financial gain: Confederate citizens captured by Federal blockaders were prisoners-of-war and could be jailed—as indeed Fehrenbach was; young Bequest, a German native, could not be apprehended in this way and, if captured on a blockade runner, would have been released.

In any event, Bequest continued his adventures as a blockade runner until virtually the end of the war. He had done quite well for himself on the Charleston-Nassau run and, according to the Capers account, had garnered sufficient financial means to start a business in Nassau. There is little doubt that the blockade runner knew what he was doing beyond the challenges of the operation. But whether he arrived with a sense of loyalty to the Confederacy, or developed one while working to supply it, is questionable. For the mature teen-ager, it was more likely the challenge of the dangers involved and the opportunity for financial gain that outweighed any nationalistic sense of actively abetting the South's rebellion. While Capers might have been wishfully thinking it in hindsight, it is hard to imagine why a young German would have felt compelled to defend the Southern aristocracy resistant to multiple pressures to change its ways to ground his activity in a romanticized patriotism. He was working for himself, and whatever ship's captain he managed to sign on with. It was not incumbent upon this adventuresome German sailor to become a committed Confederate then in order to later become a German American Charlestonian. Nevertheless, that is the implication when one looks at the remainder of the brief Capers biography. After noting that Bequest "opened a small store" and remained in Nassau until October of 1865, Capers concludes his account saying that Bequest "came to Charleston and engaged in business and planting at the town of Mount Pleasant, on the bay. Since 1885 he has conducted a successful business at Charleston, is a member of the German artillery, and has twice served as king of the German rifle club. By his marriage in 1866 he has a daughter living, Teresa L., wife of John Gishen [sic], and by a later marriage he has one son, John F." Capers saw in Bernhard Bequest an adventuresome young German who made his mark on behalf of the defeated Confederacy and who, after the war, established himself as a successful businessman, honored his German heritage, and was an upstanding family man. This somewhat myopic and Brigadier-Generalized account notwithstanding, what we have in these summary statements by Capers is a broad-brush outline of Bernhard Bequest's second-stage life in Charleston. This is when the post-Civil War stories of the Bequest brothers begin.

CHAPTER 4: RECONSTRUCTED LIVES

Toward the end of his recent magisterial biography of Queen Victoria, A. N. Wilson writes that the daily tedium of her life was in itself what he terms "a remarkable fact." "Apart from being the Queen, she had done so very little. . . .The tempting thing, when trying to make sense of any human life, whether famous or obscure, is to concentrate upon outward activities. Queen Victoria does not allow us to do that, since . . . she did not really 'do' anything. . . . So, as well as her life being that of her own times, as must be the case of a monarch in her position, her life was also that of the inner woman, of whom—from the letters and the journals—we have so vivid a sense."[1]

In the following chapters something of the opposite case obtains: the challenge of describing the lives of three men— distinctly not famous, immigrants, not monarchs—who left nothing of record to reveal their "inner" selves and whose lives we must try to fathom by looking at the things they *did* in order to somehow know who they were. Depending on the kind of record available for examination, one could argue that these two approaches are but different sides of the same coin and equally valid. The goal in any case is to make sense of their lives.

According to the Capers biographical account cited in chapter 3, Bernhard Bequest, living and operating a "small business" of an undisclosed nature in Nassau, decided to come back to Charleston. If he had returned to Nassau on the *Watson* in mid-February 1865, it was likely after Federal troops had taken

---

1. A. N. Wilson, *Victoria. A Life* (New York: Penguin, 2014), 553.

both Charleston and Columbia (February 17, 1865). Just two months later, on April 14, Robert Anderson had raised the U.S. flag over Fort Sumter four years to the day after he had surrendered in 1861. Two days later, President Lincoln was assassinated. At the end of June, President Andrew Johnson had established a provisional government for South Carolina and named Benjamin Perry the provisional governor. In September, "a convention met in Columbia and drew up the Constitution of 1865. The 'Black Codes'[2] were adopted under its authority. Article XI abolished state offices in Charleston, thereby centralizing government in Columbia."[3] Bequest, having just turned twenty-one, arrived in Charleston in October.

In view of his extensive experience as a blockade runner, it would have been obvious to the young German that, as the Union tightened the noose of the "Anaconda Plan," the Confederacy's success in defeating the blockade had effectively run its course as the war moved into 1863-64. With the loss of Fort Fisher in January 1865, and the surrender of Wilmington five weeks later, blockade running was definitively over. At some point before that, Bequest had decided to abandon his increasingly risky "job" in favor of setting up a small business in Nassau that would be only indirectly, but no less profitably, connected to the blockade. The subsequent decision to forsake his business in Nassau and to settle in Charleston likely signaled a desire to find a more stable business environment as well as the pull of the chain that had been started by Johann Rosenbohm. The *New York Times* archive contains a "Letter from Nassau" that was published in the *Charleston Courier* on June 20, 1864, and that described the

---

2. "The Black Codes, passed by the former Confederate states during Presidential Reconstruction, were part of a complex web of postwar economic, legal, and extralegal restraints designed by white conservatives to maintain broad control over the freedpeople." *Encyclopedia of the Reconstruction Era. Vol 1: A-L*, Richard Zuczek, ed. (Westport, CN: Greenwood Press, 2006), 72.

3. George C. Rogers, Jr. and C. James Taylor, *A South Carolina Chronology 1497-1992*. 2nd ed. (Columbia: University of South Carolina Press, 1994), 102.

business conditions in Nassau, some of which pertain rather obviously to the increasingly effective naval blockade of Confederate ports. It suggests why the young businessman might have thought that the tide had turned and it was time to make another move. The "letter" reads:

> To give you some idea of the business of the place, Major W. told me the other day that there were one thousand tons of bacon and pork here belonging to the Government and awaiting shipment, much of this is spoiled, and much more destined to be in the warm Summer months approaching. There are eight or ten vessels now in port loading. Three of them have just arrived from England and more are expected. It is thought that there will be twenty-five or thirty vessels running between this place and Wilmington during the coming Summer. I fear that all of our cotton will be taken away without giving back much substantial benefit, and we will be left at the close of the war without a bale for credit. There are some facts with reference to the sending out of Confederate bonds, which it seems to me should be brought to the attention of the Government. They are sacrificed out here and in Europe at about eight pence on the dollar, and as that is better than paying twenty for one for exchange, a great amount of them are sent out, and in that way our obligations at the close of the war will not be to ourselves, but in great measure to these English, who are buying them now at a merely nominal sum. The business . . . is carried on to an enormous extent.[4]

---

4. http://www.nytimes.com/1864/06/20/news/business-at-nassau.html.

Bequest must have decided to opt for what looked like opportunity in Charleston rather than risk the decline of conditions in Nassau. Although by late 1865 his first cousin Adeline Schroeder had died, his Aunt Adelheid was still there, as was Adeline's husband, and a number of other individuals in the extended family such as the Fehrenbachs. Although these individuals could not be considered close relatives, they all belonged to the group that had originated in Geestendorf and its environs, a group that collectively might have facilitated the re-entry of a young newcomer into a broken-down South and a city all but destitute. But the young Bequest would no doubt have understood that he was joining a community that had experienced the full force of the war and the turmoil that wracked Charleston, and he likely did not expect to receive much in the way of assistance from them. In many ways, the young Bequest's conscious decision to come when he did suggests that he recognized the challenges he would face. With his experience of active participation in running the blockade for almost the entire four years of the war, he was in a unique position to perceive that the disastrous conditions in Charleston offered opportunity rather than despair. It was doubtless a combination of his youth and a kind of immigrant courage that led him to appreciate that the realities of the ended war had substantively changed the character of the host city that he already knew, and that there would be sufficient opportunity to enable him to begin a new chapter in his life in the soon-to-be-reconstructed Southern city by the sea. The lure of opportunity combined with the pull of the chain established by those who preceded him must have outweighed any inclination to seek his fortune in another location offering better economic prospects. It seems safe to say that Bernhard Heinrich Bequest's decision to leave Nassau and come to Charleston at this time signaled his intention to both become a citizen of the United States—which at that point had not formally been re-united, and which had barely begun the process of healing—and to capitalize on its new beginnings. His and his brothers' postbellum story is one that clearly reflects the changes that would affect the acculturation process of the city's German ethnic community.

Those changes would transform Charleston's German immigrants into what might accurately be termed *white* Charlestonians.

There was hardly time for any grass to grow under the feet of twenty-one-year-old Bernhard, former blockade runner returned to war-torn Charleston. An excise tax record for 1865 already shows "Bequest, Bernard" of Mount Pleasant, occupation "Retail Liquor Dealer" owing taxes of $25.00. On February 8, 1866, he and Gesine Rigbers were married at St. Matthew's German Lutheran Church. Gesine was his senior at age twenty-four. Whether they were already acquainted in Germany is not known, but in light of Bernhard's peripatetic whereabouts during the previous four years, it seems likely that they met first in Charleston. Her family was from Horstkamp-Delmenhorst / Oldenburg, a town not too distant from Geestendorf.

After their marriage in 1866, with both husband and wife in their early twenties, the couple would have been intent on surmounting the challenges Charleston presented less than a year after the war. Perhaps even before they were married they knew that Bernhard's seventeen-year-old younger brother, Johann Ludwig, had arrived in Baltimore in July, 1864—some six months before the end of the war—and would ultimately make his way to Charleston. Nine months after their marriage, the couple would welcome Bernhard's fifteen-year-old brother, Carsten August, to the Bequest fold. The latter arrived in Charleston on November 14, 1866.

Bernhard's early experiences as a blockade runner and businessman in the Bahamas would now stand him in good stead. True, there were the fellow Germans in the St. Matthew's congregation, and the couple's marriage indeed took place within that center of fellow congregants and family members. But as was suggested earlier, the couple could not expect to receive much assistance from the community of immigrants who had preceded them. The post-war period was distinctly different from the earlier antebellum context, and anyone settling in the broken-down city could not realistically expect help from the war's survivors who would have had little to give, constrained as they were by concerns for their own survival and rehabilitation.

The post-Civil War City of Charleston was indeed a unique host community: the Darwinian phrase "survival of the fittest" could have served as an apt descriptor of post-war life in Charleston, as well as a warning to any late-arriving immigrant planning to begin anew with the rubble that remained after the war. In May of 1865 General Sherman had visited Charleston and written: "Anyone who is not satisfied with war should go and see Charleston, and he will pray louder and deeper than ever that the country may in the long future be spared any more war." In September, a reporter from the North had toured Charleston and described it as "a city of ruins, of desolation, of vacant homes, of widowed women....of deserted warehouses, of weed-wild gardens, of miles of grass-grown streets."[5]

By 1866, however, things had begun to look up somewhat, and Bernhard Heinrich's vision of resurgent opportunity might well have had some basis in reality:

> [E]conomic stimulus came in 1866 when the City Council passed "an ordinance to aid in rebuilding the Burnt District and Waste places of the city of Charleston" by providing low-interest loans for citizens who agreed to build in brick. . . . George Williams cleared away ruins and demolished older structures along Church, Pinckney, Anson, and East Bay streets and built fifteen large cotton warehouses at a cost of about $100,000. The city banks clustered along Broad Street near the intersection with East Bay were renovated, but much activity focused on King Street, especially where the fire of 1861 had gutted buildings. The city's Episcopalians welcomed the return of the bells of St. Michael's, which had been sent to Columbia for safe-keeping. Upon surviving the fire there of 1865 they were sent to England for

---

5. Fraser, *Charleston! Charleston!*, 273 and 275.

CHAPTER 4: RECONSTRUCTED LIVES 61

recasting in their original molds and then recrossed the Atlantic to be placed in St. Michael's steeple in 1866.[6]

In any case, by July of 1868, Bequest purchased property in the rural village of Mount Pleasant, across the Cooper River to the east of the Charleston peninsula—a town that would later become a local resort for Charleston residents, reachable by ferry from the mainland. Mount Pleasant would be the Bequest's home until the early 1880s. The following November, almost exactly three years after his arrival, he was naturalized a U.S. citizen, aged twenty-three.[7] The 1870 Federal census shows the couple as inhabitants of "Christ Church Parish" (Mount Pleasant) in Charleston County, he listed with the anglicized name of "Benjamin," age twenty-five, a merchant; she, "Sarah", age twenty-two, "keeping house." Both are officially registered as of German birth, and the parents of both "of foreign birth." The value of their/his real estate is $1,200, with a personal estate valued at $500.[8]

It was probably logical that Bernhard Heinrich should set about to establish himself as a merchant operating a "store" of some kind, possibly identical to the one he had had in Nassau. That was what so many of the North German immigrants to Charleston had tried to do, that is, fit themselves into the occupational niche of merchant that the Charleston planter-dominated and slavery-dependent society had permitted newcomers to occupy. That had been the antebellum pattern, and now, with questionable conditions prevailing in the city itself, it

---

6. Fraser, 282.

7. The official naturalization record lists his birthdate as "abt 1845." Was he himself not certain of his birth date of December 20, 1844?

8. Less that their neighbors Claus Koeper ($3000), a merchant born in South Carolina, or Mr. Schlendorff ($1500), a merchant born in Germany, but twice as much as the South Carolina-born family of Samuel Middleton, a black bricklayer ($600).

would have been similarly prudent to merchandize something that everyone needed. Bequest's store, however, was not initially in Mount Pleasant proper, but rather in Charleston, on the corner of Calhoun and East Bay Streets, so that he must have been an early commuter, crossing to Charleston by boat from his residence "across the bay."

During these first few years, the elder brother Bernhard, trying to establish his own domestic and mercantile footing, would naturally also have been mentoring the two younger brothers who had followed him. As noted earlier, Johann—now John— had arrived in the port of Baltimore in July of 1864, and subsequently made his way to Charleston. Whether he intended to try his luck in the border state of Maryland or in Baltimore itself with its significant population of immigrant Germans is unclear. He is not verifiably in Mount Pleasant until the late 1870s, but in all likelihood was there much earlier than that. Several years into the future—not until 1883—John Bequest would marry Catherine Margarethe (Mary) Rigbers, the younger sister of Bernhard's wife Gesine. He thus had ample reason to be drawn to Mount Pleasant where his brother and future sister-in-law were in residence. He had arrived in Baltimore as a "seaman," and he would later find himself working in Charleston in a job that kept him close to his maritime roots. He was still a young twenty-eight-year-old when he was naturalized in October of 1875.

The youngest brother, Carsten August, had arrived in Charleston already in 1866, only one year after Bernhard. His initial residency in Charleston is likewise unattested. Perhaps both he and John resided with Bernhard and Gesine, although that does not seem likely since neither shows up in the household in the 1870 census just cited. A notice of mail awaiting him is in the Christmas Eve edition of the *Charleston Courier* in 1869, but we otherwise do not hear of him until the 1872 Charleston City Directory listed him working as a clerk with an address on King Street. The 1872 Directory information was likely furnished sometime in 1871, because by January of 1872 August Bequest had set himself up as a merchant in Abbeville, South Carolina, where he remained, despite several set-backs, until 1879.

CHAPTER 4: RECONSTRUCTED LIVES 63

Further investigation into what the elder Bernhard was *doing* to establish himself in Charleston during the first decade after the war reveals that he and Gesine were married only six years before she died in 1872 shortly after giving birth to a daughter, Theresa Louise.[9] After her death, Bernhard Heinrich did not remain a widower for very long. The following year on July 3, 1873, he married Catherine Mehrtens. According to the St. Matthew's church record, Catherine was eighteen—eleven years Bernhard's junior. She was from Südwede, a small village in the vicinity of Geestendorf, and a member of a family that had immigrated to Charleston prior to the war.

The Bequest family's domicile in Mount Pleasant is attested by several Charleston death records. A seventeen-month-old son, Henry L. (doubtless Heinrich *Ludwig*, after his uncle), died in 1878 of diphtheria, and a daughter, Anna Meta Adeline (likely named for Bernhard's cousin, Adeline Schroeder), born seven months later in 1878 died of scarlet fever before her third birthday. In Mount Pleasant, Bernhard Bequest became sufficiently established to be referred to as a "planter." The records at the Charleston Register of Mesne Conveyance show real estate transactions for Bernhard Bequest in Mount Pleasant from July 1867 through May of 1879, verifying him as a landowner for both personal and commercial purposes, with real estate of considerable value. One of his transactions was the sale of Mount Pleasant lots and other items to a fellow German, Otto F. Wieters. That transaction references him owning a grocery store known as the "Seven Mile Store on the Georgetown Road", as well as a grist mill and a sloop. He became a citizen of sufficient civic stature that he would serve the Mount Pleasant community for eleven years as a town councilman, and for the four years between 1876 and 1879 he held office as the town's *Intendant* or mayor. Throughout this extended period of residence in Mount Pleasant, the family remained a part of the St. Matthew's German

---

9. Theresa is the daughter referred to in the Capers account who later became the wife of John Henry Gieschen—not "John Gischen" as reported by Capers.

Lutheran congregation. It was not until the early 1880s that Bernhard and Catherine left the more rural Mount Pleasant location to move into the city proper, close to where he had operated his store on the corner of Calhoun and East Bay streets. The birthplace of the couple's one surviving child, John Frederick Bequest, born September 9, 1882, is given as "Charleston."

Bernhard Bequest's story as briefly outlined here leaves plenty of room for details—the daily pursuit of "health and happiness" as an immigrant to Charleston. While those immigrants who had come to Charleston during the years prior to the Civil War had to accommodate themselves to the peculiar institutions of the antebellum city, it is important to keep in mind that the first twelve years of the Bequest brothers' existence in the defeated South coincided with the complete revision of everyday life known as Reconstruction. By the time of Bernhard's arrival in late 1865, the efforts of the Federal government to re-unite the Confederate states with the Union had already begun. South Carolina was under U.S. military command. As noted earlier, a month before he came, a convention had met in Columbia and had drawn up the state's new Constitution—adopting its version of the Black Codes—and state offices in Charleston were closed and the government resettled in Columbia. Bernhard Bequest was going to try gain his footing in Charleston as a grocer and a farmer in Mount Pleasant at the same time South Carolina was going to be resurrected from its ashes. His beginnings after the war coincided with the implementation of Presidential Reconstruction, Andrew Johnson's questionable efforts to carry out what Lincoln had initiated with the emancipation proclamation. It might not have seemed the most propitious time to undertake a new beginning, but it clearly took the grit and mind-set of a young immigrant to read the deplorable conditions in evidence as a setting for opportunity awaiting action.

Whether he was prepared for it or not, Bernhard would have immediately confronted what historian Eric Foner termed "the most critical issue of the time"—the re-creation and management of the labor force under radically changed conditions:

The ferment in the countryside and ideologies and prejudices inherited from slavery together convinced the white South that coerced labor was necessary to resume the production of plantation staples. With their personal authority over blacks destroyed, planters turned to the state to reestablish labor discipline. Laws regarding labor, property rights, taxation, the administration of justice, and education all formed part of a broad effort to employ state power to shape the new social relations that would succeed slavery.[10]

The temper of the times as centered on the labor question, together with the enactment of the Black Codes by the convention in Columbia, signaled the character and the mood of the culture that Bernhard Bequest encountered. The numerous efforts throughout the South to suppress the rights of the emancipated black population were so mean and in violation of the reigning ideology of free labor that they went unenforced or were soon declared void. Foner proposes, nonetheless, that "the legal system of Presidential Reconstruction had profound consequences, limiting blacks' options, reinforcing whites' privileged access to economic resources, shielding planters from the full implications of emancipation, and inhibiting the development of a free market in land and labor."[11]

It would be inappropriate here to try to reconstruct a history of Reconstruction in Mt. Pleasant, in Charleston, or in South Carolina in order to assess the effects that each of those contexts might have had on the Bequest family as it moved through the post-war period. So much was in upheaval that it is difficult to note even the most significant sign-posts along the

---

10. Eric Foner, *A Short History of Reconstruction. 1863-1877* (New York: Harper & Row, 1990), 92.

11. Ibid., 97.

historical road that the Bequests and the other family members who had survived the war would have to travel. Nonetheless, the following timeline suggests how the course of Bequest family events (in **boldface**) intersected with local and, state, and national history:[12]

--1865: November 13; South Carolina ratifies the Thirteenth Amendment which freed the slaves.

--1866: February 8: **Bernhard Heinrich Bequest and Gesine Margarethe Rigbers marry.**

> *December 19*; South Carolina rejects the Fourteenth Amendment.
>
> *December 20*; Legislation passed to establish an immigration commissioner to encourage immigration of European whites to offset the black majority.

--1867: November 19-20: The first election to allow the freedmen to participate fully is held to elect state and local officials.

--1868: January 14 - March 18: A convention draws up the Constitution of 1868. The convention comprises seventy-six blacks and forty-eight whites.

> *June 2-3*: The first general election held under the Constitution of 1968.
>
> *July 9*: Francis L. Cardozo becomes the state's first black secretary of state.
>
> *July 9*: South Carolina ratifies the Fourteenth Amendment.

---

12. Excerpted and adapted from George C Rogers, Jr. and C. James Taylor, *A South Carolina Chronology, 1497-1992*, 2nd ed., 1994, 101-110.

November 3: Ulysses S. Grant elected president. South Carolina casts six electoral votes for him.

November 9: **Bernhard Heinrich Bequest becomes a naturalized citizen.**

--*1870*: U.S. Census (South Carolina): Whites: 289,667; blacks: 415,814; others: 125; Total: 705,606

> *February 1*: Jonathan Jasper Wright is the first black elected to the South Carolina Supreme Court, serving until his resignation December 1, 1877.
>
> *November 28*: Alonzo J. Ransier is the first black South Carolinian to be elected to the office of lieutenant governor.
>
> *December 12*: Representative Joseph H. Rainey is sworn in as the first black South Carolinian in the U.S. Congress.

--*1871: October 17*: President Ulysses S. Grant issues proclamation suspending the writ of habeas corpus in nine South Carolina counties.

December 24: Birth of Theresa Louise Bequest

--*1872: July 19*: **Death of Gesine Margarethe Bequest, née Rigbers**

> *November 5*: Ulysses S. Grant reelected president. South Carolina cast seven electoral votes for him.

--*1873*: **July 3: Bernhard Heinrich Bequest and Catherine Mehrtens marry.**

October 7: Henry E. Hayne enrolls as the first black student at the University of South Carolina.

--1876: April 19: Bernhard Heinrich Bequest is elected Intendant of Mount Pleasant, SC.

July 8: At least one white and four blacks are killed in a race riot in the industrial town of Hamburg, SC.

September 9: Birth of Bernhard Heinrich Ludwig Bequest

September 16 - 19: At least one white and about forty blacks are killed in race riots at Ellenton in Aiken County.

October 17: President Grant issues a proclamation to place federal troops at the call of Governor Chamberlain.

November: In South Carolina, the tempestuous and disputed gubernatorial election between the incumbent Chamberlain and Wade Hampton takes place. In the national election, Rutherford B. Hayes is elected president. South Carolina's seven electoral votes are disputed but eventually are counted for Hayes.

November 28: Federal troops occupy the State House in Columbia.

December 14: Wade Hampton, disputing Chamberlain's election, takes the oath of office as governor.

--1877: April 10: President Hayes orders federal troops withdrawn from Columbia. Chamberlain concedes the gubernatorial dispute, leaving Hampton as governor.

March 1: The General Assembly passes legislation to end public executions.

CHAPTER 4: RECONSTRUCTED LIVES   69

March: The University of South Carolina is divided into two branches: whites attend in Columbia, blacks in Orangeburg.

December 10: Wade Hampton is elected to the U.S. Senate.

--*1878: February 10*:   Death of Bernhard Heinrich Ludwig Bequest

***September 16*: Birth of Anna Meta Adeline Bequest**

--1879: April: Bernhard Heinrich Bequest's Intendancy of Mount Pleasant ends.

--1880: U. S. Census (South Carolina): White: 391,105; Black: 604,332; Other: 140; Total: 995,577

--*1881: April 19*: Death of Anna Meta Adeline Bequest

--*1882: September 9*:   Birth of John Frederick Bequest

Possibly another way to elucidate the challenges facing the Bequest brothers and other immigrants—both those who survived the war and those who came afterwards—is to garner from a mix of statements by historians of Reconstruction the complexity of the prevailing conditions during the period in which the Bequests and others were being initiated into South Carolina and Charleston life:

> First, . . . postwar conservatives continued to believe in white supremacy. Second, they still detested democratic, majoritarian rule, believing instead in elite (meaning themselves) and local rule over all, including over poor whites, for whom they often showed little regard. Third, postwar conservatives carried forward the

antebellum belief that history was a living force from which a society could not escape. Antebellum conservatives invoked the past as part of their justification for continued existence of slavery. Postwar conservatives similarly defended the reestablishment of elite rule as a reflection of a historically sanctioned fact of South Carolina society. Through their particular reading of the past, South Carolina's conservatives believed that history had destined them to remain on top of a hierarchical social order, whether slave or free.[13]

Many white Carolinians would continue fighting to regain this "way of life." Conventional warfare and guerilla operations were out of the question in 1865, but there were avenues of opposition, loopholes for exploitation. Under President Johnson's provisional government, conservative reconstruction took place within a legitimate system. After the establishment of Radical rule in 1868, disorganized, locally-based resistance appeared, along with trial-and-error attempts at cooperation, abstention, fraud, and economic intimidation in an effort to weaken the state Republican machine. Over the years violence grew more coherent, political, and widespread, and so did conservative politics and political opposition. White Carolinians grew more unified and deliberate, and their resistance became more

---

13. Charles J. Holden, *In the Great Maelstrom: Conservatives in Post-Civil War South Carolina* (Columbia: University of South Carolina Press, 2002), 2.

organized, directed, and effective. By 1876 resistance had evolved into war.[14]

In late winter 1867 the Congressional Reconstruction Acts imposed military rule on the South and required a non-racial franchise. Shortly thereafter the Union Republican Party was organized in Charleston. Now any lingering hopes whites had of regaining control over the freedmen were shattered. When a constitutional convention was held in the city during early 1868, over one-half of the delegates were black. This convention instituted universal male suffrage and when the first legislative session of 1868 convened, blacks were present as elected members of the state house of representatives and senate. General Edward Canby replaced Mayor Palmer Gaillard with a white military officer. In May thirteen of eighteen aldermen were also removed and seven of their appointed replacements were black. . . . Throughout the period, except for the years 1871-1873, half the seats in the city council were occupied by black men and Charleston blacks held other important elective and appointive offices at the local, state, and federal levels.[15]

In a sense South Carolina has always been the most extreme expression of southern sectionalism: secessionist when the rest of the South was trying to remold the Union in its image, Bourbon

---

14. Richard Zuczek, *State of Rebellion: Reconstruction in South Carolina* (Columbia: University of South Carolina Press, 1996), 4-5.

15. Bernard E. Powers, Jr., "Community Evolution and Race Relations in Reconstruction Charleston, South Carolina," *The South Carolina Historical Magazine*, 101, no.3 (July 2000), 217-18.

restorationist when the rest of the south was trying to find an accommodation between the antebellum and postbellum worlds, militantly segregationist when all but the most retrograde southern states were seeking to accommodate themselves to new winds (often with the minimum amount of change but still to accommodate).[16]

After the bloody fighting ended, General Daniel E. Sickles, in September 1865, was placed in charge of conquered South Carolina. Ferdinand Gregorie, intendant of Mount Pleasant and warden of Christ Church, had to "surrender" the village to the General, who made his headquarters in Charleston. Negro troops were stationed in Christ Church Parish, supposedly to keep order. A company of Negro cavalry used Christ Church as a stable, and the church was wrecked. Doors, windows, pews, and pulpit were burned in camp fires; and it is said that the tablets of the Lord's prayer and the ten commandments on the walls beside the chancel were torn down and were seen by a horrified parishioner as part of a pig sty.[17]

The darkest days of Reconstruction were now in progress. Federal troops still occupied South Carolina, and poverty was the general lot of its people. So poor were the members of Mr. Gadsden's congregation that the vestry in 1870 informed him that a salary of $400 a year, and the

---

16. Cole Blease Graham, Jr., *South Carolina Politics and Government* (Lincoln: University of Nebraska Press, 1994), xxv.

17. Anne King Gregorie, *Christ Church, 1706-1959: A Plantation Parish of the South Carolina Establishment* (Charleston: Dalcho Historical Society, 1961), 111-12.

CHAPTER 4: RECONSTRUCTED LIVES   73

parsonage rent free, was "the utmost that the Vestry could do this year." In the autumn the vestry went further and requested him to discontinue the ancient practice of collecting alms from the whole congregation on Communion Sundays. Three years later the good rector's annual salary was reduced to $300, and all too frequently even the meagre stipend was not paid promptly. As he said of his flock, "There is here a nucleus of Episcopal families which is the steadfast element of the Parish. But our work is largely that of a Missionary in Mount Pleasant, . . . preaching the Gospel to the poor."[18]

Out of a voting population of 75,000 (white males) South Carolina supplied 71,000 soldiers for the war. Of these, 30,000 died in action or from wounds. No Northern state suffered such a percentage of loss of manpower. Last of all, and most significant, 400,000 slaves in South Carolina were set free. From March to June of 1865, thousands of former slaves deserted the Lowcountry plantations and streamed into Charleston to celebrate their new freedom. Within a few years there were 4,000 more blacks than whites in Charleston, living in filthy, miserable shanties along the waterfront. After the war, there were four million Negroes in the South, mostly uneducated. In South Carolina there were 415,000 Negroes and 290,000 whites. In Charleston County, the ratio of black to white was

---

18. Gregorie, 115.

2 to 1. There were only nine counties in the state with a white majority, all of them in the upstate.[19]

There were 124 delegates to the 1868 Constitutional Convention. Seventy-three were black. Of the fifty-one white delegates, thirty-six were native-born and fifteen were Yankee interlopers. Of the thirty-one members of the Senate, ten were black. In the House, seventy-eight out of 124 were Negroes. Blacks enjoyed the majority in the South Carolina House until 1874. Only twenty-three of the whites were Southern born. The rest were carpetbaggers. The Republican-led legislature from 1868 to 1877 was more famous for its corruption than its accomplishments. There was much buying and selling of votes.[20]

South Carolina set the pattern in 1866. The German-born Confederate general John A. Wagener planned the state's immigration movement and served as commissioner of immigration. The legislature enacted a law protecting immigrants disembarking at Charleston. At a meeting in 1867 in the hall of the Bruderliche Bund, Charleston's foreign born endorsed the state program. Although Wagener's agents were active in Germany and Scandinavia, their efforts were abortive. Most of a party of 152 who arrived in 1867 aboard a German bark soon

---

19. Mark R. Jones, *Wicked Charleston, Volume 2: Prostitutes, Politics, and Prohibition* (Charleston: The History Press, 2006), 29.

20. Jones, 33.

CHAPTER 4: RECONSTRUCTED LIVES   75

left the state. When the Radical government abolished the commissioner's office in 1868, only four hundred persons had been brought in.[21]

The campaign to develop southern economy on a base of white immigrant labor failed in two ways. First, of the millions of Europeans who came to the United States between 1865 and 1914, only an incidental number entered the South. Second, the economic interests which hoped to profit from immigrant laborers or land buyers never reconciled most of the southern people to an influx of foreigners. In fact, Southerners, though they had little experience with immigrants, in this period became as outspoken xenophobes as those old-stock Northerners who objected to the masses of foreigners actually in their midst.

Although nativism did not become a prime issue in the post-Civil War South until after 1900, Southerners were predisposed to distrust outsiders. The long history of uneasy relations between whites and Negroes made "racial" distinctions axiomatic. For a century before 1860 white Southerners had incorporated little new blood or unfamiliar culture; they were ethnically more homogeneous than the mixed northern population. Colonial Huguenots, Scots, and Germans having long since been absorbed and their distinctiveness forgotten, southern whites prided themselves on the purity of their Anglo-Saxon heritage.[22]

---

21. Rowland T. Berthoff, "Southern Attitudes toward Immigration, *The Journal of Southern History* 17, no.3 (August, 1951), 336-37.

22. Berthoff, 343.

Along with the physical destruction was almost total economic destruction at war's end. Every bank in Charleston had lost its capital assets, many industries had been destroyed, and much of the Southern railroad system was ruined. Charleston's economy was so depressed that only a small number of people were able to secure work to support themselves. The vast majority of both black and white Charlestonians were unemployed and suffering. In this labor market, where demand had so drastically decreased, whites whose wealth had disappeared with the war competed with blacks for jobs they would previously have disdained, or else they survived on government rations.[23]

Nevertheless, the black migration had a significant effect on the population of Charleston, which increased from 40,467 in 1860 to 48,956 by 1870. Rural black migrants accounted for nearly all the increase, transforming Charleston's black population into a clear majority. There had been only 17,146 blacks in the city in 1860, but their numbers had grown to 26,173 by 1870. While the black population spiraled upward, the white population actually declined, from 23,321 in 1860 to 22,749 in 1870.[24]

---

23. Wilbert L. Jenkins, *Seizing the New Day: African Americans in Post-Civil War Charleston* (Bloomington: Indiana University Press, 1998), 47.

24. Jenkins, 48.

Although in the early 1870s it seemed as if Charleston's economy might gradually recover, a worldwide depression had a devastating impact on Charleston's weak economy that would last until 1896. Capital in the city's banks, which had totaled almost twelve million dollars in 1860, declined to less than four million dollars by election day in 1872. Moreover, in 1873 some thirty-eight firms collapsed, and payments were suspended by three of the city's four state banks. The "crash" of 1873 proved to be a financial nightmare for both black and white Charlestonians. The following year brought additional financial hardships, as sixty businesses in Charleston collapsed, and the Broad Street office of the National Freedmen's Savings Bank folded and ultimately closed its doors after its parent bank in Washington, D.C., failed. The fifty-three hundred blacks and two hundred whites who had deposited their money in the bank were informed of the bank's collapse and were understandably shocked to learn that they would not get back the modest savings they had invested there.[25]

On all accounts, these were not ordinary times, and for the immigrant, doubly difficult. By the time Bernhard and Catherine Bequest's one surviving child was born, the period known as Reconstruction—generally understood to have run from 1865 to 1877—was over. Had they been privileged to a larger perspective, they could claim that they had survived the most tumultuous decade in South Carolina and Charleston's history. It is thus fair to ask: "How had the immigrant Bernhard Bequest come this far?" "What had he actually *done*?"

---

25. Jenkins, 159.

Well, he had been busy. For one thing, he had wasted no time in getting involved with the German movers and shakers who had founded the *Deutsche Schützen-Gesellschaft* (German Rifle Club) just ten years earlier. Recognized as the oldest rifle club in the United States, the Charleston club was founded in 1855 by a small group led by two members of the triumvirate referred to in chapter 2, John Andreas Wagener as President, with Franz Adolph Melchers as Secretary. Wagener led the club until he resigned in 1867; Melchers assumed the leadership in April of that year.

In his last presidential address to his fellow countrymen in January 1867, Wagener recounted the history of the German rifle club tradition going back to the year 1286 in Silesia, emphasizing that "the rifle clubs of our old fatherland were protectors of the citizens, were allowed, at least during their festivities, to wear uniforms, served in emergencies as a paramilitary police force, elected their own leaders and officers, and during shooting activities exercised legal and executive power over their membership.[26] The club's constitution was revised in 1868 and again in 1872, and sets forth in thoroughgoing detail the obligations of the officers in their respective capacities, the responsibilities and expectations—financial and behavioral—of the members, the rules of order, schedule, and language (only German) for meetings, etc. The German Rifle Club was thus a German society unto itself within the larger Charleston society. It allowed the immigrant and his family to maintain something of their heritage in what at times must have seemed like an alien world. Bernhard Bequest, aged twenty-three, was admitted as a member on April 3, 1868, joining his close-knit fellow immigrants just seven months before he became a U.S. citizen. The rifle club

---

26. "Die Schützengesellschaften in unserm alten Vaterlande bilden eine Art Bürgergarde, sind im Nothfalle zum Polizeimilitärdienst verpflichtet, dürfen, wenigstens bei Festschießen, Uniform tragen, sich ihre Führer und Officiere erwählen, und haben für die Gesellschaften während der Dauer des Schießens und auf die öffentlichen Schießstände beschränkte gesetzgebende und executive Gewalt." *Verfassung der Deutsche Schützen-Gesellschaft in Charleston, Süd-Carolina. Gegründet am 21. Mai 1855. Gesetze revidiert Mai 1868 und Januar 1872* (Charleston, 1872).

in Charleston would become a cornerstone in his life, a center and nexus of social relationships that would sustain him throughout his career in Charleston.

Thus comfortably embraced within the fold, the recently-married Bernhard was working to keep his home in Mount Pleasant and his grocery store in Charleston going. In June of 1868, with only his earlier declaration of intent to become a citizen registered, he was called for jury duty in Charleston by the Court of General Sessions and Common Pleas. His officially acquired citizenship in November of 1868 would thereafter provide a patently secure footing for his business and civic activities and telegraphed his intentions to function productively in the host society. As previously noted, even before he was naturalized he had purchased in July of 1868 a lot in Mount Pleasant. It is interesting to note that the legal document recording the transfer shows that he was using the names "Benjamin" and "Bernhard" interchangeably, and that it was "H. C. Knee" who witnessed the transaction before the notary public. The witness was in fact Johann Rosenbohm's brother-in-law, Hermann Knee, who had been in Charleston since the mid-1830s. He had acquired and occupied the Rosenbohm house on Church Street, and by this point was a well-regarded member of the German ethnic community. Clearly, the young Bequest couple had access to the Rosenbohm-related clan who had preceded them. In the following month of August, the *Charleston Daily News* carried notice of a Sheriff's Sale of various properties to be disposed of on September 7, one of which was a "lot of land, with the buildings and other improvements thereon, situate on Bennett-street, Mount Pleasant, measuring one hundred and seven (107) feet front, by one hundred and twenty-five (125) feet deep, more or less. Levied on and to be sold as the property of W. T. Pearce at the suit of B. H. Bequest." Subsequent notices of the Sheriff's Sale of the same property indicate that the purchase was postponed, and it is likely that Bequest never obtained the property—it was never recorded in the Register of Mesne Conveyance in Charleston. Bequest's "suit", nonetheless, makes it clear that he was actively engaged in acquiring property and had the means to do so.

By April of 1869, the *Daily News* was running the following advertisement: "A chance for excursion and picnic parties, target companies, etc.—The subscriber offers his Hall, at Hilliardville[27] to Excursion and Picnic Parties, and visitors generally. The accommodations are ample, and the Hall large and well ventilated. A target has been erected on the grounds for the benefit of those wishing to practice. For terms apply to D. [*sic*] H. Bequest, Mt. Pleasant." It is unclear from the newspaper advertisement exactly what property this involves, and it is questionable whether Bequest was "the subscriber" or only acting as a kind of rental agent. Nonetheless, his activity in this regard shows this new German American actively engaged in both his local and ethnic communities. By June of 1870, the Federal census recorded "Benjamin" and "Sarah," using what would have been considered "American" names, as residents in Mount Pleasant, living between Mr. and Mrs. Schlendorff and a bachelor, Eli Englemann[28]—fellow German neighbors.

Five years after the war and during the first half of the Reconstruction decade, under the duress of labor inadequacy and the enactment of lien laws, property was readily available and relatively inexpensive to all but the emancipated. For the German immigrant, ownership of land would have been a driving force and a means of achieving a status only imagined in the homeland. There and here, the "propertied" were the people who mattered. In February 1871, "B. H." Bequest bought more property, this time a 63' x 200' parcel on Pitt Street in Mount Pleasant belonging to a neighbor that extended and butted on his own property. For this

---

27. Adjacent to Mount Pleasant, the village of Hilliardville was planned in 1847 by Charles Jugnot and Oliver Hilliard. This area included the picnic ground of the popular Alhambra Hall. Hilliardville was incorporated into the Town of Mount Pleasant in 1858.

28. 1870 Federal census, enumerated without an exact address. The neighbor "Eli" is likely Eike Englemann who married another Rigbers sister, Anna Margaretha. John Bequest was one of the sponsors at the baptism of that couple's son at St. Matthew's in 1872.

transaction, Bequest did not have to rely on a fellow German: he was sufficiently established that he could call on a close Mount Pleasant, native-born neighbor, Henry Lofton, to serve as witness to the real estate transaction.

Two months later, for whatever purpose, the Bequests were financially stable enough that "Benjamin"/Bernhard could travel to New York City aboard the Steamship *Champion*, captained by Robert Lockwood of blockade runner *Margaret and Jessie* fame. "Sarah"/Gesine did not accompany him[29]—perhaps because she was pregnant with their daughter Theresa Louise Adeline, born eight months later on Christmas Eve, 1871. The 1872 Charleston City Directory lists the grocer Bequest and his store at the "E. corner Calhoun and East Bay." As noted earlier, his brother August (now twenty, with his first name Carsten already dropped) is employed as a clerk, likely in his brother Bernhard's store, living at 470 King Street.

If, despite the unsettledness of South Carolina's radicalized political, social, and economic re-construction, things were going well up to this point, Charleston life took a cruel turn with Gesine's death in July of 1872. At this point, Bernhard is twenty-eight, with a seven-month-old child, living in Mount Pleasant and commuting by ferry to run his grocery store in the city. However he managed to care for Theresa Louise (with the help of his bachelor brothers, neighbors, near-relatives, acquaintances, a freedwoman servant?), he kept his life together until he married Catherine Mehrtens less than a year later on July 3, 1873. The widowed Bernhard had probably known Catherine Mehrtens for some time. She was the daughter of Heinrich Mehrtens, likely the "H. Mehrtens" who was an officer in the German Rifle Club already in 1856.[30] After Bernhard's acceptance into the group in 1868, the elder Mehrtens would have

---

29 She, "Mrs. B. Bequest", had travelled to New York on the steamship *Saragossa* in June of 1869.

30. The 1920 Federal Census record for Catherine as the widow of B. H. Bequest indicates the year of her immigration as 1855.

been a fellow Rifle Club member whose family and daughter the widower would have had opportunity to meet and know. Together, the newly married Catherine and Bernhard—she ten years younger than he—would weather Charleston's and Mount Pleasant's last quarter of the nineteenth century.

Looking back at Capers' brief biographical account, Bernhard purportedly participated in the civic life of Mount Pleasant from the very beginning—as a councilman for eleven years and four as its mayor. Apparently it made no difference in his early civic involvement that he had not yet been naturalized. His blockade-running experiences would have seemed to his neighbors to bestow on him the aura of a southern patriot; he was young but obviously more than a neophyte; and to Mount Pleasant's bedraggled survivors of the war, he promised to be the new blood that the town could welcome.

A sense of what life was like in the small island village at that time can be culled from a letter written by Henry Slade Tew to his daughter in February 1865. Henry Tew was a storekeeper and the Intendant of Mount Pleasant from 1868 to 1870. Three mayors would serve the town between Henry Tew and Bernhard Bequest, but the character of the town changed more slowly than mayoral incumbents. The February letter was written to Emily Jenkins Tew approximately eight months before young Bequest arrived in Charleston and gives an account of the occupation of Mount Pleasant by Union troops. The passages excerpted below provide an inside view to the general sensibilities of the time and describe what Bernhard Bequest would accommodate himself to when he settled in Mount Pleasant.

> Dear Daughter,
> Your absence from home at the time of the evacuation by our troops and the taking possession of those of the U.S. was a great relief to our minds, as our apprehension of insults and violence had been excited by the reports of such conduct elsewhere, and I have prepared this narrative or sort of diary to put you in possession of such facts as transpired and in some of which I

CHAPTER 4: RECONSTRUCTED LIVES

was an actor, as may prove of interest to you at some future time may be referred to as part of the history of these eventful times. . . .

While these scenes were transpiring over here, those of Charleston must have beggared description,—to us was visible only the awful magnificence of the scene, while the terror, confusion, suffering and crime must have been appalling to the dwellers in the doomed city. The burning buildings public and private the repeated explosions, the gun boats and other vessels burning in the harbor all presented such a scene as but few ever witness in a lifetime, and surely one which none would ever desire to see repeated. Oh God! What a night of horror that memorable 17th of February was. . . .

About 12 o'clock Saturday three barges landed from the fleet and as I had been elected Intendant by the people on Friday, in that official capacity attended by some of the citizens I surrendered the town submitting to the military authority of the U.S. and was promised protection to persons and private property. The boats were commanded by Lieut. Gifford from the Flagship—they brought a small U.S. Flag ashore and hoisted it for a while on the Light house. The officers were courteous and the men quite peaceful. Many from the fleet were ashore on Saturday and Sunday but we had not yet seen any from the Army from whom we feared violence and insult. All our own blacks boisterous in their reception of the visitors but none that I am aware of had yet left their work or homes. Monday 20th we heard that the troops that had landed at Bull's Bay were marching down and about 11 o'clock the shouts of the negroes apprised us of their arrival. There were three regiments of U.S. colored troops all under the command of Col. A. S. Hartwell, who took his quarters temporarily at the light house. I called on him, told him my name and position and asked protection for the persons and property of the citizens who were mostly women and children and were greatly apprehensive at the presence of the coloured troops. . . .

Colonel Hartwell then entered into conversation with me, asked me if I was connected with the Tews of Rhode Island, and if I was favorable to secession, as he had received so many assurances from people that they were not, that he was at a loss what to think and could only judge by the manner and not the language. I told him I would reply with the upmost frankness, that if more than one man in South Carolina out of Fifty told him he had opposed secession they lied, and that for myself, tho a Union man in 1832 and in 1850, yet on the election of Mr. Lincoln I thought all hope of justice to the South in the Union was lost, and I went for secession with vote and voice. He thanked me for the frankness of my reply and said it would be better if all would be equally so. . . .

Many of the negroes from the Plantations came down in the Army train, and together with those of the village made quite a multitude of shouting wild creatures whom the thought of freedom had changed from quiet to transports of uproarious joy. I must tell you what I did for my own. A few days before I gave them $50.00 told them the money would soon be worth nothing and advised them to buy whatever they could then. I also told them that when the troops came they knew they were free to go or stay as they pleased—if they stayed, as long as I had anything to eat they should share as they always had done—Not one answered a word, and I knew of course they would go—they stayed however until Wednesday and then went off without a word of leave taking—Sary setting the example—Louis is gone also, Margaret and Zoe are still here as Elisa is with William and forbids their leaving, but I suppose they will not stay long. . . .

When orders came for the Brig. to move to the City and they left us with only six men as a guard and our negroes noisy, stealing all they could lay hands on and moving into the houses that were vacant. It was a sleepless night to us. We all sat up till 4 o'clock. Wednesday was a quiet day. . . .

March 1

The 52nd Regt. Major Hennessy Com'g now garrison Mount Pleasant. Headquarters are now established at Mr. Whilden's house and the proximity to our own dwelling is the best guaranty we can have of quiet and order. The commander seems to be determined to enforce order and maintains stricter military discipline than we have ever had over here before from the troops of *either* army. He does not appear to have much sympathy or regard for the blacks, at least he does not place them above the whites and make all claims and interest subservient to theirs. . . .

On Sunday 19th went to Church and in the pew before us was a mulatto girl with a white soldier—we heard he married her Saturday 25th. Attended the funeral of Sally Venning and on Sunday 26th that of little Eddy Royall who died of measles. The whole five of Mr. Royall's children having been taken at one time. On that Sunday the Episcopal Church was taken possession of by negro troops. Their regiment is commanded by Col. Beecher the brother of H. Ward Beecher and Mrs. H. B. Stowe, and we hear that his wife who is with him declines all acquaintance with the whites, but has called upon the colored ladies and invited them to her quarters—from this time forth until matters are settled I suppose that the Church is to be abandoned by the whites, as no one will care to subject themselves to the annoyance of having a colored gentleman or lady perhaps both walking into your pew and overpowering you with their odor or filling you with vermin.[31]

The idiosyncrasies of life in Mount Pleasant in 1865 resonate with the biases, antipathies, and prejudices endemic in the South when the end of the war left a vanquished people feeling their way out of chaos and not quite used to the new rules of order. For an immigrant such as Bequest it would have been a case of new rules twice over, although with his blockade-running past he must have had a good idea of what he was getting into. If the new order called for accommodation, he was up for it: in truth, he had little choice if this was to be his new home.

Young Bernhard Bequest actually ran for the office of Warden in the Mount Pleasant election in November 1868 when Henry Tew was elected as Intendant. In the *Charleston Daily News* report of the election results (November 13, 1868), he was one of eleven candidates for Warden: six were reported as Democrats, four were reported as Republicans and colored, and Bequest was reported as "white" and Republican. He received one vote. The following day, the newspaper ran a retraction: "MOUNT PLEASANT.—We are requested to say that the statement in the report of the Mount Pleasant election, published in our last issue, that Mr. Bequest is a Republican, is wholly incorrect."[32] The six democrats had run away with the votes, the colored Republicans—

---

31. Anonymous, "An Eye Witness Account of the Occupation of Mt. Pleasant: February 1865," *The South Carolina Historical Magazine* 66, no. 1 (January 1965), 8-14.

32. "Local Matters," *Charleston Daily News*, November 14, 1868.

doubtless "radical" reconstructionists—were defeated, and the white immigrant with a mistaken political affiliation learned something of a lesson about playing in Reconstruction politics.[33] In the next election in 1870 he did much better, tying with George Kinloch for the second highest number of votes (127) of the six wardens elected. The *Charleston Daily News* of September 13 reported that "the election passed off quietly. The parties chosen were all Reformers except the last" (S. Robertson with one vote). Running as a Reformer was obviously preferable to running as a Republican.

His 1868 political defeat was likely minimally disappointing to Bernhard, hardly any damper on his election as a member of the German Rifle Club the previous April. On the whole, 1868 would turn out to be something of a banner year for Bequest as well as the Rifle Club. Because of the war, the annual "Schützenfest" had not been held for eight years. Finally in May of 1868, a month after Bequest was voted in as an active member, the Club, with permission from Washington, again put on its festival, and the German sharpshooters paraded in full complement down the streets of Charleston amidst the acclamation of the crowds and the lively strains of the music.[34] Participating in the activities of the German Rifle Club would constitute a focus of Bernhard's social life—actually define him within the German community—enable him to establish himself as a Charleston businessman and to evolve from his immigrant status into a Charlestonian of German heritage.

The annual spring Schützenfest of the German Rifle Club had become a major event for Charleston's inhabitants. Effusive praise was the topic of the two-column article on the front page of the *Daily News* of May 8, 1869:

---

33. And Capers' "eleven years as councilman" is brought into question.

34. "...paradirten in voller Anzahl, unter dem Jubel der Bevölkerung und den rauschenden Klängen der Musik durch die Straßen Charlestons." Quoted from Alexander Melchers' 1872 address to the membership, printed in the 1872 edition of the club's constitution.

The fact that yesterday would be the concluding day of the Schuetzenfest, drew together the largest crowd that has ever been seen at the Platz. The trains, omnibuses, private and public vehicles were tasked to the utmost to convey the immense number of visitors. These were not confined to the Teutonic element. All nationalities and all classes flocked to the gay scene to enjoy the occasion, and witness or participate in its joys and amusements. The city was deserted; many stores were closed, and avenues of trade were as still and quiet as on Sunday.

The morning was spent in various pastimes; the Saengerbund and the Teutonia societies sang; the Turners, adult and juvenile, contorted themselves into indescribable shapes; the music of the band and the harps filled the air with delightful sounds, and even the quivering leaves on the overarching branches were inclined to put on airs. About midday the grounds began to fill up rapidly. Every effort was made to cause the last day to be an epoch in the history of the Charleston Schuetzen. Sugar eating, milk feeding, sack racing, greasy pole climbing, mill walking, and sliding on the waterfall caused dense masses to congregate wherever these sports were in process. The greasy poll [sic] was successfully climbed by a white boy, who cleaned the hoop of its prizes as he did last year.

The very best spirit prevailed, and all seemed to enjoy themselves. It would be unwise even to guess at the amount of lager consumed. Kegs and barrels were emptied and replaced, and these again ran dry. Yet, to the honor of the Schuetzen be it said, there was not one riotous person on the ground. So much for lager, with our good Germans to drink it. No unpleasant incident jarred the harmonies of the day. The participants were all too good humored to get vexed with anybody. In the matter of courtesy, the German hosts were masters of the situation, and dispensed their heartfelt hospitality in a free and whole-souled manner.

The shooting ceased at four o'clock, and a brass howitzer made the fact known in stentorius tones. The committee immediately set to work making out the prize list. It was completed by half-past 5 o'clock, when there was a general assembling around the tribune, where the Saengerbund and the Teutonia and their visiting friends sang a parting song as a prelude to the general distribution of prizes.

Captain Melchers then introduced Professor H. D. Meier. . . . Professor Meier delivered an eloquent address in German, speaking of the festival and the glory of the occasion, and the success that had attended it from beginning to end. He continued for some time in his usually impassioned strain, passing in review the main and incidental features of the festival, not forgetting some handsome allusions to the visiting Schützen, He was frequently and loudly applauded. Filling the Schützen horn, which can hold two bottles of wine, he drank to the health of the King. He then addressed the masses in English, and said he regretted he could not speak that language as fluently as he would like, and give expression to the sentiments that filled his heart. He thanked the people of Charleston for the generous support they had given the festival. They had sustained it in a manner that would never be forgotten. He was glad to meet Germans from all parts of the country under one banner, but the best banner to him was the banner of "free labor."

Commentary on this report might be saved for a later discussion, but it should surely be noted that B. H. Bequest was awarded one of the "Eagle" prizes, a "China tea set from Washington, D.C." After this, no one would be surprised that at every annual Schützenfest B. H. Bequest would be one of the prizewinners: he was one of the sharpest of the German sharpshooters, taking prizes not only in the "target shooting" category, but also the "Eagle" ceremony in which specific parts of the spread-eagled target were shot off with precision. It was his talent with the rifle that earned him the first prize at the 1871 Schützenfest when he became its King for the following year.

If German men were the heroes of the annual Schützenfest, it was the members of the German Ladies' Society who played an equally important social role in the ethnic community. The *Charleston News* report on "The German Fair" put on by the Ladies' Society says a lot about how the Germans were regarded by others in Charleston at the time.

> THE GERMAN FAIR / A TRIUMPH OF TASTE AND SKILL...: The sterling worth and unselfish feeling of the German citizens of Charleston are always displayed to best advantage when charity or religion appeals to the hearts which beat so warmly for God and Fatherland. They are thorough in their amusements. There is no lackadaisical enjoyment in the gala doings of the German. But when the religion of their fathers calls upon them for help and aid, their serious souls are stirred to the depths, and they labor with a zeal and devotion which no people can surpass; Happily, however, the Germans do not deem it necessary to be lugubrious because the object of their work is solemn and severe. They wreathe the garlands of innocent gaiety around the pillars of the Temple of Duty, and light up the stern

responsibilities of life with the sunny splendor of their smile. No worthy German calls upon a German and meets with a rebuff. The German, it is true, has no patience in dealing with the drone and laggard; but undeserved misfortune and unavoidable affliction claim and receive that substantial sympathy which finds expression in act more than in word. The Germans are always staunch and true, and never have their finest qualities been shown to better advantage than in the Fair of the German Ladies' Society, whose triumphant opening we chronicle today. The object of the Fair, we need hardly add, is to obtain the means of completing the new German Lutheran Church in King Street, whose tower already rears its head above the neighboring buildings.

After a lengthy description of the new St. Matthew's Church, the offerings at the fair are described in considerable detail, each table's wares sequentially portrayed as more desirable than the preceding one. Table No. 5, for example, is "under the management of Mrs. Fischer and Mrs. Bequest, assisted by Mrs. Lilienthal and Mrs. Wagener," confirming that Gesine Bequest had taken a place in the church community equal to the one her husband was acquiring in the Rifle Club. The newspaper reporter concluded that

> the opening night of the Fair of the German Ladies' Society was successful beyond expectations, but we desire to see the fair more fully attended by the general public. The Germans of Charleston are never backward in giving their help to any measure which is for the good of the community, and it is due to them that the people at large should assist them in erecting a building which is necessary for the religious accommodation of a large body of our most

valuable citizens and will be, besides, an ornament to Charleston.[35]

While it is generally agreed that it is bad form to judge the past by standards of the present, it is difficult to overlook the fact that it was indeed *judgment* that was being passed by the newspaper reporter and, indirectly, by the editor.[36] Charleston and its ruling class have not infrequently been accused of being paternalistic, and there is no lack of that in the passages cited above: "They" are a separate entity from "Us," viewed and judged from a distance, as if the viewer in the center is looking at something on the periphery, ready and able to comment on "them," "the Germans," "their serious souls," "the sunny splendor of their smile," "their finest qualities," "our most valuable citizens." Obviously, the "Germans" had for some time been making a very good impression on the natives, but even though "they" were trying so hard to become well-behaved and "valuable" members of the community, the latter would still keep them just a little marginalized—for yet a while.

The effort to navigate the waters between the margin occupied by the immigrant and the center where the native-born and the acculturated lived had begun almost a quarter of a century earlier when immigrant numbers had increased to the point that they were recognizable as a *group*. We can understand that the seemingly frenetic activity on the part of John A. Wagener was an

---

35. *The Charleston News*, Tuesday, November 1, 1870.

36. The editor by this time was the Englishman Francis Warrington Dawson. According to a brief summary about the *Charleston Daily News* (*Chronicling America: Historic American Newspapers*) Dawson, along with Bartholomew Riordan, had bought the paper in 1867. As its outspoken editor, Dawson "castigated and cheered developments in South Carolina. He argued that the state's reliance on cash crops like cotton had left its economy too vulnerable to forces beyond its control. He championed manufacturing and immigration and encouraged business and community leaders to diversify their local economies and invest in railroads. He fiercely criticized the Republican-dominated Reconstruction-era government for its perceived corruptness and ineffectiveness."

effort by an individual with leadership abilities to organize and assist what had become an immigrant *community*. The clubs and societies served to meld individuals into a mutually supportive body, the newspaper facilitated communication and offered helpful guidance, and a German fire company provided a sense of security within the context of an already overtaxed civic "service" and signaled the immigrants' willingness to contribute to the well-being of the larger community. That by 1840 Wagener should lead his community to establish a *German* Lutheran Church, however, speaks to a substantive need of the immigrant Germans and reveals something of the process by which they came to play such an important role in the life of the city. Founding a new church was an effort of great significance that extended to the entire ethnic community. Establishing St. Matthew's German Lutheran Church had meaning beyond an additional "accomplishment" to be credited to Wagener's leadership skills.

Looking back to those earlier days, it was natural enough that the growing German immigrant community in Charleston would expect to be able to practice their own religious traditions in their adoptive homeland. They were, after all, Protestants moving into what was uncontestedly a Protestant community: the United States as a whole, in fact, could consider itself a Protestant country, settled from its very beginnings by Europeans of every description seeking religious freedoms derived from the Reformation and separation from the Church of Rome. Those coming to Charleston in the nineteenth century came into a Protestant city dominated by a long-established Episcopal heritage. They would know, of course, that there was already a Lutheran church—St. John's—whose minister, John Bachman, was a New Yorker born to German parents and whose ministry at St. John's would last for almost sixty years—from 1815 to 1874. He had early on become a popular and much admired figure in the Charleston community, and his church would become known locally as the *English* Lutheran church.[37] For the immigrants

---

37. St. John's was earlier known as "the German Lutheran Church," its congregation populated predominantly by Colonial-era German immigrants. It

arriving after Bachman had begun his ministry, the English-based services would not have been all that accessible to those speaking *Platt,* nor would the esteemed civic figure have been the individual the majority of these Germans could readily identify as their religious leader.

It is admittedly beyond the scope of this volume to trace the history of Lutheranism in South Carolina: suffice it say that from its beginnings in the seventeenth century it was anything but the result of a clear and carefully planned mission to establish congregations adhering to a unified confessional body. For years it was nothing but small groups of heterogeneous believers scattered about the hinterlands, served by itinerant pastors who might or might not be trained adequately for their work. Trained and educated pastors rarely accompanied the emigrating group, the clergy unwilling to take on the hardships and penurious rewards in exchange for the more comfortable circumstances they enjoyed in their home community. Such itinerant ministers as were available, as well as the disparate flocks they served, could be *Lutheran* or *Reformed* or *Calvinistic*—however much or little those distinctions might have mattered at the time and in those

---

called a German, Jacob Eckhard, to be the organist in 1786, and "doubtless at his instigation, a new hymnal in German was obtained for the congregation, 'likewise a *Choralbuch.*'" Eckhard later became organist at Charleston's St. Michael's Episcopal Church, but "maintained a lively interest in St. John's and remained a member of the corporation until his death. He was appointed to a committee to obtain a new English hymnal for the use of the church in 1809." (George W. Williams, *Jacob Eckhard's Choirmaster's Book of 1809* [Columbia: University of South Carolina Press, 1971], xi-xiii.) The 1809 date for introducing the English hymnal suggests how subsequently the congregation would be known as the *English* Lutheran Church. Bachman was instrumental in forming in 1819 a society for securing and distributing tracts and books among members of the congregation—"The Tract and Book Society of the Lutheran Church of German Protestants, of Charleston, South Carolina, for the Dissemination of Useful Religious Knowledge." Thus while the congregation was constituted for some time primarily of German Protestants, its services and Bachman's ministry were conducted in English. Bachman's "English" ministry enabled him to begin his "notable ministry to the Negro population in Charleston" the year after he accepted the call of St. John's.

circumstances—held together by the sense that it was better to accommodate any perceived doctrinal differences than to accentuate them.

It was nonetheless recognized that since its founding the congregation of St. John's in Charleston was the largest and most coherent in the state. It also could include a mixture of the faithful: during the ministry of John Christopher Faber that began in 1787, it was reported that "Reformed and Catholic Germans worshipped at St. John's."[38] Thus doctrinal differences among the *Lutheran* congregations in South Carolina seem always to have been a factor: the distinctions came with the immigrants from Europe—these, the legacy of Luther's Reformation and its subsequent extension under other reformers such as Zwingli and Calvin. It was in fact the same throughout the entire United States, so that the various Lutheran synods that evolved in the United States during the late eighteenth and early nineteenth centuries disputed among themselves, either as adversaries or as allies, the larger question of what it meant to be a genuine Lutheran in America.

The South Carolina Synod was not founded until 1824,[39] almost a decade after Bachman had begun his ministry at St.

---

38. *A History of the Lutheran Church in South Carolina* (Columbia: South Carolina Synod of the Lutheran Church in America, 1971), 105.

39. G .D. Bernheim's *History of the German Settlements and of the Lutheran Church in North and South Carolina.* (Philadelphia: The Lutheran Book Store, 1872), 467-69, reports three salient actions taken by the founders of the Synod at their meeting on January 14, 1824: 1) On motion, it was resolved, that the Augsburg Confession of Faith be the point of union in our Church; 2) The New York English Lutheran Hymn book was recommended to be introduced by the ministers into their churches; 3) The Committee on the 'State of the Church" lamented "that whilst the harvest is plenteous, the laborers are few," having reported that "There are in the State of South Carolina twenty-four Evangelical Lutheran churches, and in the State of Georgia, two. Of those in South Carolina, one is in Charleston, under the care of Rev. J. Bachman, having 275 communicants. Three under the care of Rev. S. Hersher, having 380 members. Six under the care of Revs . . . Meetze, . . . Franklow, and . . . Dreher, having 260 members. Four under the care of Rev. M. Rauch, having 380 members. Four under the care of Rev. J. Moser, having 136 members."

John's. It was Bachman as Synod President, however, who played a major role in determining whether the South Carolina Synod would, or could, align itself with the broadly-based, interstate General Synod that had been established earlier but which was still not authoritatively recognized as the leading organizational body throughout the United States.

For South Carolina leaders, as for leaders of the General Synod, the Augsburg Confession was accepted as containing a substantially correct exposition of fundamentals of the Christian faith, but it was not assumed that one must agree with every jot and tittle of the Confession in order to qualify as a Lutheran. Freedom to approach the Bible "untrammeled by the shackles of human creeds" was assumed to be more important than complete agreement on "minor points of doctrine." While leaders of the Tennessee Synod felt compelled to stress the distinctiveness of Lutheranism as compared with other Christian groups, leaders of the General Synod were inclined to agree with Dr. Bachman's description of Lutherans and other Protestants: "Our principles are the same; our creeds differ only in minor points. These are, after all, non-essentials, and it is to be regretted that all of us could not regard them as such."[40]

Charleston's Bachman was a leading advocate for unity among the synodical bodies, convinced that Lutherans "of both the 'Old' and 'American' variety were united in things that were more important than the matters on which there were differences of opinion."[41] He was elected President of the General Synod at its 1853 convention.

It need not go without notice that while Reverend Bachman carried on an active ministry to the Negro slaves in his congregation, he was recognized as a proponent of keeping the political, anti-abolitionist arguments in defense of the *peculiar institution* of slavery separate from the ecclesiastical concerns of both the South Carolina Synod and the General Synod. The issue

---

40. Bernheim, 197.

41. Ibid., 203.

of slavery did raise discordant voices among the synods: in 1822 "the young Tennessee Synod characterized slavery as 'a great evil in our land' and expressed the hope that the government would, if possible, provide 'an antidote to this evil.'" In 1835, the South Carolina Synod passed two resolutions:

> 1) Resolved, unanimously, that this Synod express their strongest disapprobation of the conduct of the Northern Abolitionists—and that we look upon them as the enemies of our beloved country; whose mistaken zeal is calculated to injure the cause of morals and religion.
> 2) Resolved, That we will hold no correspondence with the Northern Abolitionists, and that should they send to us any of the incendiary publications, we will immediately return them.

Another resolution "expressed appreciation for the fact that no Lutheran ministers were associated with abolitionism," and warned that South Carolina Lutherans would never "countenance such doctrines." The matter did not disappear, however, and by the 1836 Convention "it was learned that there were indeed Lutheran ministers in the United States who advocated abolitionism, and who were so bold as to denounce publicly those South Carolina Lutheran pastors who held other human beings in slavery. Seeing the friction created by debates on the slavery question, the Synod resolved that it would not engage in further discussion or debate on the issue."[42] In his conviction that "Lutheran strength could only manifest itself through Lutheran unity" it was largely Bachman who was responsible for making sure the General Synod at its Convention in 1839 did not debate the subject of abolition nor take a position for or against the abolition of slavery.

---

42. *A History of the Lutheran Church in South Carolina*, 1971, 242.

Now none of these matters would have seemed particularly relevant to the immigrants coming ashore in Charleston from the 1830s on. They were hardly versed on the disputes revolving around the americanization of the Lutheran bodies already in place, nor were fine points of doctrine or the political/ecclesiastical dispute their concern. Once in Charleston in sufficient number, they would have wanted—and needed—a church of their own and a ministry in their own language. In this particular case, they were heirs of the state religion practiced in most of the northern German lands, that is, the one formed through the efforts of Prussia's King Frederick Wilhelm III, who on April 4, 1830, the tricentennial observance of the Augsburg Confession, issued an edict that united the Lutheran and Reformed churches. The records of the Bequests and many of the immigrants who left Geestendorf are contained in the *Kirchenbuch 1715-1852* of the *Evangelisch-Reformierte Kirche Geestendorf (Geestemünde)*.

That European religious heritage which the immigrants brought to Charleston would ultimately be modified by the acculturation process of adopting Charleston ways and attitudes comparable to the evolution experienced by the congregation of St. John's. But initially it would have been virtually impossible for these later immigrants to come ashore and fall in with the *southern* congregation accustomed to its English-based liturgy and hymnody, or for that matter, its americanized Charlestonian pastor. According to G. D. Bernheim's account,[43] Rev. Hazelius, the President of the South Carolina Synod, in his annual report of 1839, wrote of the "the first attempt of the native German citizens of Charleston, S.C. in establishing a *second, and altogether German, Lutheran Church* (italics mine)." Hazelius reports:

> A desire having been expressed by a considerable number of German citizens of Charleston, to have the gospel preached to them in the language of their Fatherland, meetings of the Germans were

---

43. In his *History of the German Settlements and of the Lutheran Church in North and South Carolina* (Philadelphia: The Lutheran Book Store, 1872), 529-33.

held during my stay in the city and afterwards, for the purpose of making the necessary arrangements; and I have since learned that articles of a Church union were drawn up and adopted; that $500 had been collected, and about as much had been subscribed for the salary of a German preacher. . . . They adopted a constitution for their government on the 9th of December, 1840, and soon afterwards purchased a lot on the corner of Hasell and Anson Streets, on which they erected a brick church edifice. In the election of officers, Col. John A. Wagener was chosen their first President. In the month of October, 1841, the cornerstone of this (St. Matthew's) church was laid, at which time the congregation already numbered two hundred and twenty-five members. Their first pastor was the Rev. F. Becher, who had been, up to that time, a minister of the German Reformed Church, but connected himself with the South Carolina Synod in 1841, after having taken charge of this new German Lutheran congregation.

It was inevitable, nonetheless, that when John Andreas Wagener and fellow Lutherans moved to found the St. Matthew's *German* Lutheran Church in 1840, it would not be long before it was drawn into the orbit that Bachman and other Lutheran leaders had organized. By the end of the South Carolina Synod's first decade, two of its congregations had formed missionary societies, one of them Bachman's St. John's. According to the history of the Lutheran Church in South Carolina cited earlier, the synodical constitution adopted in 1834 provided the foundation for a serious mission endeavor."[44] The increasing numbers of Germans in Charleston and in Columbia were considered territory worthy of this missionary zeal, and when St. Matthew's joined the Synod a

---

44. Bernheim, 255.

year after its founding, the Synod was more than pleased to add two hundred and twenty-five communicants to its rolls. By 1846,

> German immigrants were sufficiently numerous in South Carolina to lead the Synod to authorize the publication of one hundred fifty copies of extracts of its Minutes in German. At a Conference Meeting in Lexington District in 1850 the ministers discussed the arrival of German settlers in Pickens District (Walhalla). The conference appointed the Rev. W. H. Fink to visit these newly settled members of the German Colonization Society of Charleston. Pastor Fink found there were already forty-eight families in the settlement and more were expected. . . . The settlers were Protestant, chiefly Lutheran, and expressed their desire for a pastor who could minister to them in their mother tongue.

It is reasonable to assume that the immigrants in Charleston and in Walhalla—collectively the founders and members of the St. Matthew's congregational fold—were grateful to have the attention of the Synod and to have in both locations leaders who could minister to them in their native language. There would have been something of a sense of security in belonging to a supportive larger organizational body that had a foundation and legitimacy within the host society. As good Germans anxious to assimilate themselves into the host culture while honoring their religious heritage, their intentions fit in well with Charleston's protestant environs, and their alignment with the statewide Synod signaled their agreement with the ecclesiastical and political stance of a *southern* Lutheran Church. At the same time, they became active participants in the process of americanizing the Lutheran Church in America.

Looking ahead in time to return to the 1870 *Charleston News* account quoted earlier wherein the reporter went to such lengths to provide the context and rationale for the German Ladies' Society fair, it is clear that the German immigrant community had by that point become an important sector of Charleston's populace. Recalling when the cornerstone of the "new German Lutheran Church" had been laid on December 25, 1867—"well-nigh three years ago"—the newspaper reported that "all the streets through which the procession passed were densely crowded, and every spot around the site of the new church was occupied by eager spectators." The dimensions of the new structure are furnished in full, as if to signify the extent and importance of the congregation needful and worthy of this new and impressive "ornament" to Charleston: "It is situated on the west side of King street, south of Vanderhorst, and is 145 feet in length and 65 feet in breadth. The nave is 92 by 54 feet, and the chancel 24 by 14. . . . There are three entrance doors in front, and two on the sides. . . . The steeple will be 232 ½ feet in height, higher, by over 20 feet, than any other in the city. . . . The church is built in the pure German style of ecclesiastical architecture."[45] This addition to the Charleston landscape has remained the landmark on King Street which the Germans may have intended—an edifice that would stamp their presence on the neighborhood, one that would be noticeably German in character and unmistakably signal their significance in the civic and religious life of Charleston.

Against that backdrop of Charleston's evolved Lutheran heritage, there is little doubt that from the very beginning the immigrant Bernhard Bequest and his wife were active participants in the newly established Lutheran church community. It might in fact be a fair question to ask whether Bernhard was more avidly a St. Matthew's Lutheran or a Schützengesellschaft sharpshooter? In essence, the two were synonymous. A year before the new St. Matthew's edifice was completed, the lucky marksman was named king of the 1871 Schützenfest: "[T]he eagle was demolished, and the last piece came to the ground from a shot by Mr. Ben. Bequest,

---

45. Not incidentally, and not insignificantly, Nicholas Fehrenbach, Bernhard's companion in blockade running, a first cousin to Bernhard's first cousin, was one of the five-member Building Committee, all of whom are named on the cornerstone laid in 1867.

of Mount Pleasant." His shot was described as "the triumph of the day," and the Schützenfest itself declared by the *Charleston Daily News* (May 5, 1871) to have "become an institution in Charleston, and its annual recurrence anticipated with almost as much interest by the citizens generally as by the Germans." It seems safe to say that "Ben" aka "B. H." Bequest had become something of a popular hero to his fellow Germans, who, in turn were becoming something of Charleston's favorites.

The 1871 King of the Schützenfest must have had something of a temper. About five weeks after his titling shot, Bequest was in State Court, accused of "assault with intent to kill and assault and battery."[46] Whatever he had done or said and to whom will remain a secret. The case was continued to the next term and in February, 1872, the Schützenfest King got out of the embarrassing predicament with a twenty-dollar fine. His legal entanglement had no discernible effect on his Rifle Club popularity. The 1872 "German Jubilee" was written up with the usual effusiveness: B. H. again took a prize in the target shooting (a silver plated castor for twenty-one bull's eyes) and passed the royal title ceremoniously to the next king:

> Mr. R. Heisser then advanced, and, taking the king's chain from the neck of the last year's king, Mr. B. H. Bequest, returned it to the club with an appropriate speech. The chain is a silver one, and is adorned with silver medals, each King being obliged, by rule, to add one bearing his name and the date of his reign. It was placed upon the neck of the new king, and his majesty, taking the beautiful crown of feathers and flowers, presented him by President Melchers, placed it upon the brow of Miss Schmitt, whose coronation was hailed with cheers. His majesty then read his

---

46. *Charleston Daily News*, June 17, 1871.

royal speech, which was carefully prepared, and was received with three rousing cheers.

Bequest, we can be sure, had become a staunch member of both the Club and the Mount Pleasant community by the time he reigned as king in 1871-72. Years later,[47] what was expected of the tradition-bound office of Schützenfest King was still current:

> It should be the desire and ambition of every Rifle Club Member to become King of the Charleston Rifle Club Festival at one time or another during his membership. Being truly a position of the highest honor, it devolves no special work at his hands; but, it does require that the King should take a leading and active part in all of the Club's activities during his one year of royalty.
>
> The King should set an example to all of the Club's members in every walk of life, in order to uphold its good name, which it has enjoyed since the time of its organization in the year 1855.
>
> The Kingship does not carry with it any special power or authority; but does carry with it the highest honor and respect of every member of the Club. Congeniality should be one of the King's main traits. For such is, indeed, essential to make the King as well as every member proud of being a Charleston Rifle Club Member.

Thus honored in the 1871-72 "Fest", twenty-seven-year-old Bequest would find himself twice honored four years later: for a second time he would hold the kingship of the Schützenfest and, as well, be elected as Intendant of the town of Mount Pleasant. As noted earlier, after Gesine's death in 1872, Bernhard took only

---

47. Expressed by a member of the "Charleston Rifle Club" (the name change occurred in 1917) and recorded in the 1938 *Schutzen Journal*.

a year to re-marry, a year during which he maintained his personal and business life in Mount Pleasant. His was one of the town's established businesses. The *Charleston Daily News* ran an article under the headline "Our Suburban Resorts / Mount Pleasant / A Sketch of the Village by the Sea": "There are a number of stores where every article needed by housekeepers can be obtained at about the current rates in Charleston. Among them (not to discriminate) I will mention Messrs J. H. Patjen, B. Bequest, Witschen, Torck, Claus Koeper, and Schlendorff."

And he was still dealing in real estate. In December 1873 he sold (and Catherine renounced her right and claim of dower) a large piece of land (518' x 1680') between Mount Pleasant's Division and Center Streets for $1,000. Real estate records are silent on when and how Bequest originally acquired this property, and since there is no mention of built structures on the property, it seems likely that it was land that Bequest was farming.

By the time the annual spring Schützenfest was announced in 1874, the newspapers were calling it "The People's Festival." "What was once known in Charleston as the German Schutzenfest (the umlaut dropped) has, of late years, assumed so cosmopolitan a character that it is now more appropriately called the People's festival."[48] The "People's Festival" was described in the sub-headline as "a Grand Military Pageant": the parade, it seems, included every para-military organization in the City of Charleston and then some, in the following order: social Mounted Club, German Hussars, The Fusilier Band, Carolina Rifle Club, Charleston Rifleman, Washington Artillery, Sumter Rifle Club, Palmetto Guard, Washington Light Infantry, Wagener Artillery, Irish Volunteer Rifle Club, Color Guard, National Zouaves, Irish Volunteers, German Fusiliers, Montgomery Guards, Guard of Honor, the chariot containing the eagle target. Then the various carriages: "in the second carriage behind the eagle target rode Major Melchers, editor of the *Zeitung*, and Ex-Kings Melchers,

---

48. *News and Courier*, April 21, 1874. The *News and Courier* was the successor to the combined (1873) *Charleston Daily News* and the *Charleston Courier*.

Dunnemann and Bequest, of the Charleston Schutzen Club, and visiting Schutzen in citizens' dress. . . . The streets through which the pageant passed were thronged with spectators, who occupied windows, balconies and the sidewalks." Lest it be forgotten, this blatant military pageant/display marching through the streets of Charleston was a white show of force during some of the darkest days of Reconstruction. The jovial, well-behaved, civic picnic that had been re-started in 1868 had taken on a different attitude, and the Germans were very much in the center of the action.

In mid-1874, Bernhard Bequest was receiving shipments on the South Carolina Railroad of wood and lumber, evidence that he was working to establish himself in another business undertaking while continuing to operate his store in Mount Pleasant. Possibly he also maintained a footprint in Charleston at Calhoun and East Bay—although it seems unlikely that he could have managed three operations at once both in Mount Pleasant and in the city. What he was starting in 1874 ultimately became his Charleston wood and lumber yard business on East Bay Street, his signature occupation until his death in 1899. The wood yard was established on East Bay Street by February 1879, but Bernhard and Catherine did not move to Charleston just yet. He was still a Mount Pleasant "planter" of sorts with enough land to raise hogs and possibly other livestock. On January 28, 1875, the *News and Courier,* with a little tongue in cheek, notified its subscribers that its correspondent, "Kappa,"

> says Hadrell's Point, of which Mount Pleasant is an integral part, has been dubbed 'Hungry Neck' but the same is now proved to be a misnomer. On Tuesday morning Mr. B. Bequest, the ex-Schutzen king, slaughtered a hog, which weighed after dressing off the hair 397 pounds, and measured from the snout to the root of the tail six feet two inches. And the whole length with the tail extended, seven feet six inches. The animal was a sow of the Berkshire breed, and was raised in Mr. Bequest's yard in the Village. When she fell

victim to the knife she had reached the immature age of about two years and ten months.[49]

Mount Pleasant's B. H. Bequest, at least for the local citizenry, was a champion in more than one regard. As one of the town's leading merchants, he had become a man of recognized means and talents, and only ten years after his arrival, was not a stranger to anyone—in Mount Pleasant or in the city proper.

In May, the Mount Pleasant Bequest store was burglarized. On the twelfth, the *News and Courier* found the theft sufficiently newsworthy to report:

> On Sunday night last, the store of Mr. H. Bequest, on Mount Pleasant, was forcibly entered through the windows and robbed of a trunk containing several hundred dollars in bonds, several hundred dollars in checks, and over three hundred dollars in gold amounting in all to over $1,500. The thieves, James Armstrong, colored, and James Hudson, a young man formerly a clerk in the store of Mr. Bequest, were arrested yesterday, and the bonds, checks and eighty-five dollars in money recovered. The case will be investigated before Judge O. R. Levy to-day.[50]

With the partial recovery of his assets, the burglary was apparently not a major financial setback, but the theft may have given Bequest pause to think about the viability and liabilities of the store in Mount Pleasant and whether his plans for the wood business might be a safer and more lucrative business venture. Ten years after the war and still struggling under the demands of political reconstruction, the city's efforts to construct and/or reconstruct private and public spaces and places continued for years to always be "work in progress." Charleston had to be rebuilt

---

49. *News and Courier*, January 28, 1875.

50. The $1,500 valuation represents, in current dollars, about $215,000.

from the ground up, and Bequest, as suggested earlier, was one who had a mind to find opportunity in the bleakest circumstances. As Walter Fraser describes it,

> [t]he carpentry and contracting firms of the city were busy repairing, renovating, and constructing public buildings and both black and white churches. In the area of Meeting Street so devastated by the fire of 1861, the Circular Congregational Parish Hall went up in 1870, and the rebuilding of the Circular Church, a project that was to take twenty years to complete, began. Work on the U.S. Customs House resumed and went on for many years. St. Matthew's German Lutheran Church on King Street...was an imposing Gothic Revival structure with a tower and spire that soared 297 feet, the highest in the city. It was completed in 1872. The Freundschaftsbund, or Friendly Alliance, a social club for German immigrants, was the most significant structure of its kind built after the war.... But hardly any capital was going into the construction of private homes, and along the west side of Bay Street between Elliott and Tradd streets the once handsome eighteenth-century residences and prosperous shops became barrooms, bordellos, tenements, and boardinghouses. Drunkenness, brawling, gambling, and stabbings became common in this neighborhood, which the local press described in the early 1870s as 'the filthiest and . . . wickedest' in Charleston. Here and elsewhere in the city blacks and whites lived in close proximity. One writer observed that in Charleston 'the magnificent and the mean jostle each other very

closely in all quarters of the city; tumble-down rookeries are side by side with superb houses."[51]

Before long, Bernhard would be operating, more or less full-time, a lumber yard just a little north of Charleston's "filthiest and wickedest" neighborhood.

The 1875 Schützenfest was, as usual, even better than the one the preceding year. Not unexpectedly, the second prize in the target shooting went to B. Bequest, "one handsome silver plated water cooler and waiter." It was a fitting honor to mark the anniversary of his first decade of residence in Charleston's "village by the sea." And with this much noticeable success behind him, he had more than enough of a platform that he could, either by virtue of his own ambition or because he was encouraged by friends and acquaintances, run in 1876 for election as Mount Pleasant's mayor. The four years he would hold that office are the beginning of B. H. Bequest's second decade in Charleston and warrant a separate chapter. To all appearances, this Bequest brother had reached something of a pinnacle in his Charleston trajectory, so that at this point his story can be left to rest until the following chapter brings to light what his younger two brothers were *doing*.

---

51. Fraser, *Charleston! Charleston!*, 290-91.

CHAPTER 5: DIFFERENT PATHS FOR THE YOUNGER TWO

The two younger brothers of Bernhard who followed him to Charleston came with less preparation than that which Bernhard's blockade-running experiences had given him. As was noted earlier, seventeen-year-old John had landed in Baltimore before the war was over and before his older brother had left Nassau. Exactly what his plans were is unclear: he may not have known that his elder brother had been working in the blockade or when the latter would take up residence in the Charleston area. But if he was on a ship destined for Baltimore, either as a member of the crew or as a passenger (at his age, more likely employed as one of the crew) he must have realized that Maryland was not a Confederate state and that if he stayed there he would be among the "enemies" of his extended family in South Carolina. With no record of his activities between his arrival in 1864 and his documented existence in Charleston in the 1870s, his first six years in the United States are a blank. What is known of his later life in Charleston suggests that he was indeed the "quietest" of the three brothers, not ostensibly inclined to social or political ambitions and not particularly inclined to assume any position of leadership.

In any event, it is easier to think that he went to Charleston sooner rather than later. If for whatever reasons he had stayed in Maryland after his arrival, by the time the war was over the following year, he would have experienced enough of its final months' turmoil to look southward and see his brother's residence in Mount Pleasant as a logical destination as well as a kind of haven. As a young North German seaman with a brother already in place in the maritime environs of Charleston and Mount

Pleasant, he would have had every reason to try his luck there rather than anywhere else. The fact that his younger brother August would arrive in Charleston in November of 1866 suggests that there may have been some sort of plan that the three of them had had for some time—that they should all re-start together in the same place, as soon as they could manage to make it to the city in the South that so many others from Geestendorf had made their home.

For the entire decade of Charleston's highly unsettled years of Reconstruction, quiet John Ludwig Bequest lived a completely unremarkable life. He is not accounted for in the 1870 Federal census in either Maryland or South Carolina, so at age twenty-three was not sufficiently permanent anywhere to be counted and certainly did not yet own property. He was naturalized in October 1875 in South Carolina, indicating that he had declared his intention to become a citizen three years prior. The two "subscribers" to his naturalization, in fact, state that he had lived in Charleston for the past *five* years. In that case, he was in Charleston by 1870, and through luck, or by fortitude, or with help from his brother(s), he managed to keep himself out of the alms house. However much on the quiet side, the young immigrant cannot have been oblivious to the social, economic, and political contexts that defined Charleston and South Carolina at the time. He would have been aware that Ulysses S. Grant had been re-elected president in 1872 and that Daniel H. Chamberlain had been elected South Carolina's Republican governor in 1874. In 1875, he willingly, knowingly, purposefully, became a United States citizen in a state in which the white population was unsettled, angry, and again rebellious, and in which the black population would exceed 60 percent within the next five years.[1]

Apparently without a pre-conceived plan of how he would make his way in the post-Civil War re-United States, John Bequest would have had to take whatever income-earning opportunity came his way. There was no dearth of competition—all those earlier emancipated were now in the labor pool along with the

---

1. 1880 Federal census.

CHAPTER 5: DIFFERENT PATHS FOR THE YOUNGER TWO

other immigrants looking for work. He surfaces in the public record for the first time in 1878, when the Charleston City Directory listing shows him working for his brother Bernhard as a clerk and living "e[ast] end of Calhoun." He is one of three *Bequests* listed: his widowed Aunt Adelheid, mother of his cousin Adeline, is "boarding" at 64 Meeting Street (next door to her widower son-in-law Frederick Schroeder), and his brother, "Benjamin" aka Bernhard, is a "wood merchant e[ast] end Calhoun, r[esides] Mount Pleasant." It seems clear that John is being supported by his older brother and, on the basis of the indefinite address, likely living above the store that Bernhard had earlier established at the corner of Calhoun and East Bay Streets. His elder brother, at this point in 1878, is serving as Mayor of Mount Pleasant, resides there, but is establishing his lumber business in town, and now has two operations going in that Charleston neighborhood.

By 1884, John, somewhat less adrift, was working as a driver for the Palmetto Brewery. This was employment that undoubtedly came his way by virtue of his German friends and/or relatives: one of Charleston's leading German businessmen, J. C. H. Claussen, had started the Palmetto Brewery in the 1870s and was more than willing to find employment opportunities within his business domain for fellow Germans. In April of the previous year (1883), John and Catherine Margarethe Rigbers had been married by the Rev. Louis Mueller, pastor of St. Matthew's Evangelical Lutheran Church, so that John was now head of a household. Their first child, C. Adeline Therese—another child named for the late Adeline Bequest Schroeder—was born the following January and baptized at St. Matthew's. A son, Johann Ludwig, was born exactly a year later in 1885. Despite the additional mouths to feed, his employment at the Palmetto Brewery was apparently not anything permanent. In 1886 he is in the City Directory as a "Stableman." Still in search of something more secure, he changed jobs again and by 1888 was working at the Morris Island Light House. That at least was work more attuned to his background as a seaman, allowing him to work a boat of some kind and be close to the water. He and Catherine were living in the city at this time, but twenty-four years after his arrival in the U.S. John Bequest was not yet propertied: in 1888 the couple was boarding at 38 Calhoun Street, not far from his elder brother's residence at 335 East Bay.

Doubtless in pursuit of a more rural environment, possibly to acquire a home of their own, he and Catherine undertook to move to Mount Pleasant—the reverse of what Bernhard and his wife had done after his Intendancy had ended in 1879. They had left the village and moved to a location close to Bernhard's wood yard on East Bay Street, just a few yards south of Calhoun. The younger couple and their children were resident in Mount Pleasant by 1889.

In August of 1889 there occurred an "incident" in Mount Pleasant, and John Bequest, now a Mount Pleasant resident, was deputized by the sheriff of the village to assist in handling the situation. It involved "the race issue." The incident as reported in the *News and Courier* of August 24 and 25, 1889, was headlined "Reviving the race issue / An exceedingly ugly affair at Mount Pleasant." Three-and-a-half columns reported on "[t]he accidental shooting of a negro woman by a white boy . . . the calling out of the State troops, the fiendish work of black viragoes, the law triumphant." In summary, the negro woman, Moisie Holmes, had just purchased some soap and bacon in Tiencken's store where the owner ("one of the most prominent, popular and conservative citizens of Mount Pleasant")'s seventeen-year-old brother-in-law was clerk. The young Fred Scharfner had just cleaned his loaded gun, which was lying on the counter. Although warned to be careful, Moisie accidentally brushed against the gun, the gun discharged, and Moisie was mortally wounded in her left side and her left arm shot off. The young clerk, with the help of Jimmie Davis, a negro man with a cart, got her to a doctor, then "went to Claus Koeper and gave [him]self up." By the time Scharfner had turned himself in to Sheriff Hale, the angry crowds were forming. It took no time before the situation was known in Charleston:

> The news spread with lightning rapidity, and the truth of the rumor, so far as the sheriff's appeal for aid, was speedily verified. Gen. Huegenin,

CHAPTER 5: DIFFERENT PATHS FOR THE YOUNGER TWO

commanding the 4th brigade, was soon in communication with Governor Richardson, and as the result of the telegraphic correspondence, orders were at once issued to Col. Magrath, commanding the 1st battalion of State Volunteer Troops, to detail two companies of his command with orders to report to Sheriff Hale. . . . The detail was promptly made, the German Fusiliers and the Sumter Guards being designated, with Major J.C. Von Panten to command the battalion.

The military promptly arrived in Mount Pleasant with the afternoon ferry and, as might have been expected, the situation got worse before it got better. A few excerpts from the newspaper account tell the story:

[I]t is difficult to imagine how any civilized or even semi-civilized people could have made the tragedy the pretext for a threat to lynch.

The negro women of Mount Pleasant, however, like their sisters of Cainhoy, Edisto, or other places along the seacoast are very excitable. They at once sounded the war whoop, and in an incredible short space of time had all the black vagabonds of the village in a state of rage that threatened a rupture of the peace.

[A] number of the white residents of the Village, whose business brings them to the city every day, appeared on the wharf. Most of them were armed with Winchester rifles and were anxious to get to their homes, where their families were comparatively unprotected and at the mercy of the black fiends who were heading the intended riot.

About half-past ten o'clock the German Fusiliers, about twenty-five strong, marched into the Ferry slip under the command of Lieut. Schroder. The men were attired in the handsome fatigue uniform of army blue and wore patent cartridge belts, each belt lined with twenty rounds of ammunition.

[T]he Sappho steamed up to the Mount Pleasant wharf. The disembarkation was the work of two minutes, and then the battalion, with fixed bayonets, loaded muskets carried at the right shoulder and at quick step, marching in columns of fours, was on its way to the scene of the supposed battle.

The jail is at some distance from the Court House. . . . Near it are several houses with double piazzas, all of which were crowded with women—the men in that vicinity being gathered into groups of four or five. They were as sulky, as ugly and as brutal a set as could be gathered together anywhere in the State. The women were engaged in cursing, swearing, blaspheming, shouting, and shrieking; the men stood with lowering looks and sulky mien. It was altogether an ugly, treacherous, brutal crowd, which might, under the tongue lashing of the black viragoes, have caused considerable trouble but for the timely arrival of the soldiers from the city.

But as was the case on Mount Pleasant, the women were the loudest and the most indecent in their denunciation of the white race. These flaunted their skirts in the faces of every white woman or child who passed them without escort and indulged in obscene and abusive language.

CHAPTER 5: DIFFERENT PATHS FOR THE YOUNGER TWO

It will of course be understood that the colored persons who so disgraced their race last night constitute a small and a most disreputable part of the colored population of Charleston, but the crowd that assembled at Market wharf about seven o'clock made no effort to conceal their bitter hatred of the white race. It mattered not to them that there had been no murder done, that the young lad whose gun had accidentally killed a colored woman was as unhappy as he was unfortunate. It simply gave them opportunity of exhibiting their hatred to the white race.

The people who were arrested yesterday by Sheriff Hale were Maria Alston, Amelia Simons, Handy Washington, the ring leader, John Edwards and Jim Brown. There will be a number of other arrests.

Mr. Pollte, a prominent colored lawyer, also assisted in quieting the negroes by his coolness. He was aided by the Rev. J. S. Singleton and the Rev. J. F. Lite, both colored preachers. They advised the negroes to keep quiet and obey the law.

John Bequest had been present throughout: "Early yesterday, when the mob was gathering, Sheriff Hale deputized John Bequest and A. Danton, and they with Charles Lafayette, a colored deputy sheriff, and Isaac H. Harris, the colored jailer, rendered assistance to the sheriff in preserving the peace." [2]

This newspaper account reveals how little had changed in Mount Pleasant—and in Charleston—between 1865 and 1889, how ineffective the efforts to reconstruct the region had been, how

---

2. *News and Courier*, Saturday Morning, August 24, 1889.

endemically the racial divide persisted, and not the least, how unmistakably Charleston's Germans had become a prominent, and dominant, force in the city's citizen soldiery.

A more personal tragedy struck when in June of 1890 the couple's four-month-old son, Johann Frederick, died of "inflammation of stomach bowels." And two years later (May 28, 1892), after having borne four children in nine years, the immigrant Catherine Margarethe Rigbers Bequest (Catherine Mary Sophie), aged thirty-eight, born in Germany, Charleston resident for seventeen years, died of "erysipelas facia." Her death notice in the *News and Courier* indicates that the couple had moved again—from Mount Pleasant to a house in town on the northeast corner Spring and Norman streets. That evidence would suggest that John Bequest, by now aged forty-five, was still not propertied in Charleston. Like his elder brother, nonetheless, the widower John would take another wife in little more than a year. With three children under ten, he married Mary Emma Condon, a younger woman from Pennsylvania, and moved back to Mount Pleasant.

A memorial obituary that appeared on the one-year anniversary of Catherine's death suggests that John's elder brother Bernhard Heinrich, was still there for him, for the memorial in the *News and Courier* was signed "Sister and Children." The "sister" could only be Bernhard's wife, Catherine née Mehrtens; the children would have been Catherine and Bernhard's son John Frederick and the widowed John's own surviving three: C. Adeline Therese, aged nine, John L[udwig], aged eight, and Heinrich L[udwig], aged six. Even if Mary Emma Condon was already in the picture as his future wife—they married in July of 1893—it was more than appropriate that the brother and his wife remember the late sister-in-law. Did it matter that in neither the 1892 funeral notice nor the 1893 anniversary memorial John's younger brother, Carsten August, was not mentioned among the bereaved? That question can possibly be answered by stepping back in time to look at what Carsten August Bequest had been doing to establish himself after *his* arrival in post-Civil War Charleston.

CHAPTER 5: DIFFERENT PATHS FOR THE YOUNGER TWO

If indeed there had been a plan for all three brothers to settle in Charleston, or if, on the other hand, the younger two had left Geestendorf on the invitation of Bernhard Heinrich suggesting that there was ample opportunity in the defeated city for all of them, the most junior of this threesome seems to have felt early on that there was perhaps not enough room for all of them in the same place. As was noted in the previous chapter, August (*Carsten* had been dropped almost immediately) came to Charleston as a fifteen-year-old in 1866 and was first accounted for as a clerk in his elder brother's store at Calhoun and East Bay. By some point in 1871 he took himself—an independent twenty-year-old—to upstate South Carolina where he opened a grocery store in Abbeville, SC. Why Abbeville? Not likely because it was nearby that the famous nullificationist John C. Calhoun had been born; equally unlikely did the town call out to him because it was in one of its houses that Jefferson Davis had acknowledged the final defeat of the Confederacy. More likely because there was a German Lutheran community in Abbeville, and because he may have been influenced to try his luck there in light of Charleston's St. Matthew's Lutheran community's missionary zeal to settle immigrants and establish congregations in other parts of the state. John Andreas Wagener and others (among them Hermann Knee) had been instrumental—already by 1850—in organizing the German Colonization society and founding the town of Walhalla, populated primarily by the North German immigrants who had arrived over the years on Wieting's ships. The latter were encouraged to be even more pioneering by moving to the more rural location in the fertile northwest corner of the state where competition with the locals for employment would be less of an issue. In any case, Abbeville was not that far from Charleston, was indeed a more rural, less competitive environment, and given its size, could well accept a(nother) dry goods/grocery/liquor store. At the time, one could get there on the Blue Ridge Railway that connected Charleston with the town of Hamburg on the Georgia border.

August's start in Abbeville was stymied by two "great" fires that caused him significant losses. The first fire, reported in the *Charleston Daily News* on January 22, 24, and 26, 1872, had occurred the previous Friday and, in addition to the Court House and the Marshal House—a hotel, had consumed "the stores of J. Knox, Trowbridge & Co., Traeger & Bequest, and Kapshan & Sklarz." Traeger & Bequest managed to save the "larger portion" of their stock in their storeroom in the lower story of the Marshal House. They were reportedly not insured. The *Abbeville Medium* hoped "that [Abbeville's] citizens will see the importance of a body of organized firemen, and that they will go to work, raise a fire company and buy an engine." It offered condolences to "the sufferers in this great and melancholy catastrophe."

The Bequest partnership with Traeger apparently did not survive the conflagration: another "great" fire, almost exactly a year later, found an "easy victim" in the grocery store of sole proprietor A. Bequest. This time, "Bequest's loss is partly covered by insurance in the Richmond Banking Company to the amount of $1500. He saved a small portion of his stock of goods."[3] Surviving these two set-backs, August was advertising in the business section of Abbeville ("estimated population 1,600")'s 1876 -77 City Directory as "A. Bequest / Dealer in / Dry Goods, Groceries, Provisions & Liquor / Abbeville, S.C." By that time he was married (December 7, 1876, at St. Matthew's, Charleston) to his second cousin, Augusta Catherine Rohde. Augusta apparently at first remained in Charleston while August was in Abbeville: their first son, Heinrich Christian, was born in Charleston in October of 1877. A second son, Bernhardt (for his uncle!), however, was born in Abbeville two years later. The infant lived only sixteen days according to the church record. By the time a third son arrived in January of 1881, the couple was back in Charleston. Exactly when it was decided to call it quits and return to Charleston remains unclear, but the Abbeville enterprise had run its course. With a wife and two young sons, August, now approaching the age of thirty, started a grain mill on Queen Street. That enterprise did not originate as a hare-brained idea or an arbitrary decision: there was already a Hanoverian

---

3. *Charleston Daily News*, February 1, 1873.

CHAPTER 5: DIFFERENT PATHS FOR THE YOUNGER TWO

immigrant family in Charleston who ran the Blohme Milling Company manufacturing flour, grist, and meal. Whatever the exact nature of this *German* connection, the Blohmes were good friends, compatriots, and mentors to the Bequest couple. The latter's fourth son, born in 1883, was named August Blohme Bequest.

It should not be forgotten that, by the time the August Bequests are starting over in Charleston (about 1880), the Abbeville experience had taken place during the middle years of Reconstruction in rural, upstate South Carolina. The politics there were undoubtedly more straightforward than in the larger cities like Charleston and Columbia, but the aversion to Radical Reconstruction was no less intense, possibly more so. The activities of the Ku Klux Klan[4] were more noticeable and demonstrative of the racial divide in the rural areas than in the urban setting of the cities. August and Augusta were married just after the disputed gubernatorial and presidential elections of 1876, and would have been witness to the less nuanced rural politics that brought an end to Reconstruction in South Carolina. When they returned to Charleston, August's elder brother was ending his term as elected mayor of Mount Pleasant, and Charleston with the rest of the state was on its way to being "redeemed":

> After 1877 white Democrats controlled state and local government and claimed to have redeemed South Carolina from the Republicans; neither black nor white Republicans were elected to Charleston's City Council or the state legislature for decades. The local white Democratic "Redeemers," or ex-Confederates, now controlling the election machinery prohibited blacks previously supporting the Republicans from voting in municipal elections. Haunted by the potential political power of the black majority,

---

4. Founded in Tennessee in 1866, the Klan had chapters widely spread throughout the southern states. The Klan was very strong in South Carolina during the 1870s.

whites depicted Reconstruction as black-dominated, corrupt, inefficient, and barbaric government that must never be allowed to recur.[5]

From this point on, August's activities reveal characteristics that mark him as the more aggressive Bequest brother. If with hindsight an observer would see Bernhard Heinrich evolving as the methodical, careful, well-respected businessman and civil servant, and the less organized, less ambitious John following a directionless course, the youngest brother August could be seen developing into a driven, Type-A businessman looking to move up, rub shoulders with the bigwigs, and willingly engaging the rapids of the local political river.

In December of 1884, August's name, along with those of numerous other Germans, appeared on the list of signatories to a call for a *Democratic* demonstration in support of the Grover Cleveland-Thomas Hendricks Democratic victory in the 1884 presidential election:

> To the Citizens of Charleston: Believing it eminently proper that Charleston should publicly display her appreciation of the late Democratic victory, and as the various trade organizations as well as our worthy City Council seem undecided in the matter, we the undersigned merchants and citizens being of the opinion that such a display should be had and that it be made worthy of Charleston, would request that the citizens hold a mass meeting for the purpose of determining the advisability of such demonstration and that the same be held at the German Artillery Hall, Wentworth street, at half-past 8 P.M. on Monday, December 1, 1884.[6]

---

5. Fraser, *Charleston! Charleston!*, 301.

6. *News and Courier*, December 1, 1884.

CHAPTER 5: DIFFERENT PATHS FOR THE YOUNGER TWO

Clearly, as one of the "undersigned merchants and citizens," the German immigrant August Bequest was firmly in the Democratic camp. It is not too untoward to suggest that, being white, he could hardly have been anything else. Without venturing too far afield, it should be noted that the "democratization" of German immigrants had begun much earlier during the 1870s:

> Formal political mobilization started at the second "Taxpayers' Convention," held in late February 1874. In 1871, conservatives had begun forming state "tax unions," a network of cells that replaced the onerous "Democratic" title but performed the same function. The Taxpayers' Convention of 1874 was really a pre-Democratic state convention, with state leaders discussing options for the upcoming campaign. For a time, discussion centered around a tactic proposed by the president of the convention, William Dunlap Porter, and Edgefield's cavalry hero, Martin Witherspoon Gary. After the failure of violence (the Klan), cooperation (1870) and abstention (1872), conservatives sought a new approach. Porter and Gary's plan was simple, legal, and fairly inexpensive: bring white immigrants to the state to shift the voting balance and secure a Democratic victory. Gary, chair of the convention's committee on immigration, had no doubts that Germans would make good Democrats, for he believed the difference between Democrats and Republicans was "race, not party." Those who favored drawing the "white line" in society and politics were already hard at work. Five thousand dollars had been raised thus far, and Gary had hired an agent in Germany. Immigration into the United States and the trip south was to be handled by an agent in New York, Tilman R. Gaines. Gary argued that since ten South Carolina counties had white majorities, and twelve were split rather

closely, "the introduction of a few hundred immigrants" into each of the marginal ones would bring Democratic control of the legislature, and possibly even the executive. Gary's immigration plan had many supporters, but his open emphasis on race was the spark that electrified whites. The editor of the *Charleston News and Courier* agreed with Gary, that "it was entirely a question of race." The paper quoted Gary's convention speech at length and voiced its approval with the belief that "God had destined the caucasian race to rule the other, and if the white men of this state would be true to themselves, they could speedily release themselves from their troubles. The great trouble was that the white men did not unite among themselves." The *News and Courier* applauded the war hero for vowing to restore "the dominance of the white race" and attempting to "protect his self-respect and restore his race to their natural rights."[7]

This brief look at the situation in the early 1870s and afterwards does not, of course, mean that a comparable *use* of German immigrants for political purposes was applicable a decade later, but it does bring to the forefront how easily August Bequest and other Charleston Germans could find themselves aligned with the resurgent Democratic Party. There can be no doubt that it was "entirely a question of race" that encouraged them in their whiteness to covenant with the Southern white society of which they were now a part. That covenant had been in place for many a year—already in antebellum times when the immigrant had virtually no options to cross the racial divide.

---

7. Richard Zuczek, *State of Rebellion: Reconstruction in South Carolina* (Columbia: University of South Carolina Press, 1996), 137.

CHAPTER 5: DIFFERENT PATHS FOR THE YOUNGER TWO

In Charleston, August worked diligently to quickly become a known entity in the business community. The *News and Courier*[8] could report on an accident "at the grain mills of Mr. A. Bequest in Queen street" without having to offer any further identification to its readers. It could report in its column, "Police Court," with a little tongue in cheek, that "three persons, all colored, constituted the cast of the performance at the police matinee yesterday. R. Lewis was charged with being drunk and disorderly and with ringing the doorbell of the residence of Mr. A. Bequest. Mr. Bequest appeared in Court and asked leave to withdraw the charge, as Lewis had satisfactorily explained the matter to him. Lewis was thereupon dismissed."[9] No address or further identification necessary for the understanding Mr. Bequest. The understanding businessman was not so conservative that he would retreat from modernization: his grist mill was one of the first to be listed with the Charleston Telephone Exchange.[10] Acting on every opportunity to connect and be noticed, the German Lutheran could even donate one of the prizes for the Cathedral Chapel Picnic for the benefit of the catholic church's Sunday-school.

By mid-1885, August had become sufficiently engaged in Charleston's business enterprises that he would be named one of three creditors on a creditor committee in the bankruptcy case of the S. A. Durham & Co. Financially, he was doing well enough to buy a parcel of "Pine land,"—some 525 acres in neighboring Colleton County—"a portion of the Spring Grove Plantation in what was formerly Saint Paul's Parish" from James L. Platt for five thousand dollars. As for his social life, he apparently kept his distance from the Rifle Club crowd in which his brother was so

---

8. *News and Courier*, January 30, 1885.

9. *News and Courier*, February 11, 1885.

10. An innovation that had been in existence only since 1879. It was the first telephone exchange in South Carolina and one of only eleven in the nation.(Fraser, *Charleston! Charleston!*, 302).

firmly ensconced, but found his place in the German Artillery. They, too, held great parties:

> There is not one perhaps of all the events of social and fashionable life in Charleston which is looked forward to with more of the anticipation of fun and frolic and delight than the masquerade ball of the German Artillery. That gallant command are far-famed for their brilliant success in the field of beauty as well as on the field of valor, and Charlestonians are always assured that whatever they undertake will be done with equal taste, judgment and discrimination. They have already scored a long list of successes, and last night's brilliant affair was a most notable occasion even compared with its famous precedents.
>
> The committee of arrangements has, as usual, made the entertainment and accommodation of their guests an object of their special care and attention. They had left nothing undone that would make the evening one of perfect and exquisite enjoyment.[11]

August Bequest was one of "the gentlemen to whom a very large share of the credit for the occasion is due."

If the term "wheeling and dealing" might be applied without its pejorative connotations, it would be an apt descriptor for August Bequest during the period after his return from Abbeville into the 1890s. The grist mill operation planted him firmly in the business world, and he had a social circle in which he could extend his connections both within and outside the ethnic

---

11. *News and Courier*, January 21, 1886. It should not pass without notice that here, as was so often the case, what the *Germans* did was so much appreciated by the *Charlestonians*, as if they comprised two distinct groups. After the party was over, were the Germans grateful for the positive review of the event but not aware that they were still not members of the establishment?

CHAPTER 5: DIFFERENT PATHS FOR THE YOUNGER TWO

community. He was financially stable enough to buy and sell property, as well as invest in things that, even with risk, looked promising of a positive return. He was becoming something of an operator, seizing opportunity when it knocked. With the help of his friend J. C. Blohme, for example, August had extended credit to C. L. Schmancke, a store-owner on upper King Street. In October 1886, the "estate" of C. L. Schmancke was sold at auction with August Bequest "under deed of assignment" as recipient of the proceeds. Auctioned items included a dray mule, wagon, cart, iron safe, platform scale, desk, 20,000 lbs. husks, 5,000 lbs. chips, soap, lard, flour, hay, corn, and oats. It was to be cash on the barrel, with "goods to be removed immediately after the sale."[12] Doubtless it was only Mr. Schmancke who suffered a loss.

With their daughter Annie Agnes Catherine added to the household in mid-July of 1887, it was nonetheless hardly the case that the family of six was resting comfortably in the lap of luxury: August and Augusta repeatedly advertised—along with numerous others seeking additional income—in the Visitors Guide for the annual "Gala Week" goings-on that they took in visitors: "A. Bequest, 236 King street, meals to order, rooms on application."[13] But August kept on the move. Along with two other dealers, he advertised rather pleadingly for Charlestonians to buy lime for their building projects at their very competitive prices:

> LIME, $1 PER BARREL, AT N.E. / RAILROAD DEPOT, OR $1.10 AT STOREHOUSE. We beg to give notice that we are better prepared than ever to offer inducements in price of Lime, and will name prices that will defy all competition. Quality guaranteed for any Lime sold in this State. A trial of our Lime is all we ask or require to convince the most prejudiced advocate of Northern or Eastern Lime. The new H. L.

---

12. *News and Courier*, October 19, 1886.

13. *News and Courier*, January 28, 1887.

> Kimball House at Atlanta, Ga., was built and plastered with Southern Lime; also the Insane Asylum at Morgantown, N.C.; the elegant Mansion of Mr. Geo. W. Williams, and the Bagging Factory at Charleston, S.C. The new State Capitol of Georgia, at Atlanta, is now being built with it, and will be plastered with it. The famous Eagle and Phenix Cotton Mills at Columbus, Ga., were constructed with it. Give us a trial order. Apply to Fleming Bros, 151 East Bay st. / A. Bequest, 22 Queen st. / or H. L. Townsend, 26 & 28 Market street, Charleston, S.C.[14]

Whether or not there was much success in selling the new "southern" lime at the grist mill, August Bequest was not above trying a new tack. He was apparently sensitive to Charleston's limitations as a trading center and was among those advocating improvements to the city's railroad service. He was signatory to the following petition to the South Carolina Railway Company, Northwestern Railroad Company, and Charleston and Savannah Railway Company:

> We, the undersigned, respectfully petition that your roads will unite in building union depots for passengers as well as freight; that you will increase the facilities for handling, transferring, and storing cotton, naval stores, heavy freights, grain, etc. at such depots by the erection on the water front of all necessary buildings. By these changes and improvements we feel assured of our ability not only to retain our present trade, but also

---

14. *News and Courier*, February 2, 1887.

CHAPTER 5: DIFFERENT PATHS FOR THE YOUNGER TWO

to bring into this city a vast volume of new business.[15]

More than likely reacting to those limitations that directly impacted his supply of stores for the grist mill, August assessed his options and decided to try something new. He bought a restaurant. Announced in the *News and Courier*'s "All About Town" column on February 8, 1887[16], the purchase must have presented itself as an opportunity to play a different role on Charleston's business stage, possibly a more up-scale and socially advantageous operation than the rather pedestrian grist mill operation on Queen Street.[17] And before anyone had time to notice, by the end of 1887 "Bequest's restaurant" was a *place*. When in November of that year Charleston hosted the "Pilot Boat Regatta," "the visiting pilots [were] entertained at a supper at Bequest's restaurant in King street."[18] Everyone knew where that was.

The new restaurant owner could now continue his involvement in Democratic politics in a somewhat more social setting, hosting the downtown crowd at tables while discussing the issues of the day. He was registered in Ward 3 and in late 1887 was one of twelve delegates to the Nominating Convention. On another front, he was a stockholder in the "recently chartered" Consumers' Coal Company. The *News and Courier* reported on the stockholders' meeting of November 9, 1887:

---

15. *News and Courier*, June 12, 1887.

16. "The King restaurant, on King street, has been purchased by Mr. A. Bequest from the last owner, Capt. J. S. Connor."

17. He did not give the mill up immediately: In October of that year, the newspaper reported a fire on Chalmers Street that "reached the shed which covers the engine and boiler of [Bequest's grist mill], which shed was partly consumed." That reference, nonetheless, is the last mention of the Bequest grist mill in the *News and Courier*.

18. *News and Courier*, November 3, 1887.

> The stockholders met...and organized last night at the German Artillery Hall under very flattering conditions. Over one thousand shares of the capital stock of $50,000 were represented, a set of by-laws, carefully prepared, were read and adopted and the following board of directors elected: Henry Schachte, E. H. Jahnz, A. F .C. Cramer, A. Bequest, H. A. Heiser, Henry C. Wohlers, H. Sahl. The board will meet on Monday afternoon and elect officers. An assessment of 20 percent was called for and met with a ready response.[19]

It seems clear at this point that August had moved into the circle of Germans who were playing a major role in Charleston's economic development and determining the city's future.

As might have been expected, there was some messy business along the way. Being on the board of the Consumers' Coal Company did not keep him out of court: he was involved in a case before the State Supreme Court involving 5,000 bushels of mixed sacked corn that had been purchased by H. Bulwinkle & Co. from Cramer and Blohme, (German from German!) and later found to be defective. A. Bequest—in an unspecified capacity—had signed the receipt for Bulwinkle's payment of $4,400 to Cramer and Blohme. Bulwinkle was suing for $1,136.70 (the corn had subsequently been sold at auction). The case was remanded to the Court of Common Pleas for a new trial, but was not further reported on by the newspaper.

As restaurant owner, August was no longer concerned about the State's railroads' ability to handle shipments of heavy freight and/or grain, but he now had trouble with the "Sunday Law," "blue laws," the "Sunday cocktail" issue. The newspaper quoted him extensively on the matter in December 1887, Bequest saying he would fight aggressively if the campaign to have

---

19. *News and Courier*, November 10, 1887.

CHAPTER 5: DIFFERENT PATHS FOR THE YOUNGER TWO

barrooms and restaurants close on Sundays to avoid selling beer or liquor became law.[20]

Owning and running a restaurant in Charleston cannot have been easier in the late nineteenth century than it is now in the twenty-first. If it gave August Bequest a kind of stage on which to act in several roles, it must have consumed him almost completely. Apparently "Bequest's restaurant" was almost a 24/7 kind of operation. In January of 1889, the *News and Courier*[21] reported on the burglary of "Dr. Eckel's Drug Store" on King Street:

> The burglary was committed between the hours of 1 o'clock and 5 o'clock in the morning. At the former hour the door was tried and found closed and secure. It was found open four hours later. How the burglars entered the store through the front door, facing on King street, and directly under a gas lamp, and in plain view of Bequest's restaurant, which is kept open until an early hour in the morning, and how the large desk could have been taken out of the store and carried through the streets without exciting attention is a mystery.

Besides the long hours, there was a constant turnover of employees, to say nothing of the quest for supplies. Over and over, there could be found an ad in the newspaper wanting either one or two new waiters or, almost as often, one or two "good milk (often "Milch") cows." Sometimes, the help stole from him: Alfred Jones was in Police court in May of 1890 for stealing "a lot of dishes and tray from A. Bequest." Jones either paid his fine of fifteen dollars or spent thirty days in jail

Restauranteur Bequest did manage enough time off to take one of his sons with him to New York on the steamship *Seminole* in August of 1890. Every fall, however, there was work to be

---

20. *News and Courier*, December 17, 1887.

21. *News and Courier*, January 20, 1889.

done for the annual "Gala Week," working on the organizing committee, collecting donations, etc.: A. Bequest was one of the "representative business men" who took "hold of the scheme...to make [the 1891 Gala Week] a glorious celebration. It is going to be a $10,000 exhibition."[22] By October, the Gala Week decoration fever was reported as "contagious along King street. The boulevard is now a pretty and bright picture and is one ceaseless sea of gaudy banners, fluttering flags and veri-colored tissue festoons. . . . Bequest's restaurant was covered with a multitude of lanterns, which were hanging from lines of tissue festoons."[23]

All this activity did have its rewards. The Bequest family, August, now 40; Augusta, 34; Henry 14; John 10; August Blohme 8; and little Annie Agnes 4, could afford to spend the summer at the seashore on Sullivan's Island. The family was named among those "families . . . moving over every day to add to the colony of pleasure and health seekers."[24] Their departure in September was also duly noted, and from the list of names, one could conclude that the Sullivan's Island summer community included a large colony of Charleston Germans—essentially the ones who had achieved economic success.

Well-off enough to afford a summer rental on Sullivan's Island, the owner of Bequest's restaurant was cocky enough to risk ignoring the prevailing liquor laws. In April of 1892, A. Bequest, 226 King Street, was one of four "saloon-keepers" arraigned before the Recorder in the Police Court, charged with selling liquor on Sunday:

> Mr. Anspach at first appealed for a jury trial and was referred by the Recorder to the Court of General Sessions. Later in the day, however, he appeared at the Central Station and stated that he

---

22. *News and Courier*, August 20, 1891.

23. *News and Courier*, October 28, 1891.

24. *News and Courier*, June 12, 1891.

CHAPTER 5: DIFFERENT PATHS FOR THE YOUNGER TWO

had reconsidered his appeal and was ready to pay the fine. He accordingly deposited twenty dollars. Mr. Bequest also settled up later in the day. . . . Chief Martin said last night that hereafter there would be a slight change to the methods now pursued in dealing with the violators of the Sunday liquor law. Hereafter as soon as the cases are lodged against the parties they will be taken immediately into the Sessions Court, where they will be finally disposed of.[25]

If in Court one day, five days later he was elected treasurer of Democratic Ward 3, Club 2. Meeting throughout the city, all of the club meetings "had been called for the purpose of perfecting the reorganization of the local Democracy for county purposes, and in every instance were largely attended."[26] August Bequest was now positioned to mind the finances that would be used to reorganize some of the local Democratic forces. This would not be the only time he would serve as a treasurer responsible for an organization's money. To whatever degree the city's democrats reorganized themselves, they were surely in charge of its politics, and August Bequest's name could frequently be found as a signatory to various actions taken by his Club or the Party on public questions or concerns.

By this point, the youngest Bequest brother had pretty well climbed into the top echelons of Charleston's business leaders. He had made it his business to become a popular German: he had his finger in as many pies as possible, operated a restaurant that was something of a city landmark, and held office in the local Democratic club in control of the political pulse of the city. He was forty-one years old when in early 1893 he became a U.S. citizen. Whether he had kept in close touch with his two brothers is debatable. As noted earlier, he had not been among the

---

25. *News and Courier*, April 5, 1892.

26. *News and Courier*, April 10, 1892.

family mourners when his sister-in-law Catherine had died in 1892—as if he were otherwise too occupied on various fronts to devote time to his relatives. Perhaps any familial estrangement is purely hypothetical. But given August's noticeable rise in social status, his two brothers nonetheless might have wondered what they should have done differently: possibly they were envious of his having met with so much success so quickly; maybe they acknowledged that it was his gregarious personality that allowed him to move easily among the influential people; maybe they thought he was on the moving train that they had somehow missed. Whatever his older brothers thought, it seemed clear that August Bequest was destined to move further along the road to success. Who could know what opportunities lay ahead?

CHAPTER 6: THE MAYOR OF MOUNT PLEASANT

The previous chapter detailed the course of August and John Bequest's lives in Charleston after their post-war arrival up to the early 1890s. This one steps back more than a decade to follow the path taken by the men's older brother. Back in the mid-1870s, Bernhard Heinrich was, quite literally, minding his business in Mount Pleasant, serving on the town council, and quite possibly thinking about running for the office of Intendant of the village by the sea.

The story of how this naturalized American, resident in Mount Pleasant for only a decade, came to be elected mayor of this Charleston suburb seems to border on the unbelievable, although it does not exactly fit the rags-to-riches pattern. Bequest himself left no written record of his experiences. There is no publicized account of a platform by which he presented himself for office, no *News and Courier* report of the election results, no comment on his "ticket" or his party affiliation, virtually nothing to verify that he, in fact, held the office. The *History of Mount Pleasant, South Carolina* by Petrona Royall McIver, nonetheless, lists him as the town's Intendant from 1876-79. According to the ordinances governing Mount Pleasant[1] as amended and adopted between 1837 and 1883, it was public record that

> the Intendant and Wardens, before entering upon the duties of their respective offices, shall take the

---

1. *Acts of Assembly relating to, and Ordinances in force of the Town of Mount Pleasant from the Act of Incorporation to the Present Time, also Rules for the Government of Council. Printed by Order of Council* (Mount Pleasant, 1883).

oath prescribed by the Constitution of this State, and also the following oath, to wit: "As Intendant (or Warden) of the Town of Mt. Pleasant, I will equally and impartially, to the best of my ability, exercise the trust reposed in me, and will use my best endeavors to preserve the peace and carry into effect, according to law, the purpose for which I have been elected: So help me God."[2]

For the duly-elected Bequest, preserving the peace and carrying into effect…"the purpose for which [he had] been elected" would have included:

--being "vested with all the powers of Justices of the Quorum of this State within the limits of the said Town";

--having authority to "appoint . . . such and so many proper persons to act as Constables";

--being charged to "ordain and establish all such rules, by-laws and ordinances respecting the streets, ways, markets and police of said Town, as shall appear . . . proper for the security, welfare and convenience of said Town, and for preserving the health, peace, order and good government within the same";

--having "power to abate and remove nuisances . . . and to classify the inhabitants liable to patrol duty, and to require them to perform such duty as often as occasion may require";

---

2. *Acts of Assembly*, 13.

CHAPTER 6: THE MAYOR OF MOUNT PLEASANT

--being "required to issue warrants against all offenders, and cause them to be brought before him . . . and, upon due examination, shall either release or admit to bail . . . or commit to jail such offenders as the case may require";

--being duty-bound "to keep all roads, streets and alleys open and in good repair";

--having "the full and exclusive power of granting licenses for billiard-tables, to keep taverns, or retail spirituous liquors within the said Town"[3]

Thus for Bequest on a personal level, and for the residents of the village of Mt. Pleasant,[4] the office involved considerable responsibility, and Bernhard Bequest's election as the village mayor says a lot about how in a short time he had won the respect of his fellow citizens—a trustworthy immigrant businessman and property owner with leadership capabilities, chosen to manage the affairs of the town. Given the absence of records, however, it is difficult to offer a judgment on what might be considered his administration's accomplishments.[5] They might have been entirely routine, although the fact that records are lacking does not mean that nothing of note was the order of the day. The year Bequest was elected, in fact, was anything but "routine." The Mt. Pleasant mayoral election would have taken place approximately at the same time the state and the nation witnessed the disputed

---

3. Cited in *Acts of Assembly*, 14-16.

4. The "Act to renew and amend the Charter of the Town of Mount Pleasant, February 28, 1871" states that "the said town shall be called and known by the name of Mt. Pleasant," making the usage of the abbreviation *Mt.*, rather than *Mount*, official.

5. Despite every effort, the author has been unsuccessful in locating any official records of Mt. Pleasant during these years.

presidential election of Rutherford B. Hayes, during which South Carolina was embroiled in its own disputed gubernatorial election in which the Democrat Wade Hampton unseated the Republican Governor, Daniel Chamberlain. The determined efforts of the Democrats in 1876 to oust the Republicans' Chamberlain effectively marked the state's "redemption" from the throes of Reconstruction.

It has indeed been noted as part of Mt. Pleasant's historic landscape that "in 1876, an election which overturned Black Republicanism and restored white Democrats to power in the district, state, and region so inflamed the town that black Republicans seized the streets for an entire night and fearful white Democrats along with a handful of black political allies barricaded themselves in their homes." [6] It would be legitimate to question how much of a role Bernhard Bequest played in "overturning" Black Republicanism and "restoring" white Democrats to power. Was he, eleven years after his immigration, elected to office because he had become a *white* Democrat? It is not at all unreasonable to view Bequest's being elected to the office of Mt. Pleasant's Intendant as the culmination of a process that had begun when he decided to leave Nassau to settle in Charleston.

One historian's analysis of "how the Germans became white southerners"[7] claims that German immigrants were "a middleman minority community, occupying a middle tier on the racial and ethnic hierarchy below white southerners and above African Americans," who after the Civil War "increasingly exhibited their desire to become white southerners." As a post-war resident landowner in Mt. Pleasant since his immigration, Bequest would have had a similar agenda. By the latter years of

---

6. "The Historic Landscape of Mount Pleasant: Proceedings of the First Forum on the History of Mount Pleasant." Amy McCandless, ed., (Mt. Pleasant, 1993).

7. Jeffery G. Strickland, "How the Germans Became White Southerners: German Immigrants and African Americans in Charleston, South Carolina, 1860-1880," *Journal of American Ethnic History* 28, no. 1 (2008), 52-69.

Reconstruction most native white southerners would have acknowledged that it was really the mercantile Germans who were the backbone of Charleston's economic revival after the war, and Bernhard Bequest legitimately could have been counted among the successful members of that merchant league, in the same company with Oskar Aichel (John Hurkamp & Co., wholesale and retail grocery), Otto F. Wieters (wholesale liquor business), J. C. H. Claussen (baker), and Frederick W. Wagener (wholesaler in naval stores and cotton). It is fair to say that the progression of Bequest's acculturation—from his naturalization to his serving as Mt. Pleasant's Intendant during the same years that the Democrat Wade Hampton represented and monopolized the South Carolina political scene—was nothing other than this particular German immigrant's path in becoming a "white southerner."

As the Germans had gone through stages of asserting their cultural heritage on the local scene, for example, establishing the Schützen-Gesellschaft and other paramilitary "social" organizations, they had represented a middle ground by inviting the attendance and participation of African Americans, while at the same time displaying martial uniforms and guns in their exhibitionary parades—the latter affirming the sense of white superiority assumed by the non-African American crowds in attendance. With their increasing social and financial ascendancy, the Germans by 1868 were becoming increasingly attuned to the platform of the Democratic Party. By 1871 they were sufficiently politically organized to nominate one of their own, John A. Wagener, a "former Confederate general and slaveholder," to run for mayor of Charleston. In that election, enough white southerners would endorse Wagener's candidacy that he would win a two-year term. By that point in the middle of the Reconstruction era, the Germans were already standing on modified footing. African American Republican politicians lashed out at the Germans for their efforts on behalf of the Democratic Party. Lieutenant Governor Alonzo Ransier, an African American, considered it "the basest ingratitude in General Wagener and the Germans to support a ticket in opposition to the rights of the colored people." Ransier argued that the Germans had betrayed the African American community: "So far as the negro is concerned—let the Germans remember when they came here in their blue shirts—you patronized them, traded with them, and through your patronage they are enabled to-day to raise their heads and now desire to govern us."[8]

As for Bernhard Bequest's election to Mt. Pleasant's Intendancy in 1876, he was surely but a small fish in the much larger political pond. Nonetheless, it is patently clear that he was elected as a *democrat* and that his electors thought of him as a white southerner. To his own and the general population of Mt. Pleasant's satisfaction, he served a three-year term: with only two exceptions, his predecessor mayors had all served one- or two-year terms.[9] To all appearances, he had come a long way in the ten years since he arrived in prostrate Charleston. He had indeed seized every opportunity that had come to him and could now present the public persona of a well-adapted Mt. Pleasant businessman and civic citizen.

As a German southerner, nonetheless, he cannot have completely forsaken his German heritage and forgotten who he still, by nature, was. That he was still an immigrant German grocer in the second year of his Intendancy is attested by an officially recorded "Agreement and Lien on Crop" with a February 22, 1877 date. The document stipulates that the German grocer was providing "the necessary seed and provisions" to one Frank P. Wallace, the latter sharecropping a parcel of land in Christ Church Parish (Mt. Pleasant) belonging to a Dr. Dawson, with Wallace entitled to two-thirds of the crop(s) planted and harvested. Wallace, in exchange for the seed and provisions, agrees to give "B. H. Bequest a lien of his entire two thirds part or shares of said crop or crops so planted and harvested...excepting always such crop or crops as shall be planted and harvested upon a certain part

---

8. Strickland, 62.

9. The first Intendant, Andrew Hibben, served ten years, from 1844 to 1854, and Joshua Toomer had served three, from 1859-1862.

CHAPTER 6: THE MAYOR OF MOUNT PLEASANT

or piece of said land containing about one and one half (1 ½) acres...being now under lease for one year from the date first mentioned (16 December 1876) to and cultivated or intended so to be by the said B. H. Bequest separate and apart from the portion planted by said Frank P. Wallace."

There is nothing in the document to reveal exactly what kind of seed Bequest was supplying to Wallace, but it was very likely that Wallace was going to plant cotton, and Bequest was acting as a creditor within the crop lien system that governed agriculture in the postbellum South. The crop lien system was a system of credit that

> allowed the farmer to place a mortgage on his future crop with the person or persons who advanced him supplies for his operations. Normally those who made advances only accepted liens on an easily salable crop which was inedible and difficult to steal. . . . No other crop planted in the lower South so completely satisfied these requirements as did cotton. Thus, Southern agriculture became more and more dependent on it.[10]

The lien system had been in place ever since emancipation and all too many farmers had become dependent on it. The lien law was repealed in 1877, but reinstated in 1878 and was in effect throughout the 1880s. While the law enabled the farmer without resources to try to eke out an existence by mortgaging his expected harvest in exchange for the necessities to plant the crop, it invariably put the southern farmer "into a state of helpless peonage to the merchant who had become his creditor."[11] The 1878 law also protected the landlord leasing land for agricultural

---

10. William J. Cooper, Jr., *The Conservative Regime: South Carolina, 1877-1890* (Baltimore: The Johns Hopkins Press, 1968), 135.

11. Ibid., 136.

purposes: the landlord held "a prior and preferred lien for rent" on at least one-third of the value of all crops raised on his land.

So here one witnesses Bernhard Bequest—himself a kind of "sharecropper" farming a leased 1 ½ acre plot[12]—providing supplies on credit to a less fortunate sharecropping citizen of the new, postbellum South. In view of what is known about Bernhard Bequest, there is every reason to absolve the naturalized German immigrant—in his capacity as one of the town's retail merchants and now mayor of the town—of anything usurious in arranging this transaction: he was, at the time, a man of his time in South Carolina, a merchant playing a role that was expected of him. As "furnishing merchant," in fact, Bequest represented "the most direct means by which the lien laws were made to work as a source of credit and banking for his community." His Mt. Pleasant store was "both a source of supply and a market facility" and like most store owners, he was "to all outward appearance a stable citizen . . . and a decisive voice in . . . community affairs."[13] Economically, the German farmer/merchant Bequest occupied a higher position on the social ladder than the native southern sharecropper Wallace.

The fact that Bequest had set himself up in Mt. Pleasant as the owner of a "store" had much to do with the role he came to have as one of Mt. Pleasant's leading citizens. In his crossroads/center-of-town general store, the merchant who offered the local people everything they had been denied during the four years of the war became one of the lead actors on the town stage:

> Thus it was that the store became more than a market for produce and a place in which to buy supplies. Its stove in cold weather and its porch and shade trees in spring, summer and fall were

---

12. A lease from a landlord that did not exceed the one-third value of the crop did not require a written agreement.

13. Thomas D. Clark, "The Furnishing and Supply System in Southern Agriculture since 1865," *The Journal of Southern History* 12, no. 1 (February 1946), 44.

CHAPTER 6: THE MAYOR OF MOUNT PLEASANT

places of general assembly. Merchants were busy long hours each day with the affairs of the community. Inside their little latticework doors and beside the tall breast-high shelf-like desks, they worked at their books, and held whispered conversations with their debtors. . . .

Country storekeeping was one-half orthodox merchandising and the other half sizing up the capabilities and honesty of customers. It was a highly personal sort of enterprise which required a generous amount of giving and taking, and a keen sense of humor and understanding of all the frailties of mankind.

Few country merchants ever heard of statistics, but they were always well informed as to the crop every customer had planted and as to its general state of cultivation from week to week. They knew the approximate size of shoes, the length of legs, chest measurements and girths of most of their customers. From week to week they took mental notes of goods which they showed, knowing full well that most customers would go home and debate the matter before making a purchase, and would then send a note. They were philosophers who weighed five pounds of sugar, cut off huge pieces of fat meat, pumped five gallons of kerosene or dished up buckets of lard while they kept up a steady flow of advice or lamentation. Working hard, living closely and paying all debts was ever a cardinal rule of economy with them. Their whole philosophy of the credit system was one of strict control and constant retrenchment for the debtor. Paying one's debts was ever a virtue which gave customers high standing at the stores.[14]

While not the only merchant in town, Bequest doubtless played his role well enough to earn the esteem of his customers who, after ten years of watching him on the Mt. Pleasant civic stage, would chose him to manage the affairs of their community

The merchant-mayor, of course, had a personal life that took its own course. As noted earlier in chapter 4, his and Catherine's seventeen-month-old son Bernhard Heinrich Ludwig (Henry L.) died on February 10, 1878, of diphtheria. That loss was doubtless assuaged by the birth of their daughter, Anna Meta Adeline, in September. In addition, he was enthusiastically active in several of the ethnic community's fraternal organizations. "Intendant B. Bequest" won the "race for the pig" at the picnic of the German Artillery in June "amid loud shouts from the bystanders."

By 1879, the Mt. Pleasant merchant was able to get the wood business that he had dallied with on the side firmly established in Charleston proper. The *News and Courier* carried the following advertisement on February fourteenth:

> In connection with present business, I will keep always on hand prepared moss, cleaned by machinery recently purchased for the purpose of cleaning moss of all dust, which I will roll in quantities to suit purchasers. B. H. Bequest, Wood Yard, East end Calhoun street.[15]

---

14. Thomas D. Clark, *Pills, Petticoats and Plows. The Southern Country Store* (New York: Bobbs-Merrill 1944), 52-53.

15. The 1878-79 Charleston City Directory lists the wood yard at 8 Washington Street, a location just south of Calhoun, with "Benjamin H. Bequest" residing "Mount Pleasant."

CHAPTER 6: THE MAYOR OF MOUNT PLEASANT

Since he was still running his store and living in Mt. Pleasant, he managed both businesses by employing his younger, unmarried brother, John L. as a clerk at the wood yard near the corner of Calhoun and East Bay.

Forecasting his intention to move from the town of Mt. Pleasant to Charleston where he had established his wood business, in May of 1879 Bernhard sold three lots of land in Mt. Pleasant, along with a variety of equipment—five cotton gins, a grist mill, a 10hp engine, and a sloop—as well as a store "known as the Seven-Mile Store on the Georgetown Road"[16] and all its "stock in trade" to a fellow German, Otto F. Wieters, for the sum of $10,000, payable in two installments of $5,000 with annual interest of 7%. Shortly thereafter, in mid-July of 1881, he turned around and purchased for three thousand dollars four parcels of land from an "old Charleston" resident, Charlotte Smith, the entire purchase amounting to a substantial acreage: the first, a parcel of 2,758 acres known as "Clayfield Plantation"; the second, an adjacent 170-acre property known as "Baldwin's Old Field"; thirdly, a neighboring parcel of 1,455 acres known as "Hampton"; finally, a one-acre plot with a barn, Reserved and excepted from this conveyance were two parcels, one of 632 acres which had previously been conveyed to Robert M. Venning, and another of 233.4 acres of the Clayfield Plantation, which Charlotte Smith conveyed to an African American Mt. Pleasant farmer by the name of Friday Reed (or Reid) on the same day for $500.00. We can assume that in 1881 when Bequest acquired these properties he envisioned the pine-forested land as a source of the wood he would be retailing from his wood business on East Bay Street.[17] Absent any record of how and/or whether this

---

16. This was not Bequest's store in Mt. Pleasant's center, opposite the Courthouse. See earlier mention in chapter 4.

17. The plantations in Christ Church and St. Thomas Parishes were known from colonial times for the lumber that could be harvested there and sold on the Charleston market. See Suzannah Smith Miles, *East Cooper Gazetteer* (Charleston: The History Press, 2004), 75.

arrangement/business plan worked, a decade later all of this property was lost to Bequest in a Master's Sale auction in 1891 through a suit brought against "Bernhard Bequest and others" by the Germania Savings Bank in the Charleston Court of Common Pleas. Clayfield (2,758 acres), Hampton (1,455 acres), and the one-acre lot with the barn were sold by the end of 1891 for $2,800.00.[18] The same properties were up for auction four years later, again under pursuit by the Germania Savings Bank. The *Evening Post* in November, 1896, stated that "Clayfield, Hampton, and Baldwin, Old Field and others, in Christ Church Parish" were sold for $1,700. Clayfield and Hampton were again available for purchase as late as 1920, advertised as "Country Lands," "about 18 miles from Mount Pleasant and on the McClellanville-Georgetown Road. Good pasturage and large acreage of excellent planting lands."[19]

The 1881 purchase of the Clayfield and adjacent properties was a real estate transaction completed after the couple had moved into the city. In the 1881 City Directory, they had taken up residence at 11 Middle Street, not far from the original Bequest footprint at the corner of East Bay and Calhoun. The move into town would have occurred in late 1879 or early 1880: the 1880 Federal census (dated June 1880) confirms the family of Bernhardt [*sic*] Bequest living at 305 East Bay Street.[20]

Rather peculiarly, the City directory for 1882 includes what looks like four Bequests: Bernhard's widowed Aunt Adelheid (mistakenly recorded in this listing as "Adeline") is "boarding" on Meeting Street; brother August (returned from his sojourn in Abbeville) is employed at "D. Rohde & Co" and living at #4

---

18. *News and Courier*, December 4, 1891.

19. *The Sunday News*, Charleston, S.C. August 8, 1920.

20. The 1880 census, for whatever reason, does not account for the daughter, Anna Meta Adeline, born in September of 1878, who died 1881 [April 19th] of scarlet fever: the official death record for the two-and-a half-year old stipulates her "place of residence" as "East Bay near Calhoun."

CHAPTER 6: THE MAYOR OF MOUNT PLEASANT

Morris Street; Benjamin H., a planter, resides at 305 East Bay Street; and Bernhard A., in "wood," resides at 11 Middle Street. The four individuals are really three. It has already been clarified that *Benjamin* and *Bernhard* had become interchangeable names for the Mt. Pleasant farmer/grocer/mayor, and here the confusion likely derives from the information for the Directory being reported orally. The German *A* (ah) and *H* (ha) are easily misheard or misunderstood, and the re-located wood dealer may intentionally have been using one name for his business and another within the confines of his home. #305 East Bay and #11 Middle Street were no more than a block apart from each other, and it was doubtless not the responsibility of the Directory canvasser to distinguish which individual was living or working under one name or the other at either location. Admittedly, the accuracy of these Directory listings is somewhat suspect: the 1884 listing has the "planter" Bequest's residence at #309 East Bay. While the houses on East Bay may have been re-numbered at some point, it is likely that the Bequests moved three times before settling into the house that stood as #335 East Bay—acknowledged in the 1885 Directory listing. The last move to #335 in 1882 was the final one for Bernhard and his family. [21]

Once back in the neighborhood of Calhoun and East Bay, the ex-mayor of Mt. Pleasant devoted himself to his business in wood. Given the general agricultural depression that affected everything and everyone in the postbellum South, the move had been Bequest's purposeful transition from merchandizing in the rural, agriculture-based environs of Christ Church Parish to the more urban setting in Charleston in which he would merchandize a commodity necessary to the re-building of a city doing its best to recover from the past and take its place in the "New South." It was not incidental that the opportunist Bequest recognized that

---

21. #335 was where Bernhard and Catherine's son John Frederick was born and raised and where, after Bernhard's death in 1899, John Frederick continued to live with his mother. John F. moved back to the house after his marriage in 1904 and raised his children there.

lumber milling was developing as a major industry in the Carolina Lowcountry,[22] and that wood and associated products would be needed and used to build and maintain what had previously been destroyed.

The move to Charleston to establish a new business was not without personal trauma. The couple had had a son, Anthony, born in Mt. Pleasant mid-1879, so that they moved into town with three children: ten-year-old Theresa Louise, Bernhard's daughter by his first wife, three-year-old Anna Meta Adeline, and Anthony, a toddler, aged two. But both of the younger children had died at tender ages by the middle of 1881. Theresa Louise was an only child when the couple's son, John Frederick, was born in September, 1882.

Despite these personal tragedies and the stresses of making a go of his new business, the German wood-dealer, as could have been expected, continued his involvement with the Schützen. The *News and Courier* of May 9, 1885, reported that among that year's Schützenfest prizewinners "B. F."[sic] Bequest had won a box of cigars. The reporter went on to relate how very much the men of the rifle club had become integrated into their *home, sweet home* Charleston:

> The prizes, the total value of which was 2600, were awarded by Capt. Alex Melchers, who briefly thanked the company for the interest they had taken in the festival. It was thirty-one years, he said, since the Schutzenfest was introduced into the United States. Though for centuries it had been observed in Germany. To Charleston belonged the honor of forming the first rifle club in this country. After the distribution of the prizes, the games were proceeded with until sundown. The cadets were about the last to leave the grounds, and on their way to town in their

---

22. By 1883 there were at least a dozen sawmills operating in the city (Fraser, *Charleston! Charleston!*, 309).

wagon regaled all who came within sound of their voices with "Way down in North Carolina," "Barney McCoy," "Wait till the clouds roll by," the German ditty "Schnick, Schnack der doodle sack," "Der Deutscher Rhein," and as they neared town, "Home Sweet Home."

Modeled after the German Schützengesellschaft, the Charleston Rifle Association was formed in 1883. In 1885 it held a contest between its sharpshooters and those of the Savannah club. The executive committee of the Charleston Association requested that B. H. Bequest be on its team. He and his fellow team-members—"experienced rifle shots, the best in the city"—regrettably lost the contest to Savannah: the high score for the Charleston team was 41. Bequest came in second high with 40.

That was in May. On the fourteenth of July, Bernhard Bequest left Charleston on the *City of Atlanta* for New York. He was on his way back to Germany, one month shy of his forty-first birthday. This trip back to his home would last for three months: he did not arrive back in New York until the middle of October as a passenger on the North German Lloyd's *Donau*. He was back in Charleston by the nineteenth. Just what the reasons were for such an extended absence remain unknown. His three sisters were more than likely still in Geestendorf, as well as his mother, Tette, who would have been a sixty-five year-old widow. Perhaps she had died[23] and there were estate matters to be settled. Perhaps it was simply time to recharge his batteries—there was no doubt that the past two decades had been draining. Becoming a native southerner in the era of the Civil War and Reconstruction would have tested the mettle of the best of the North German immigrants. But some reason of personal significance must have lain behind the wish or necessity to leave the Bequest wood yard in the hands of his employees or someone else. Again, the absence of any record leaves only the option of conjecture.

---

23. A verifiable date of death is lacking.

The wood yard, in fact, may have suffered some degree of mismanagement during his extended absence. In the archives of the South Carolina Historical Society there is a letter from the Charleston wholesale dealer of boots and shoes, D. O'Neill & Sons, dated November 1885 (one month after Bequest's return from Germany), in which the firm's lawyer had determined that "there [was] an amount of interest unpaid and an alleged credit for wood tickets for which no wood was delivered." The letter references Bequest's attorney, suggesting that the debt and the payment had been in dispute at some time previous: "Your lawyer in making the partial payment to Mr. Mordecai left out these items which together amounts to $36.00. It will be necessary for you to pay this before your note can be delivered up. Please call on Mr. Mordecai and arrange the matter with him before further proceedings entail more expense to you." The politeness of the letter does not obviate the fact that the wood merchant was in some bit of legal trouble, whether by his own hand or because someone else had made a mistake during his absence. At some point, Bequest must have paid his debt since there is no record of "further proceedings," but the dispute, nonetheless, had cost him something. Paying legal fees to settle a debt of thirty-six dollars suggests the complex scenario of a cash-flow problem—the purchase of shoes and boots on credit for what must have been "personal" needs—as well as possibly sloppy bookkeeping according to the unique "personal" method of the individual merchant. It seems unlikely that the upstanding Lutheran Bequest would have purposefully tried to scam Mr. O'Neill and then engaged legal counsel to defend his actions. It was undoubtedly the case that operating in the local business world of 1885 had become more complicated than it had been twenty years earlier, and the immigrant still carried something of an extra burden in navigating the multiple demands of family, business, and Charleston society.

The earlier bulk sale to Otto Wieters of various property did not include the Bequest store in "downtown" Mt. Pleasant. It was for rent at the end of 1885, an asset Bequest had wisely held onto and that would now serve as a source of extra income: the advertisement in the *News and Courier* described the store "opposite the Courthouse, formerly occupied by B. H. Bequest, one of the best stands in the town." Henry Schachte, the Broad Street real estate and insurance agent, must have been successful on behalf of his client: the "To Rent" advertisement only ran twice.

If the Bequest wood-yard had previously been located on East Bay Street close to where the family was living, the 1886 City Directory indicates that the wood lot had been relocated adjacent to the north of the residence. There he was closer to Calhoun Street and the wharf at its eastern end where some of his products could be off-loaded. He could advertise, for example, that he had "2,000 bushels Pon-Pon gravel. I will deliver at $1.75 per load from Marshall's wharf. East end Calhoun street."

We can assume that running the wood business during this period in Charleston would have required a fairly vigilant eye on the competition: the Bequest operation was surrounded by twelve other wood yards of various sizes and popularity, so that the former Mt. Pleasant farmer/merchant was only one of many in the business of "wood." All the wood dealers in town would have taken more than usual notice of each other in late summer of 1886. On the last day of August, Charleston suffered "a terrible earthquake," "the most disastrous event in the city's history." The city's Bequests were not named among those injured or killed, nor were either Bernhard's or August's business operations cited for extraordinary losses.[24] But, as the newspaper headlines suggested, "the whole city [was] injured." The local group of wood dealers would have been cognizant of the extent of each other's losses, although their wares stored in open lots were probably less susceptible to damage than others' structures or the goods warehoused in them. Whatever the damages caused by Charleston's famous earthquake, wood-merchant Bequest, like everyone else, had little choice but to pick up and keep going. The earthquake may actually have been good for the city's wood dealers.

---

24. Ninety-two people died.

Trying to be successful as one of Charleston's wood merchants seems to have noticeably diminished Bequest's involvement with his fellow Schützen. For a number of years his name is noticeably absent from the list of prizewinners in the newspaper columns covering the annual Schützenfest festivities: only in 1891 is he mentioned as fourth-prize winner in one of the target competitions. His all but complete disappearance from the annual target contests seems to argue that something had changed in his relationship with his fellow Schützen. Had something personal occurred so that he purposefully avoided the company of his compatriots? Had he felt that his skill as a marksman was not what it had been earlier? Perhaps the Club itself was changing in ways that he did not approve of; perhaps he recognized that as times were changing the festival itself was losing some of its aura. The newspaper report in May of 1886[25] did seem somewhat reticent, with more attention paid to the *Platz* than to the festivities themselves:

> The Schutzenfest of 1886 was inaugurated yesterday with becoming military and Terpsichorean honors. Like everything else that is undertaken by Capt. Melchers and his command, the festival of 1886 promises to come up to the high standard of the Gesellschaft. . . . The park, which, as everyone knows, is situated just north of the city boundary, and on the banks of the Ashley, is one of the best arranged and most suitable pleasure grounds in the vicinity of the city. The Gesellschaft have spent thousands of dollars in its improvement, and have made it a beautiful and attractive resort. The booths built under the tall pines are handsomely decorated; the poplars planted some years ago have attained a fine growth. And the freshly painted and picturesque buildings gaily decorated with bunting,

---

25. *News and Courier*, May 13, 1886.

CHAPTER 6: THE MAYOR OF MOUNT PLEASANT

representing the flags of all nations, give the place a holiday appearance which is suggestive only of mirth.

In any case, it would have appeared to the newspaper reader that the twice-honored Schützenfest King had backed away from the kind of involvement that had been his signature in earlier years. The Schützenfest nonetheless continued to be the major spring festival in Charleston during the years through the turn of the century, although the newspaper accounts marking each year's celebrations seem to get shorter, the enthusiasm somewhat formulaic, the "Capt. Melchers well-planned program" giving way to new entertainments that had little to do with the original agenda, and new names—a younger crowd—among those responsible for the *Platz* and its program. It was the case that the city and its citizens, including its Germans, were in a different place and of a different mood than where they had been twenty years earlier.

But perhaps none of these conjectures about his relationship with the Schützen explain why Bequest's name is absent from the public record of the annual Schützenfests. It is not entirely incidental that in 1886 a new lodge of the Fraternal Order of Knights of Pythias was formed in Charleston. In January 1887, the *News and Courier* seemed pleased to report that

> [a] meeting of Palmetto Division (uniform rank) of the Knights of Pythias was held at Pythian Hall last night. The principal business of the meeting was the measurement of the Knights for their uniforms, the orders for which have been sent to the Pettibone Manufacturing Company of Cincinnati, who will forward them to Charleston within a month. The uniform is said to be very handsome and imposing. It consists of black frock coats and pants, white helmets and plumes and gilded belts, with swords and side arms. Palmetto Division has recently been organized here with the assistance of Mr. Knight R. M.

> Haywood, colonel and aide-de-camp of Brunswick, Ga. Its membership numbers forty, and its first parade will be made probably in November or December next.
> The following are the officers of the division: A. A. Kroeg, Sir Knight Commander; D. M. Kirk, Sir Knight Lieutenant Commander; George M. Trenholm, Sir Knight Herald; B. H. Bequest, Sir Knight treasurer; W. B. Gross, Sir Knight recorder.
> The members are all connected with the Order of Knights of Pythias, of which there are several lodges in this city and in other parts of the state.

Bequest's role in organizing this new division of the fraternal order and his serving as its treasurer suggests that he was not so much downplaying his affiliation with the Schützen fraternity, but rather expanding his circle of contacts and involving himself in a different fraternal association.

Even at first glance, the similarities between the Schützen and the Pythians seem obvious: if in the previous year the Schützenfest was reported to have begun with "becoming military and Terpsichorean honors," the Pythians founding the Palmetto Division were comparably thrilled with their splendid uniforms—"very handsome and imposing"—and the prospects of marching in a parade displaying their finery, swords, and side arms. It is not unimportant that it was the "military department" of the Order that was referred to as the "Uniform Rank."[26] This new Pythian affiliation would command Bequest's attention over the course of the coming years. It was not that there were anything like distinct differences separating the two fraternities—much the same group

---

26. The website (kophistory.com) notes that the Uniform Rank (UR) "came into being in 1878. A great many Pythians were Civil War Veterans and some lodges formed their own military drill teams. This would in time evolve into the Uniformed Ranks. The Pythian UR was sometimes known as the Army of the Lily."

of individuals belonged to both and they were "connected" in more ways than one. But during the years after 1886 Bequest's name is more often in the record in connection with the Pythians than with the Schützen. Was he more comfortable in the company of the one group dedicated to friendship, charity and benevolence as he transitioned into the Charleston at the end of the century? Had he thought that the arc of the popularity of the Schützenfest had reached its high point so that its ethnic-sponsored "mirth" might no longer be the right mechanism for accomplishing a more complete acculturation to Charleston ways? Was it that he wanted to exchange his German sharpshooter image for one that was defined by membership in a somewhat less militaristic, more Americanized, brotherhood of citizens "pledged to the promotion of understanding among men of good will as the surest means of attaining Universal Peace"?

The "Thirty-Three Knights Knocking Around Charleston" headline in the *News and Courier* in December, 1887, gave a full explanation of the "benevolent and charitable organization," but also described the impressive uniform and requisite amount of military training "so that in case of necessity every member of the Uniform Rank could take his place in the volunteer army of the nation with some practical knowledge of the duties of an officer and soldier."[27] The next year (1888) the Knights and their guests had a "grand time" at their first annual picnic at the Schützenplatz where B. H. Bequest took sixth prize at the 100-yards ring target. In 1889 Sir Knight Treasurer Bequest was one of some seventy Charleston Knights from the city's two divisions of the Uniform Rank (Charleston and Palmetto) who travelled by train in their full regalia to attend the annual meeting of the Grand Lodge, Knights of Pythias, of South Carolina. At the June 1889 "second annual summer's night festival of Palmetto Division" Bequest took first prize—$10 in gold—in the 200-yards Ring Target competition. He took another prize in 1890, travelled with his fellow Knights to Milwaukee in a special railroad car furnished by the South

---

27. *News and Courier*, December 11, 1887.

Carolina Railway,[28] and was re-elected treasurer in both 1893 and 1894. It would appear that the fifty-year-old had settled into another niche that suited him just fine.

All the while, of course, the wood yard kept him busy. The yard had been expanded southward along East Bay, almost to Hasell Street. The 1891-93 City Directory claims wood *yards* in the plural, at Palmetto wharf and 288 East Bay. Along with his competitors, he advertised constantly in the *News and Courier*—ads that varied just slightly in message and in size. He sold pine and oak blocks, gravel, molding, white and yellow sand, red clay, lightwood and yellow pine—"cut to any length. 6 inches up, just as you want it, for stoves, fireplaces or grates. Delivered promptly." His office was at the corner of Hasell and East Bay streets, his telephone number, 272. During the Christmas season in 1894, the *News and Courier* ran a column of "Christmas Tide Comforts," offering suggestions to holiday shoppers of what to buy and where to buy it. "Among the gentlemen and firms in heterogeneous flourishing professions, trades and business in and about town who are deserving of public commendation through the columns of the News and Courier as well for their business integrity as for their unquestioned success in their respective lines are the following:...B. H. Bequest...numbered among the first-class supply yards for fine gravel, brick, etc. is the firm name of the above named gentleman."[29]

In his capacity as wood merchant, Bequest was under contract with the city as early as 1890 for work, the nature of which is never specified: between 1890 and 1893 there are a number of City Council reports that show the city approving invoices for minor amounts ($16.25, $19.50, $23.90, $22.50, $7.50, etc.), usually listed in the Council's report under

---

28. "The entire car was draped in red, blue and yellow, the colors of the Order. From each side of the car hung banners, on which were printed in colors the words: 'Palmetto Division, Uniform Rank, Knights of Pythias, of Charleston, S.C. to Milwaukee, Wis. The South Carolina Railway, The Old Reliable.'" *News and Courier*, July 4, 1890.

29. *News and Courier*, December 19, 1894.

CHAPTER 6: THE MAYOR OF MOUNT PLEASANT

"Commissioners Public Lands." He was doubtless a known entity to the City Council: he tried in 1892 to sell his "second-hand fifteen-horse power boiler, in good order" that he had at his location at Palmetto wharf, and when it failed to sell, he had his fellow Pythian, A. A. Kroeg, who served as alderman, bring his petition to the Council in 1893 "to remove steam engine to 288 East Bay Street." The petition was "referred to committee on steam engines with power to act." He kept the engine for years at his other location.

The suggestion was made earlier that Bequest's affiliating with the Pythian Order signaled his effort to expand his circle of acquaintances and to be associated with an organization dedicated to manifestly admirable goals. The Pythians and the Schützen were so similarly oriented, however, that becoming a Pythian did not move Bequest much beyond his already recognizable groove. In his circle there were hardly any groups of Germans with which he did not enjoy some relationship. Although there is no evidence that he was formally a member of the German Artillery, he had more than a simple ethnic bond with the men who comprised the membership. This particular group of Germans had their origin in the militia company organized by John Andreas Wagener already in 1841. In 1892 the members of the organization—the venerable old and the sentimental new—celebrated the organization's "semi-centennial" in October, an event that received a lot of coverage in the local press, once again certifying that the Germans were held in high regard by the local citizenry. The event was a torchlight parade from the Artillery Hall on Wentworth Street up King Street to the square in front of the Citadel and across the street from St. Matthew's German Lutheran Church. If the columns in the *News and Courier* are accurate, most of Charleston's citizens turned out to admire the marchers in their very impressive finery and the adults, at least, to reflect on what the German Artillery stood for. Before the parade got underway, Theodore Melchers presented a custom-designed badge to the group's leader, Capt. Frederick Wagener:

> It is your untiring exertion which has made this company what it now is: it is through your

influence and your work that to-day it owns this magnificent armory, second to none in the Southern States, and it is your untiring zeal which has made this day such a success. This beautiful jewel has been chosen with special care to commemorate your various services. You here behold the shield or battle flag of the "Lost Cause," surrounded by rays of glory, surmounted by the emblem of the Artillery, crossed cannons and the eagle—above which you see our national colors and those of Germany, united and held together by the coat-of-arms of our beloved State, South Carolina. These emblems are to denote that you fought as a true and brave defender of the "Lost Cause": that you are a true son of the Fatherland, a loyal citizen of the United States, and a prince (a merchant prince) of South Carolina. Wear it near your heart as a perpetual memento of the love and esteem which your comrades bear you.[30]

In the spectacle of the torchlight parade that moved among the throngs down Wentworth and up King Street, there were eight carriages "filled with veteran members of the company and their guests." In the second carriage were Levi Wetherhorn, J. F. Stelling, Capt. A, Melchers, and B. Bequest. More than likely a guest of Alexander Melchers, Bernhard Bequest was surely proud to be in such company. He cannot have been the least uncomfortable celebrating the accomplishments of Frederick

---

30. *News and Courier*, October 19, 1892. Frederick Wagener was a younger brother of John Andreas, the leader of the ethnic community's early triumvirate that worked so hard to integrate their fellow German immigrants into the native community. It is possibly gratuitous to note that the newspaper was sufficiently capable of forgetting the recent past so that its reporter could casually, but incorrectly, refer to the late German leader as "Julius A. Wagener" in his column's second paragraph.

CHAPTER 6: THE MAYOR OF MOUNT PLEASANT

Wagener, a Confederate war hero who had fought bravely for the "Lost Cause" and then become one of Charleston's leading businessmen.[31] After all, Bequest was a friend of almost everyone on the podium or in the parade. His path to acculturation was in parallel with theirs, and he would probably have been just as proud to be in uniform and carry one of the torches had he not been invited on this occasion to ride with one of the city's leading Germans. And he could shoot with the best of them: at the Artillerymen's June 1894 picnic in Summerville in the park by Wagener's Pine Forest Inn ("eleven packed coaches bore the picnickers from the Line street depot") Bequest took second place at Target No. 1—"which was a pay target, the prizes were a percentage of the total receipts"—winning 15 percent. At Target No. 2, his marksmanship enabled him to carry home a somewhat less impressive box of canned peaches.

While trying to glimpse the nature of Bernhard Bequest's Charleston life during the years leading up to his fiftieth birthday in 1894, not much attention has been paid to the political climate and whether it impacted him, and if so, to what degree. At the national level, James Garfield was elected president in 1880, but South Carolina had cast its electoral votes for his Democratic rival, Winfield Hancock. In '84, Grover Cleveland came to power with South Carolina's nine electoral votes behind him. South Carolina's democrats were out of step in 1888 when Benjamin Harrison was elected. Cleveland came back in 1892, again with the help of the state's electoral votes. Locally, supremacist

---

31. "Frederick W. Wagener's contribution to Charleston's economic development was profound and indisputable. Wagener arrived at the height of German immigration to Charleston. He began his business career as a retail grocer like so many other Germans. Upon returning to Charleston in 1865 after his service in the Confederate Army, he partnered with other Germans to form a wholesale grocery establishment that grew into a significant business in the community." Quoted from Jeffrey Strickland, "Frederick Wagener, 1832-1921," *Immigrant Entrepreneurship: German-American Biographies 1720 to the Present*, 2015 (http://www.immigrantentrepreneurship.org/entry.php?rec=24 accessed January 21, 2016).

southerners were managing the political scene with the "Eight Box Voting law"[32] that was in place by 1882. After that, the most political excitement revolved around renegade Benjamin Tillman who started making noise already in 1885 when he "made a stunning speech on the plight of the farmer at Bennettsville before the State Grange and the State Agricultural and Mechanical Society."[33] Tillman kept at it, and was successful in ousting South Carolina's old conservative regime by winning the governor's race in 1890. He was the state's governor from 1890 to 1894, and one of its U.S. senators from 1895 to 1918. His words in his inaugural speech suggest the political road traveled since the end of the Reconstruction era:

> The citizens of this great commonwealth have for the first time in its history demanded and obtained for themselves the right to choose her Governor; and I, as the exponent and leader of the revolution which brought about the change am here to take the solemn oath of office.... Democracy, the rule of the people, has won a victory unparalleled in its magnitude and importance.... The triumph of democracy and white supremacy over mongrelism and anarchy, of civilization over barbarism, has been most complete.[34]

It is difficult to believe that the German immigrant would have come so far as to subscribe to this kind of rabid political

---

32. This constituted a literacy test, requiring voters to put ballots in separate ballot boxes. Illiterate voters—the targeted black population—would require "assistance" to put their ballot in the proper box.

33. George C. Rogers, Jr. and C. James Taylor, *A South Carolina Chronology 1497-1992*. 2nd ed., (1994), 111.

34. Francis Butler Simkins, *Pitchfork Ben Tillman, South Carolinian* (Baton Rouge: Louisiana State University Press, 1944), 170-71.

radicalism, although it was the distinctive flavor of the political soup of the time, not easily dismissible, but not easily swallowed by a non-native. One non-race-related issue during Tillman's governorship would have been of particular interest to the beer-loving Germans—the question of prohibition. South Carolinians passed a non-binding referendum in 1892 calling for prohibition. Tillman managed to subvert the teetotalers by having a Dispensary law enacted, effective July 1, 1893, that prevented the private sale of liquor and required that it be sold between sunrise and sunset in sealed packages which could not be opened on the Dispensary premises. After resistance to the law led to rioting in the city of Darlington in 1894, the state Supreme Court declared the law unconstitutional. Within a year, Tillman managed to replace one of the Supreme Court judges, and the court subsequently declared the 1893 law constitutional.[35]

The Charleston Germans would surely not have signed up to be prohibitionists, so the alternative was to be *for* the Dispensary law. Within weeks of the law's initial passage, the *News and Courier* furnished a list[36] of those freehold voters who had signed the petition of Henry A. Meyer—doubtless a German—to be appointed dispenser for Charleston County. B. H. Bequest was one of the signatories. It was questionable how conscientiously the law would have to be followed, and it might have been assumed that with a fellow German as the Dispenser, there would be some wiggle room. It did not seem to matter much to anyone that twice in 1896 B. H. Bequest was subjected to "police raids" that found him at 288 East Bay harboring "a demijohn of whisky and 15 bottles of palmetto beer."[37]

---

35. The law was in effect until 1907.

36. *News and Courier*, July 18, 1893.

37. *Evening Post*, February 6, 1896. The police also raided C H. Hutmacher, P. J. Hilson, and C. F. Klencke, all of whom were guilty of having a few bottles of beer. In April, "Under the Post's Eyes," "a demijohn of whisky was seized yesterday at Bequest's place on East Bay." [*Evening Post*, April 24, 1896].

If the 1886 earthquake had left the wood yard at 288 East Bay Street relatively undamaged, the hurricanes that visited their fury on Charleston in 1893—one hit in late August, another in mid-October—also seemed to have had little effect on the Bequest operation. The *News and Courier* reported on the extensive damage[38] and "what all is going on to restore and repair," but assured its readers that "Broderick's coal and wood wharf is again in good condition," and that "H. Bequest's wood yard is again stacked with logs and blocks."[39]

When back in 1879 Bequest had sold lots in Mt. Pleasant along with other items to Otto Wieters, one of the items sold was a sloop. At the time, it was not worth noting that the Mt. Pleasant grocer with a nautical background and extensive sailing experience, living in a village on the shore across the river from Charleston, owned a boat. But having divested himself of that vessel, at some later point he acquired something larger, a schooner which he named *Lenore*. Exactly when or how that acquisition had come about is unclear, but in April of 1894 there were legal notices in several issues of the *News and Courier* in which he stated that as "Half Owner" he would "not be responsible for any debts contracted by the Captain or Crew of the schooner LENORE." There is nothing in the record to reveal what this apparent dispute involved, or who the other owner of *Lenore* might have been. But between this point in 1894 and 1899 Bequest became the sole owner of the two-masted sailing vessel: it was listed as one item in the inventory of the wood yard after his death. No matter how much of a Charlestonian he had become, the North German Geestendorfer with a yearning for the water had remained true to his heritage.

Bequest's wood yard was one of three of the city's "firms" that in 1894 was awarded a government contract:

---

38. Between the two storms, "over 1,000 lives were lost in the coastal areas." (George C. Rogers, Jr. and C. James Taylor, *A South Carolina Chronology 1497-1992*, 2nd ed. [1994], 113.)

39. *News and Courier*, September 2, 1893.

CHAPTER 6: THE MAYOR OF MOUNT PLEASANT

> Three city firms in luck. / Government contracts awarded for furnishing coal, wood and provisions. / Washington, April 9.—Special: The Secretary of the Treasury has awarded the contract for furnishing fuel for vessels for use in the 6th light house district for the fiscal year ending June 30, 1895 for coal to Johnson & Co. of Charleston, and for wood to B. H. Bequest, of Charleston. The contract for furnishing provisions in the same district and fiscal year for vessels to Welch & Eason, of Charleston.[40]

He must have felt that the government contract carried with it a modicum of prestige and an affirmation of his success in the business. His ads during the summer months of 1895 projected confidence: "The best dry oak and pine blocks in the city. Oak $1.95, Pine $1. Mixed $1.10, delivered. B. H. Bequest, Wood yard corner East Bay and Hasell. Telephone 272."

During the 1890s the Americanized wood dealer started playing baseball. Baseball in Charleston at that time was a new recreational outlet for the still-recovering city, apparently something the athletic sharpshooter wanted to try his hand at. In 1894 he was a team member of the "amateur baseball club," the "Osceolas." The competition with other Southern teams, for example the "Clippers" from Nashville, was important enough to civic pride that the newspaper kept the public informed of wins and losses: before the age of television was even conceived, one could follow the games in local establishments: "Two league games to-day. The Mobile and New Orleans games to-day will be given by innings at Mollenhauer's King street restaurant this afternoon."[41] The previous afternoon, the Osceolas had played the

---

40. *News and Courier*, April 10, 1895.

41. *News and Courier*, May 27, 1894.

Clippers and won: "McClure and Bequest held the points for the Osceolas, McMillan and Scherlock for the Clippers."

By early 1895 things had become more organized: there was a "Charleston Base Ball Club" that played neighboring towns and was part of the South Atlantic League. The *News and Courier* followed its team closely, and in May announced that "on next Thursday the club will give the people of Charleston a chance to see what they are made of, as a game will be played with the club from Orangeburg. Arrangements have also been made with the Independents of Birmingham, Ala, for a series of three games early July and some games with Savannah in the latter part of June." The fans were assured that "all the players on the Charleston Club have been working on the diamond for several years and some of them have held positions in the South Atlantic League three years ago."[42] B. H. Bequest among them; he was the Club's secretary and treasurer. His involvement in the Club was a sufficiently important aspect of his leisure-time interests that it extended to his son, John Frederick. In the summer before his eleventh birthday, he was playing first base on the "Young Sea Gulls" team. The *News and Courier* in May 1893 ran a letter "To the Editor of the News and Courier: The Crack Base Ball Club of the city has been practicing in the Park every afternoon since last Wednesday, and is now in fine trim, and the manager feels confident that they can wipe up the diamond with any club in the city who has not a player over 17 years old." John Frederick would follow in his father's footsteps as a newsworthy member of a number of Charleston teams, carrying on the legacy of his German father whose talents and skills extended beyond those of the Schützengesellschaft's sharpshooter.

The year 1895 would turn out to be an important one for the senior Bequest. At age fifty-one, he still had it in himself to undertake a new business enterprise, demonstrating the same kind of entrepreneurship that many of his German colleagues had brought to the Charleston community. One senses that he was never in a position to be idle, even though he seems to have found

---

42. *News and Courier*, May 27, 1895.

CHAPTER 6: THE MAYOR OF MOUNT PLEASANT

enough leisure time to engage in sport. In December, the *News and Courier* featured a rather lengthy column describing what the German Mr. Bequest had been doing while managing his wood business:

> Mr. B. H. Bequest, a progressive and enterprising citizen of Charleston, who has for a long time been engaged in the wood business on East Bay, had recently visited his old home at Bremerhaven, Germany, and there discovered a process of smoking fish that he thought could be worked to advantage in Charleston. Upon his return to the city Mr. Bequest went to work at once and yesterday turned out the first batch of smoked whiting from his new smoke house. The fish were caught on Tuesday, cleaned and placed in pickle Tuesday night and smoked four hours yesterday. They were then taken out on the long spits and hung up on frames to cool. A reporter for The News and Courier tasted one of this first batch half an hour after it was taken out and found that they had lost none of the delicate flavor, the flesh being firm and white. The skin of the whiting is tinged a golden brown by the smoke and it is ready for the table after being warmed.
>
> Whiting, the most delicious of pan fish, are not easily kept after being taken from the water, unless packed on ice, but by this process of smoking they will be easily transported, dry, into the country and kept for a week if necessary.
>
> The smoke house is located on Mr. Bequest's premises, 335 East Bay, and is a neat and substantial two-story brick structure. On the first floor are a set of seven large smoking ovens, with double iron doors 4 by 6 feet. In these ovens are racks and the fish spitted through the heads, hung in rows of a dozen to twenty. In the bottom of each oven a fire is kept up with hickory chips and

large flues carry off the smoke after it has passed through the pendant tiers of fish.

Mr. Bequest has not yet fully arranged the other parts of the building, but there will be a cooling and packing room and other accessories.

The industry bids fair to be a prosperous and successful one, and Mr. Bequest is to be congratulated upon introducing it in Charleston. He will probably have the fish on sale in a few days at the principal grocers, and will also be ready for orders from the country. The capacity of the smoke house is several hundred pounds of fish per day, and several varieties, other than whiting, will also be available. The price will likely be 10 to 12 ½ cents a pound for smoked fish, which is comparatively cheaper than the undressed fish, which have to be used the day caught or kept on ice.[43]

While there is no record of the "recent" trip back to Bremerhaven, it is entirely possible that Bequest had been hatching the idea for as long as a decade, ever since his three-month sojourn ten years earlier. But when he got the idea is less important than what the idea was.

It was to all appearances a brilliant concept. Fish—most noticeably what the locals referred to as "whiting"[44]—had long been a staple in the coastal city, prepared in a variety of ways but not smoked. It took a European immigrant to see the advantages of pairing an abundant resource of the host community with a method of preservation long known to the ethnic community to produce an innovation with considerable appeal to the needs and

---

43. *News and Courier*, December 5, 1895.

44. *Menticirrhus americanus* (Carolina whiting), abundant along the Atlantic and Gulf coasts, was similar to *Merlangius merlangus* (English whiting) known to inhabitants along the North Sea and the east coast of Britain.

tastes of the Charleston citizens living in the New South. Putting the idea to work, to be sure, had taken capital, as well as ingenuity. It had not happened overnight: he had figured that he had found a new use for the wood he already had on hand; he had planned the space to locate the ovens; had conceptualized how they were to be built; had investigated and recruited the sources of supply; engineered the production operation and schedule; and was prepared to undertake the marketing and distribution operation for what was to be a thriving wholesale business.

Five days after the initial story, the following appeared under "Special Notices":

> The European Fish Smokery, 335 East Bay / The public can now be supplied with all kinds of smoked fish. / Florida, Mullet, Whiting, &c, smoked fresh every day. / F. W. Cappelmann, J. H. Hesse, C. Muller, P. von Oven, F. Heinsohn, are now supplied with Fish from this smokery. / B. H. Bequest, / Proprietor / Telephone 272.[45]

Bequest's outlets were obviously some of his German grocer-friends who were more than happy to lend their support. And the operation immediately got the attention of those who advocated any new undertaking that might stimulate the local economy. Before the week was up, the newspaper called on the business community to step up to the plate and support what Bequest had initiated:

> The announcement of Mr. Bequest's success in curing fish for market and his intention to develop the industry on a considerable scale meets with a hearty and encouraging response from the farther side of the State. In his letter, which is printed this morning, Mr. W. R. McCreight, of Camden, hails the new industry as 'a great thing for Charleston,' and a very gratifying one for a good

---

45. *News and Courier*, December 9, 1895.

many ichthyophageously disposed people in all parts of the State, and expresses the opinion that if some of our enterprising business men will take hold of the business and catch and smoke fish for sale regularly they will be public benefactors and make money besides.

We think Mr. McCreight is right. There is an abundance of good fish to be had for the catching near Charleston and all along the coast of the State. The supply and the consumption in the State are far greater than most of the people of the State or even of the city and the coast region know or imagine....

If they will buy fresh fish they will buy smoked fish, which require no ice, and cost considerably less for transportation and have the especial merit besides of "keeping" until they are ready for the table. Mr. Bequest has proved that our fish can be smoked quickly and cheaply in Charleston, and that when so prepared they are quite good enough to sell themselves for ever afterward to any person who is fortunate enough to try them once. His smoked whiting are in the nature of a luxury. He could sell them by the ton if their merits were widely known and he could supply them by the ton. Other kinds, similarly prepared, are quite or nearly of as good quality. The industry of catching and preparing and selling them only needs a little money and push for its speedy development to large proportions here and at other points along the coast. It should receive at once the kind and degree of encouragement it needs. Mr. Bequest has demonstrated what can be done. Some of our enterprising business men should see to it that it is done for the comfort and profit of all concerned. Why should we buy salt mackerel and herring and cod from far States and countries when we can supply ourselves with better fish at home and make money by selling some of them besides? Can anybody say? If Mr. Bequest will give a smoked fish dinner and offer a subscription list for a joint stock smoking company to his invited guests, after they have dined, we will answer for the rest. The industry will be fairly under way before some of the very conservative business men can make up their conservative minds to inquire "what all the row is about?"[46]

A fairly large ad ran repeatedly in the *News and Courier* for the next five months, into May of 1896, worded: "A New departure for Charleston. A smokery which fills orders for air-dried and smoked fish roes, geese, eels and fish of all kinds. Try them. They are fine. For sale by all grocers. Country orders solicited. Address: The European Fish Company, Charleston, S.C., B. H. Bequest, Proprietor." For the first year, success seemed imminent:

> Mr. B. H. Bequest, who has recently put up a set of smoking ovens on his premises, 335 East Bay, and begun the drying and smoking of fish, etc. said to a reporter yesterday that the ovens were proving a success and he had every reason to be gratified with his work.
>
> Just at this season, he said, that fish suitable for smoking and drying were not plentiful in the Charleston market, and his supply came mostly from Florida. Besides smoking fish Mr. Bequest has cured and smoked hams and tongues most successfully.
>
> As yet Mr. Bequest has sent but little fish out of the city, the local trade having taken all he could

---

46. *News and Courier*, December 11, 1895.

furnish. In a short time, however, he will begin to cure and smoke sturgeon, and this can be secured in such quantities that he will have plenty for out of town shipments and will likely send a good deal to New York. The process used by Mr. Bequest is one learned by him in Germany last summer."[47]

In the Fall of 1896, his neighbor grocer, F. Wehman Sons at 309 East Bay at the corner of Laurens Street, was advertising Bequest's smoked fish: "If you have not tried them yet try them now....We get them fresh daily...smoked mullet, large, fine, 10 cents each. Smoked whiting, 20 cents a pound. The most palatable delicacy served cold."[48]

After that year, it is unclear just how long Bequest kept the smokery operational. The Bequest ads in the newspaper from March through July of 1897 were all modestly-sized ads for the wood lot selling dry oak and pine blocks. There were, noticeably, no advertisements for smoked fish. He may have kept it up, however, as a sideline to the wood yard. In an article summarizing Bequest's successes in Charleston that appeared in June of 1898, the reporter wrote: "Mr. Bequest also has the latest European fish smokery, an idea obtained in Germany two years ago. He can supply the city with delicious smoked fish at any time." [49]

One might wonder how what looked to be such a promising undertaking could in relatively short order turn sour. In hindsight, the entire venture may not have been such a brilliant idea. Had Bequest thought through the seasonal nature of his supply? How often would he have to bring fish from Florida, rather than from local waters? Other than his ethnic neighbors, were local housewives likely to cease frying freshly caught

---

47. *News and Courier*, January 13, 1896.

48. *News and Courier*, October 23, 1896. The ad ran through November 11th.

49. *Evening Post*, June 11, 1898.

whiting to plan meals around the smoked version? Were commercial fishermen going to sell their catch to other markets so that there would be no competition for the new delicacy? How complicated could the distribution of the new product become? It was one thing to deliver an order of wood chips to a buyer, quite another to get a perishable commodity to a widely distributed network of retail markets on a schedule determined by supply and demand. How much labor would it involve to generate the supply sufficient to the demand? If the wood lot had been manageable by a single proprietor, a production line would entail a number of employees and require a different kind of management. These and other questions may have been beyond the business acumen of the single entrepreneur of foreign birth bringing a new commercial idea into a culture almost paralytic by nature—more than one man, however honest and enterprising, could handle. The newspaper's insight into the fact that Bequest's initiative could be scaled up only with the backing of "enterprising business men" interested in "the comfort and profit of all concerned" is telling. In truth, Charleston in the 1890s was not the place to find many enterprising businessmen interested in capitalizing a new business in smoked fish. Whatever forethought was lacking in Bequest's entrepreneurial spirit, it would be reasonable to think that his European smokery fell victim to the soft economy that prevailed at the time. In his *Charleston! Charleston!* Walter Fraser explains that Charleston in those years had become a "commercial backwater." After northern interests had bought up failing South Carolina railroads and consolidated them into a southwest-northeast oriented line, shipping that had previously run through Charleston was directed elsewhere. Other cities in the region, such as Atlanta, Augusta, Columbia, and Charlotte developed while Charleston languished:

> The volume of trade through the harbor fell from $98.5 million in 1890-91 to $29.5 million a decade later as Charleston's share of the total United States export trade dropped below 1 percent. The taxable value of Charleston real estate declined from $25 million in 1895 to $19

million in 1904 and the city's population relative to other American cities continued to decline: in 1870 it ranked twenty-sixth among urban centers, in 1890 fifty-third, and by 1910, ninety-first. . . .

Two hotels had been refurbished by October 1894 to attract the tourist trade, but by this time local capitalists regarded Charleston enterprises as too risky. Both the old money and the new wealth made in phosphates by the Smyth, Pelzer, Jervey, Frost, Bee, and Chisholm families were being invested in upcountry textile mills, Alabama iron foundries, and street railways and utilities in cities like Nashville and Atlanta. At the same time ambitious and capable young men with prominent, local family names like Hayne, Barnwell, Rhett, Smith, and Huger were leaving Charleston for southern cities that offered them more opportunities.[50]

All factors considered, it had turned out that the vision behind the Bequest fish smokery had not materialized in the right place at the right time.

In spite of this glum context descriptive of the odds that Bequest was up against, the careful reader of the *News and Courier* of December 21, 1895 might have noticed on the first page a column headlined "A Commercial Pot Pouri / Some of the city's best business houses / Men who have done much to build up Charleston's credit to home and abroad " that went on to propose that "there are in Charleston many firms in flourishing professions, trades and businesses. Not all of them deal, strictly speaking, in holiday goods, but in a review of the prominent commercial houses of the city and of the men at the head of them it seems scarcely fair to omit those who have added so largely to the old city's prosperity." Two of those mentioned were "The European Smokery"—"under the proprietorship of B. H. Bequest...the work

---

50. Fraser, 327-28.

is done in the most thoroughly satisfactory manner and a most appetizing article is offered to the housekeepers of the city"—and the "Equitable Fire Insurance Co."—"with an authorized capital of $500,000...controlled by the following efficient business men of Charleston: Mr. James F. Redding, in capacity as president, with Mr. W. G. Mazyck acting as secretary and treasurer; and Mr. A. Bequest as vice president." Both Bernhard and his younger brother August might have felt some satisfaction in being recognized in the same column suggesting that both had "added so largely" to Charleston's prosperity. But by the middle of the next year (1896) Bernhard and his European smokery would have happily avoided association with August and his vice- presidential office in the Equitable Fire Insurance Company. By July of 1896 the Bequest name would suffer a considerable amount of bad press, and it is not unlikely that the success and/or popularity of Bernhard's smokery suffered under the negative news that would soon surround his younger brother

With the fish smokery on questionable footing, Bequest kept the wood lot going as in the past. Whatever negativity August brought to the family name starting in 1896[51]—the details follow in chapter 8—Bernhard retained his good name and reputation. For its "Deep Water Edition" of June 11, 1898, the *Evening Post* condensed the biography of the wood dealer into a lengthy column headlined "Success / Is the reward for the efforts of that well known and popular gentleman and citizen / B. H. Bequest / Wholesale and retail dealer in oak and pine wood, oak and pine blocks, gravel and white sand / Office and plant located at 288 East Bay Street, telephone / 272":

> In mentioning our citizens who have made a success by energy and business ability the name of B. H. Bequest stands among the leaders of Charleston's prosperous men.

---

51. It was also in 1896 that Bernhard lost the properties that he had purchased in 1891 from Charlotte Smith when the Germania Bank foreclosed on him.

Mr. Bequest is a native of Germany, where he was reared and educated. In 1861 he entered Charleston harbor in the bark Goss under Capt. Vieting, that well known seaman (now deceased). The morning he entered the harbor the confederate flag was flying over Fort Sumter, and a short time after, Mr. Bequest, true to the cause he believed right, entered the Confederate service and experienced some thrilling adventures in the blockade service under Capt. Moore steamer Fannie. He was on the Stonewall Jackson/Sirene with Capt. Black, and others.

Mr. Bequest is an old and tried seaman, having serviced in England, Scotland, Russia, Mexico, West Indies, etc.

After the war Mr. Bequest started in the grocery business on a very small scale at Mount Pleasant, remaining there for sixteen years. He was one of the leading citizens and enjoyed the confidence of the people. He was honored by the people, serving in the city council and four years as mayor.

In 1885 he came to Charleston and established his present business, which at that time was on a very small scale. But when, as before, hustling, coupled with untiring energy, and strict honest business principles won, and Mr. Bequest was enabled gradually to build up his now large and lucrative business. His plant is large and commodious, covering an acre of ground. He is wholesale and retail dealer in oak and pine wood, oak and pine blocks, gravel and white sand, wood sawed and delivered to any part of the city. Vessels supplied at low rates. Mr. Bequest has all the modern conveniences for the successful prosecution of his work, the capacity of the plant being fifteen cords per diem.

CHAPTER 6: THE MAYOR OF MOUNT PLEASANT

Eight wagons are run and ten men given employment. To say that he has made a success is but to read the above.

Mr. Bequest stands high both commercially and socially in the city. He is a member of the German Artillery, a K. of P., Uniform rank, having been treasurer for many years. He is also a member of the German Rifle Club, having been king twice.

Mr. Bequest is also a member of several other organizations of the city, and a public spirited, progressive gentleman who believes in pushing Charleston and the Palmetto State to the front.[52]

Several comments are in order: First, there is a remarkable similarity between this account and the one by Brigadier General Ellison Capers that was cited in chapter 3, so much so that it is difficult to know who is plagiarizing whom. The Capers account in the *Confederate Military History* volume has a publication date of 1899, but was obviously composed prior to that. Was the *Evening Post* reporter somehow privy to the Capers account, or did Capers embellish the newspaper account for his account of Bequest's adventures as a blockade runner? Did either or both accounts derive from an interview with the "well known and popular gentleman and citizen" whose memory of his earlier escapades might have been embellished? Nothing is known, for example, of his adventuresome activities in "England, Scotland, Russia, and Mexico." Second, the Capers account contains more detail about the blockade-running activities, while the newspaper reporter furnishes more information about the Charleston wood dealership: we learn for the first time that the lot was a sizable piece of East Bay property, that the per diem turnover was substantial, and that Bequest employed persons other than himself in running the business. Third, if the reporter is accurate, Bequest was actually a *member* of the German Artillery, not just a guest of

---

52. *Evening Post*, June 11, 1898.

Capt. Wagener when he rode in the 1892 parade celebrating the Artillery's semi-centennial. Finally, by the end of the century, the reporter can be forgiven for misspelling the name of Heinrich Wieting's ship *Gauss* that brought Bequest to Charleston, as well as the name of the Captain himself.

This laudatory account was published a month after Bequest, now aged fifty-four, had participated rather laudably in the May Schützenfest—the annual "three successful days of fun-making." "Ben" Bequest placed in the Target of Honor competition and won a keg of Bartholomay beer. Apparently getting back into his earlier form, he took three prizes the following year: "Ring target B, best score, marble clock with figure, B. H. Bequest…; Centre targets C, D, and E, 250 yards, resting shots, best score, handsome couch, B. H. Bequest;…Silver medals were awarded for every 75 points, gold medals for every 150 points and very handsome gold medals for every 200 points made on Targets C, D, and E, as follows: B. H. Bequest, 250 points."[53] These wins would be the last demonstrations of his marksmanship. Less than six months later, in the early morning hours of October 28, 1899, he died unexpectedly in his home at the age of fifty-five.

The funeral was held the next day—Sunday—at St. Matthew's German Lutheran Church at 3 o'clock in the afternoon. The funeral notice in the Sunday morning *News and Courier* included the call to the Palmetto Company of the Pythians to attend "in citizens' dress," as well as to the Pythian Stonewall Lodge, No. 6, whose members were to assemble at Pythias Castle Hall "at 2:15 sharp, to pay the last tribute of respect to your late brother Member, B. H. Bequest." There was to be a Pythian service at the cemetery. On Monday, October 30th, the *News and Courier* commented in its "All around Town" column:

> The funeral services of the late Mr. Bernhard H. Bequest were held at St. Matthew's German Lutheran Church yesterday afternoon, and the

---

53. *News and Courier*, May 6, 1899.

CHAPTER 6: THE MAYOR OF MOUNT PLEASANT

remains interred at Bethany Cemetery with Pythian ceremonies. Mr. Bequest was an estimable citizen of Charleston, and had been for many years in business here. His death at his residence on East Bay street Saturday morning was a surprise and a shock to his friend [sic], for he had been at his office quite recently and was not thought to be seriously ill. He was a member of Stonewall Lodge, Knights of Pythias, and also a member of Palmetto Company, U. R. K. P. Both of these organizations attended the funeral yesterday.

Doubtless still in shock, his forty-three-year-old widow Catherine fulfilled her duty and appeared on the thirty-first before Probate Judge H. L. P. Bolger to request that she be appointed administratrix of the estate and effects of her late husband. A number of creditors came forward in response to the published notice of probate: $6.75 worth of groceries had been charged in October at G. Abrams' "Choice Groceries"; the Standard Oil Company had delivered a bucket of light axle grease on the twenty-fifth of October; E. Wierman's "Ship and Family Groceries" presented a bill for $3.18 for some loads of gravel and white sand; there was $3.50 due to George J. Phillips for five shoeings of horses and mules during October (prior to Bernhard's death) and November (after he had died); the same horses and mules had been fed with oats and hay from the C. D. Gartleman Co. in September and October whose bill came to $38.93; Albert Bischoff, dealer in "Hay, Grain and Mill Feed" had also delivered "merchandise" in the amount of $14.86 in September and October. These bills were all paid, and two days before Christmas 1899, there was an auction sale notice that announced:

Under order of the Probate Judge of Charleston county, South Carolina, will be sold on Thursday, the 4th day of January 1900, at No. 288 East Bay street...at 11 o'clock a.m. the Engine, Boiler,

> Belting, Shafting, Saws and all machinery appurtenant to the wood yard business carried on by the late B. H. Bequest in said city of Charleston.
>
> Also the carts, three sets of harness, three horses, one mule, tools, one wagon, wheelbarrows, window shades, desk, stove and office chair, clock, and stock of oak and pine wood. The foregoing to be sold as a whole.
>
> At the same time and place one buggy and harness and the schooner Leonore.
>
> Terms – cash. Above property may be treated for a private sale, on application to the Auctioneer.

Bernhard's widow Catherine had lost three children in their infancy and now had their one surviving child, John Frederick, aged seventeen, to raise and depend on. Her stepdaughter, Theresa Louise, had married[54] John Gieschen in 1896 and was now in charge of her own household. On the one-year anniversary of her husband's death, the *News and Courier*'s "Sunday News" carried three memorial obituary notices that formulaically, but poignantly, articulated the loss they all felt:

> BEQUEST.—In loving remembrance of our husband and brother, Bernhard H. Bequest, who departed this life October 28, 1899, in the 54th year of his age.
>
> Oh, dearest father, thy gentle voice is hushed, / Thy warm, true heart is still. / And on thy pale and peaceful face / Is resting death's cold chill. / Wife, son and daughter.

---

54. *News and Courier*, November 28, 1896: "At the residence of the bride's father...by the Rev. L. Muller, Theresa L. M. Bequest, only daughter of B. H. Bequest, to John H. Gieschen."

CHAPTER 6: THE MAYOR OF MOUNT PLEASANT

BEQUEST.—In loving remembrance of B. H. Bequest, who entered into rest October 28, 1899.

Fold him, oh Father, in Thine arms / And let him henceforth be / A messenger of love between / Our human hearts and Thee. / Wife and children.

BERNHARD H. Bequest.—Died on the morning of the 28th of October, 1899, my beloved father, B. H. Bequest, in the 54th day of his age. / May he rest in peace.

As for Catherine's late husband, the auctioned "appurtenances" at 288 East Bay Street were a meagre validation of a thirty-four-year-long struggle during the hard times of Reconstruction and the fading of Charleston into the backwash of the South by a man whose career had begun with daring adventure, a vision of opportunity, service to the public good, and dedicated efforts as seaman, landowner, merchant and entrepreneur. It would have to be the praise, respect, and honors that he had won while he was yet alive that would bring satisfaction and comfort to those he left behind.

CHAPTER 7: THE QUIET SEAMAN

The 1893 memorial obituary marking the death of John Bequest's wife the previous year included a short poem. The two stanzas would seem to say less about her and more about the character of the family she left behind:

> Jesus, while our hearts are bleeding
> O'er the spoils that death has won,
> We would at this solemn meeting,
> Calmly say, "Thy will be done."
>
> Though cast down, we're not forsaken,
> Though afflicted, not alone,
> Thou didst give and Thou hast taken,
> Blessed Lord, "Thy will be done."

Although Catherine's husband John was not named among those remembering the deceased, his sister-in-law and his children surely spoke for him in expressing their loss with such Lutheran resignation and acceptance of Divine intent. From what has been revealed about John Bequest thus far, it is not unreasonable to think of him as a man willing to bow to something higher, accept whatever destiny had in store for him, and trudge on. Resigned to his wife's premature death, but with three children under ten, he soon enough found Mary Emma Condon and married her on July 13, 1893.

When Catherine Rigbers Bequest died, the couple and their children were sharing a house at 186 Spring Street with Catherine's younger brother, Frederick H. Rigbers. In the 1892 City Directory Frederick is listed as a grocer and saloon keeper at the Spring Street address. Forty-five-year-old John was

Frederick's senior by twenty-four years, so with the loss of connection through Catherine it was not an ideal arrangement. Both men must have agreed that each should go his own way as soon as possible. Once married, John and Mary Emma went back to Mt. Pleasant, and after marrying Maggie Lee Copeland in August of 1895, Frederick moved to the Atlanta region. He had settled his Charleston estate in April of 1893, less than a year after his sister had died.[1]

How John supported his family once back in Mt. Pleasant is undocumented prior to early 1894. But by that time he had found his calling as a member of the life-saving crew stationed on Sullivan's Island.[2] It was entirely appropriate that with his rather checkered employment history the quiet German seaman should find this way to earn a living: he could hardly have found a better match for the hankering for the sea that he brought with him from his native Geestendorf. It would turn out that the sea off the coast of Charleston would twice give added definition to the character of John Bequest. Otherwise, his life would have gone unnoticed by all but his own family and his closest acquaintances.

Any number of readers of Charleston's *News and Courier* of January 24, 1894, would have been alarmed to read the column headlined "Cast up by the sea / Small boat with two corpses thrown up on the beach at Morris Island":

> George Simons, a colored fisherman, made a ghastly discovery yesterday afternoon. He was returning from the fishing banks about 5 o'clock

---

1. Legal notification in the *News and Courier*, April 9, 1893.

2. The coastal barrier island proximate on the north to Mt. Pleasant. When John Bequest first took the job is not known; his "official" employment with the U.S. Treasury Department in its "Life-Saving Service at Large" is not documented until 1897. A 1915 act of Congress merged the Revenue Cutter Service with the U.S. Life-Saving Service. The latter, to which John Bequest belonged, consisted of "dozens of stations placed around the nation's coastlines that were manned by dedicated crews willing to risk their lives to save those in peril on the sea." (http://www.uscg.mil/history/web/USCGbriefhistory.asp)

when he saw a small boat lying high and dry on Morris Island beach. He pulled in to shore and the sight that met his gaze was enough to make him get back to Charleston as fast as he could.
In the boat lay two dead white men. One was in the bow, while the other was wrapped in the sail.
As has already been intimated Simons lost no time in reaching the city and reporting the matter to the proper authorities.
No further information could be gained last night, but Coroner Rivers will have a thorough investigation to-day.

The following morning a more thorough account was available, though that was of little consolation now that the identity of the victims was known:

A Tragedy of the Sea / A crew of life-savers drowned in the harbor / Of six men two bodies found and four missing—meagre details of the calamity /
Only meagre details of one of the most distressing accidents that has occurred in the waters around Charleston in many years reached the city yesterday. In this case the victims are all white men, and it is not yet known but that six lives were lost.
Monday afternoon last a small cat-rigged boat left Sullivan's Island with supplies for the Morris Island life-saving station. The passengers were Fred Miller, of Sullivan's Island, Harry R. Campsen, of Charleston, Capt George Campsen, of the life-saving crew, John Bequest, of the life-saving crew, Walter Croft, of Charleston, and a German boy, whose name could not be learned. Nothing more was seen or heard of any of the men till Tuesday afternoon, when a colored fisherman

discovered two bodies on the Morris Island beach. As has already been mentioned in The News and Courier the information was given to Coroner G. H. Rivers, and that official promptly commenced an investigation.

At 9 o'clock yesterday morning Deputy Coroner Daniel L. Sinkler, than whom there is not a more reliable or trustworthy man in the public service, started out for Morris Island. He went in the fishing boat Puritan with Capt George Jenkins and a competent crew. Mr. Sinkler spent the entire day working on the case and success crowned his labors. This is the story exactly as he told it:

'We rowed over to Morris Island, reaching there about 11 o'clock and landing at a place called by the fishermen 'Schooner's bank.' We went up the sound and soon discovered the sunken boat turned upside down. We immediately took off the sails and righted her. She was a cat-rigged bateau, not more than twenty feet long with open cockpit. She was painted white with nothing to show her name, and is supposed to belong to the captain of the life-saving crew. After thoroughly searching the boat and finding no bodies, we went out to look around for bodies. After three hours' search we found the body of Mr. Fred Miller in the water about thirty feet from the boat. In the boat we had found a pair of shoes (which doubtless belonged to Mr. Harry Campsen), a waterproof coat, a pair of pants, a coat and Mr. Miller's hat.

After finding Mr. Miller's body we recommenced the search, and after about an hour more we found the body of Mr. Harry R. Campsen in a pool of water about one hundred yards from Mr. Miller. In looking around we found one shoe in the marsh, and this caused me to think that other bodies must be near, but a further search revealed nothing more, and we returned to the city, arriving about 5:30 p.m.

The bodies of Messrs. Miller and Campsen were brought back to the city, and the odd shoe was identified as that of Mr. Walter Croft.

There is scarcely a doubt that all of the six persons who left Sullivan's Island in the ill-fated boat were lost. Nothing has been heard of any of them except in the melancholy manner already described, and it would be raising false hopes to indicate a probability of the safety of any of them.

Mr. Fred Miller was known and liked by everybody. He was an expressman on the Island, and a member of Christ Church Lodge, Knights of Pythias. He was 55 years old and leaves a wife and one son.

Harry R. Campsen was about 30 year old. He followed the sea for a livelihood and had been all around the world. He had recently returned from a cruise to South America. Capt George Campsen, of the lifesaving crew, was a brother of Mr. Harry Campsen. John Bequest was a member of the crew and in the summer time was mate of the steamer Sappho.[3] He was a brother of Mr. August Bequest, cashier of the German American Trust and Savings Bank. Mr. Walter Croft was formerly purser on the steamship Kiawah. He was about 28 years old.

How this terrible accident came about will probably never be known. The only indication of the exact time the boat overturned is given by Mr. Miller's watch, which stopped at 11.12 o'clock. Nothing more can be learned and it seems that the

---

3. The well-known steamer of the Mt. Pleasant ferry company that carried passengers from downtown Charleston to Mt. Pleasant.

tragedy of January 22 will long remain a mystery of the sea.

Coroner Rivers will hold an inquest over the body of Mr. Miller at the City Hospital this morning at 9 o'clock. Immediately thereafter an inquest will be held over the other body at 29 Hasell street. A party will leave the city this morning to search for the other bodies.

One might imagine that on reading this account in the newspaper Mary Emma would have been frantic if, in fact, her husband John had not returned home the day before George Simmons made his "ghostly discovery." She was one of the few who were able to read of the tragedy in the newspaper while knowing that John Bequest was not one of the six in the life-saving crew lost to the sea. Everyone else had to wait yet another day until the twenty-sixth to find out that John Bequest had not drowned. That made little difference to the other survivors, but at least for the Charleston German community there was some "cheerful information":

> The Morris Island tragedy / Holding an inquest on the bodies of two of the victims—two of the men supposed to have been lost were not in the boat /
> Inquests over the bodies of Fred Miller and Harry Campsen, who were drowned last Monday night, were held yesterday morning. The first was held over Mr. Miller's body, at the City Hospital, at 9 o'clock, and the other at 29 Hasell street two hours later. The verdict in each case was simply that "the deceased came to his death from drowning in Morris Island Sound on the night of January 22, 1894, in Charleston harbor.
> Mr. D. L. Sinkler, deputy coroner, was the only witness examined and he could only repeat the sad story told in the News and Courier yesterday.

Mr. Campsen's funeral services were held in the city yesterday afternoon.

Residents of Mount Pleasant and the Island speak of Mr. Fred Miller in the highest terms. He was kind, polite and obliging, and a better hearted man never lived. His funeral will take place at Mount Pleasant to-day under the auspices of the Knights of Pythias.

The cheerful information was received yesterday that all of the six men supposed to have been drowned were not lost. Mr. John Bequest and the German boy were not in the ill-fated bateau, but were on duty at the life-saving station. Mr. Bequest was down on the beach Monday night, and he says that a strong wind was blowing and the sea was very high shortly before midnight. This gives a plausible explanation of how the bateau foundered. It is probable that a flaw struck her and in the high sea the crew could not manage her.

Mr. Charles Croft, a brother of Mr. Walter Croft, and a party of friends went down in a launch yesterday morning in search for the bodies of Walter Croft and Capt George Campsen. They dragged for a considerable time, but found only a coat, shoe and handkerchief belonging to Mr. Croft. The search will be kept up for some days and every effort will be made to recover the lost bodies.

Not until the twenty-ninth, a week after the accident, were the bodies of Campsen and Croft found in Schooner's Creek. John Bequest was a member of the search party that discovered the bodies and brought the drowned victims to the city for their respective inquests.

The mystery of who the young German boy walking the beach with John Bequest that fateful night seems never to have been solved. The boy's identity, one can suppose, seemed inconsequential in view of all the other questions that needed to be answered. Long after the fact, it would be reasonable to think that the boy was likely one of John's sons, either the younger Heinrich Ludwig, aged seven, or John Ludwig, Jr., aged nine. It may have been a fortuitous decision for the father to take along one of his sons that particular day when the former went on duty for his shift.

The experience of his fellow crew members' drownings would undoubtedly have been sobering for John and his family, although it was not the first time a Bequest had been lost to the sea.[4] His was an admittedly dangerous vocation, and it would be only four years later that he would have another close call with the sea, but again not be its victim. On August 20, 1898, the Sullivan's Island Life-Saving crew was involved in the heroic rescue of a young swimmer. The *Evening Post* reported the drowning of Charles M. Coste[5], one of the guards who tried to save "young Ned Schachte":

> The cry of distress was heard by the life saving crew and Coste, one of the best swimmers of the crew, made for the water and quickly swam out to Schachte, who was almost exhausted from the terrible struggles with the waves. Guard Coste was followed by Capt. Adams, Guards Bequest and Tapio. Captain Martin, who was out horseback riding at the time, heard the cries of young Schachte and dismounting he quickly threw off his coat and removing his shoes swam out towards Coste, who had Schachte trying to bring him in, reaching the two men about the same time as Capt. Adams and Tapio. Capt. Adams was the first to relieve Coste, Capt. Martin and Guard

---

4. Accidents at sea had earlier claimed several Bequest ancestors from Geestendorf.

5. The newspaper corrected the name two days later at the request of R.R. Coste: the guard was twenty-five-year-old James L. Coste.

CHAPTER 7: THE QUIET SEAMAN

Tapio assisting him. They spoke words of encouragement to the boy, telling him they were out for a little fun and would soon reach beach.

A BATTLE WITH THE WAVES. Suddenly the swimmers reached a point where the current sweeps around the jetties like a mill race. It was a flood tide and the sea was choppy. Ned Schachte became frightened and seized Capt. Adams around the throat with a death like grasp. Capt. Martin released the boy's hold just in time to save them both, as Capt. Adams had become considerably exhausted. In fact all of the men were, as the battle of the waves and strong tides was a terrific one.

Guard Bequest in the meantime came with life belts and Schachte was delivered to him. He had not had the boy long before he cried out that he was being swept out to sea by the strong current. A boat from the life saving station had been launched and in a short time picked the men up and started for the shore.

Tapio had become very weak and was seen to go down once. The boat reached him just in time to save him from a watery grave. The water was only waste deep but the poor fellow had completely worn himself out and his strength had about left him when he was picked up. He was in an unconscious condition when the shore was reached. Some time was spent in restoring him to consciousness. Tapio is an expert swimmer.

COSTE GOES DOWN. Capt. Martin and Capt. Adams, after seeing that young Schachte was all right, made their way for the shore. They gave no thought to Coste, as they knew him to be an expert swimmer and had seen him make for the beach after he had been relieved of Ned Schachte. Instead of following the current, which forms an eddy around the rocks at that point, and swimming to shore, he attempted to swim across and it swept him away.

All of the men who took part in the rescuing of Schachte displayed remarkable bravery and coolness. Not once did any of them lose their head or become nervous, and it is not an easy thing either for a man rolled and tossed by a choppy sea, trying to save the life of another, to keep cool throughout. . . .

To-day Capt. Martin and Capt. Adams and the life saving crew have been the recipient of many congratulations.[6]

One hundred and fifteen years later—on April 27, 2013—the 1898 rescue was commemorated with an award ceremony at the old Coast Guard station on Sullivan's Island during which James L. Coste was posthumously awarded the Silver Lifesaving Medal for Heroism.[7] It was on that occasion that it was revealed that the young swimmer rescued was the grandfather of Joseph P. Riley, Jr., Charleston's mayor from 1975 to 2015.[8]

The August 1898 publicity was enough to keep the name of John Bequest in the public's mind for some time—to remind the Charleston community of the identity of one of the life-saving

---

6. *Evening Post*, August 20, 1898.

7. An article by Suzannah Smith Miles about the award ceremony that ran in the *Moultrie News* of April 25, 2013, explained that "[t]he Silver Lifesaving medal is one of the oldest decorations for heroism in the United States. Established in 1874, this medal of honor is bestowed by the U.S. Coast Guard upon someone recognized for endangering his or her own life by 'saving, or endeavoring to save lives from perils of the sea, within the United States, or upon any American vessel'."

8. In affirmation of the theory of "six degrees of separation," young Ned Schachte's father, Capt. Henry Schachte, was a business associate of both of John Bequest's brothers.

crew members responsible for keeping them safe from the ever-present dangers of the local waters—and also to identify that fellow whom they frequently saw on the ferry *Sappho* when they went across the river to Mt. Pleasant. Not one to seek out any further publicity, John and his wife and children lived quietly in Mt. Pleasant, none of them doing anything to attract the attention of the newspaper or their neighbors. Their oldest child, C[atherine] Adeline Therese was confirmed at age sixteen at St. Andrew's Lutheran Church on Wentworth Street in April of 1900, suggesting that the family had changed its membership from either the St. Matthew's or the St. Johannes congregation sometime prior to that.[9] Eight years later, on Christmas Day in 1908, Adeline Therese was married to Ira Dwight Scarborough at 129 Coming St. by Rev. M. G. G. Scherer.[10] With her marriage to Scarborough, Adeline indirectly managed to affirm her father's seafaring heritage: her husband was a ship's carpenter by trade who could doubtless find much common ground with his father-in-law. The young couple moved to Jacksonville, FL, and lived there childless until they died, she in 1957, he two years later.

The 1910 Federal census indicates that John Bequest owned his home in Mt. Pleasant (#42 Greenwich Street), and that he worked "on his own account." At age sixty-three, he was obviously no longer working for the Coast Guard on Sullivan's Island—and had not been so employed for some time.[11] Most likely he was "retired" and farming whatever small amount of land he had at his disposal. In 1910 the couple began receiving "rent for a white school," paid to them quarterly by the County

---

9. The daughter was christened at St. Matthew's in 1884, but her widower father had attended the 1893 annual "fair" sponsored by the congregation of St. Johannes, suggesting that he and his late wife had joined that congregation sometime earlier. After his marriage to Mary Emma Condon, the couple had become members of the St. Andrew's congregation.

10. Marriage notice in the *Evening Post* of January 11, 1909.

11. He was last documented in the "Life-Saving Service at Large" in 1901.

treasurer. The published treasurer's report always specifies that the three months rent payment of $19.50 is to "Mrs. J. L. Bequest." These payments were made over a five-year period: the last one recorded is October, 1915. There is no way to know exactly what the Bequests were doing—whether they were renting part of their home for use as a Mt. Pleasant schoolroom, or whether they owned another property that was vacant and adaptable for such a purpose. It may not be incidental that the Bequests sold what was identified simply as "lot plat No. 229 Moultrieville" on Sullivan's Island to Margaret Theresa Blanchard for $650 in 1915. The Moultrieville property would have been close to where the life-saving station was located, but whether the property had a dwelling that could have been used as a schoolroom is unknown. Despite no confirming evidence, it is appealing to think that Mary Emma Bequest may have been a school teacher for some of the white children in Mt. Pleasant or on Sullivan's Island. She doubtless would not have reflected on the fact that the rent she received for providing space for the education of "white" children articulated the post-Reconstruction era's legacy in Mt. Pleasant.

With their sister married in 1908 and shortly thereafter moving with her husband to Jacksonville, FL, the Bequest sons approached their maturity only two years apart. By 1903 John L. Jr., aged 18, was employed by the Federal War Department ("Engineer Department at Large") as a laborer at Fort Moultrie on Sullivan's Island. He was apprenticed as a boilermaker at the Charleston firm of Valk and Murdock, and later worked in that trade for the Riverside Iron Works. He subsequently married and moved to Florida, first to Gainesville by 1915, then to Jacksonville where his sister was located. John Sr. and Mary's younger son, Heinrich Ludwig, had already followed his sister to Jacksonville by 1910. He too is recorded in the Federal census as a boilermaker. Both men would die young, Heinrich in 1914, John, Jr. in 1918, a victim of that year's influenza epidemic.

John Sr. did have his name in the newspaper one more time: in October 1916, the *News and Courier* found it sufficiently newsworthy to report that "Mr. John L. Bequest brought to the

News and Courier office yesterday a sweet potato vine on which there were no fewer than twelve potatoes, all of them large and well formed and one of them thirteen inches in length. The potatoes were grown by Mr. Bequest at Mount Pleasant. On another of his vines Mr. Bequest states that he found eight potatoes and on yet another vine ten potatoes."[12] The news-desperate newspaper editor might have added that John Bequest was simply a local man carrying on the tradition of his ancestors who had been both sailors and farmers in the coastal strip of North Germany known as Land Wursten.

With their children following their own paths some two hundred miles to the south in Jacksonville, John and Mary Emma had only a few years together before she died on March 4, 1919, in Charleston's Roper Hospital. "John L. Bequest and family" thanked "their many friends for their kind sympathy and beautiful floral offerings sent them in their recent bereavement" with a "Card of Thanks" in the *News and Courier* of March 9.

By now—at age seventy-two—John Bequest had outlived both of his wives, an infant and two adult sons: his elder brother had died almost twenty years earlier, and his younger brother was still operating at high speed after having disgraced the Bequest name a quarter century earlier. We can imagine that the immediate issue was how he would manage by himself in Mt. Pleasant with what surely were limited resources. That must have been the concern of his daughter Adeline Scarborough living in Jacksonville. Whether his health was an issue is not known, but within two years he left Charleston to live with Adeline and her husband, Ira Scarborough, until he died at age eighty in 1925. On his death certificate, he is "John Louis Bequest," a widower, a retired "seaman." As the "informant," his daughter Adeline was unable to furnish the names of her paternal grandparents, although she knew at least that they were born in Germany. She buried her father in Jacksonville's West Evergreen Cemetery, undoubtedly a less German, less Lutheran, cemetery than Charleston's Bethany.

---

12. *News and Courier*, October 17, 1916.

As suggested by this chapter's heading, the immigrant German John Ludwig Bequest lived quietly among his South Carolinian hosts and, except for the part he played in the rescue of a young swimmer in the waters off Sullivan's Island and his own near-drowning, *unnotably*. Perhaps his second marriage to an American woman helped in the process of erasing his German heritage. Living beyond the end of the First World War when anti-German sentiment made German origins a liability, there was little reason for him to harken back to the past, no reason to commemorate one's ethnicity, no reason, even, to connect one's children to the heritage stamped on their parents. By the time John left Charleston, his children had already left the coastal city that had allowed a North German seaman to transform himself into a southern American. Charleston would not hold onto them, nor they onto it. Thus at the end of the first quarter of the twentieth century very little significance could be ascribed to the story of John Bequest as a German immigrant to Charleston, beyond the fact that it was so typical of all of those whose heritage evaporated in the process of acquiring an American, southern, identity indelibly marked by the culture unique to Charleston.

CHAPTER 8: THE RISE AND DOWNFALL OF AUGUST

If the term "mover and shaker" was not yet in the vernacular during the last decade of the nineteenth century, it would nonetheless have been an apt descriptor for the proprietor of Charleston's restaurant known to most as "Bequest's." August Bequest was a man on the move. Having already transitioned six years earlier from grist mill operator to restauranteur, he was ready by 1893 for something bigger. For one thing, he had finally made his application for citizenship and would be formally admitted as a citizen in February, just short of twenty-seven years after he had set foot in Charleston. But a month before he was admitted, he and several of his friends were granted a commission to incorporate The Charleston Improvement Company "doing a general industrial business, as well as dealing in real estate and personal property." The capital stock was $100,000 divided into one thousand shares.[1] The businessmen/friends were J. Fred Lilienthal, John D. Cappelmann, and J. C. Blohme. They were all successful Germans: Lilienthal was secretary and treasurer of the Germania Bank and Loan Association, John Cappelmann was an attorney, and Blohme was August Bequest's friend, mentor, and one of Charleston's largest grain dealers. It would appear that the restaurant owner could comfortably call these men "associates": he must have had sufficient resources to contribute to the capital investment, and the four of them together must have felt confident that they had enough collective acumen to run the newly formed enterprise. Cappelmann was probably the only one who had been

---

1. *News and Courier*, January 5, 1893.

formally trained in his profession—the others were self-made men.

It would seem that August Bequest intended to do more than just put his toe in these business waters. Less than two weeks later, the Secretary of the State of South Carolina[2], Hon. J. E. Tindal, granted a commission to I. V. Barden and August Bequest—the Board of Corporators—to open the books of subscription to the capital stock of the German-American Trust and Savings Bank. The potential subscribers would find the books at the "office of A. Bequest, 226 King street, second floor, Telephone 323." Overnight, the restaurant owner became a banker. The local press was enthusiastic. This was good news for Charleston:

> Under a call issued by Messrs I. V. Barden and August Bequest, board of corporators in the matter of the incorporation of the German-American Trust and Savings Bank, a large and representative body of citizens assembled last night at the German Artillery Hall for the purpose of effecting the organization of the new bank, the election of a board of directors and the adoption of by-laws, etc.
>
> Mr. August Bequest, one of the board of corporators, called the meeting to order and requested Mr. H. M. Bennett to act as secretary of the meeting. On the call of the subscribers it was ascertained that three-fourths of the shares subscribed were represented either in person or by proxy. On motion Mr. J. D. Cappelmann was thereupon requested to act as chairman of the

---

2. "Prior to 1886, incorporation of any manufacturing enterprise in South Carolina required a special act of legislature. In 1886 the legislature, with little fanfare or opposition, enacted a general incorporation law that allowed the South Carolina Secretary of State to grant a charter to any applicant who fulfilled the requirements of the law." (William J. Cooper, Jr., *The Conservative Regime: South Carolina, 1877-1890* [Baltimore: The Johns Hopkins Press, 1968], 121.)

CHAPTER 8: THE RISE AND DOWNFALL OF AUGUST

meeting and Mr. H. M. Bennett was appointed secretary.

Mr. J. F. Lilienthal proposed a series of by-laws, which were first read and afterward considered section by section and the same as amended adopted as a whole. This was followed by the election of a board of directors, consisting of Mr. J. Fred Lilienthal, Henry Schachte, Henry C. Wohlers, B. J.[sic] Simmons, N. A. Hunt, J. N. Hesse and Aug. H. Fischer.

After the business of the meeting had been concluded, resolutions of thanks were passed to Chairman Cappelmann, Secretary Bennett and the board of corporators for the manner in which they had discharged their respective duties. . . .

The board of directors is composed of some of our most progressive and energetic and active citizens, selected especially from the younger generation, wide awake to the true interests of the city. The board of directors just elected, it is understood, will meet on Saturday next for the purpose of electing a president, vice president, cashier, solicitor, and such other officers as may be determined on, besides the important question of the proper location for the office of the bank.[3]

The following week August Bequest was elected cashier of "the latest addition to Broad Street." The board of directors had met at the office of Solicitor Cappelmann, chosen the "Sheppard Building" at No. 58 Broad Street to house the new bank, and elected officers: A. Bequest as cashier, W. D. Nelson as outdoor clerk, J. Fred Lilienthal as president, J. N. Hesse as vice president, J. D. Cappelmann as solicitor. The directors remained as elected

---

3. *News and Courier*, January 20, 1893.

at the meeting the previous week.[4] It was not for lack of ambition that August Bequest had achieved status among some of Charleston's "most progressive and energetic and active citizens" working for the common good. It seemed not worthy of mention that so many of those "most progressive and energetic and active" businessmen were German immigrants.

On the restaurant front, there were continuing issues that commanded Bequest's attention. On January 24, 1893, there was a convention of South Carolina liquor dealers that met to "devise the ways and means of fighting the . . . dispensary law." With representatives—"prominent liquor men"—from different areas of the state, "the proceedings were conservative and business-like. No mention of politics was made, everyone seeming to be intent only upon the subject under discussion—testing the constitutionality of the law and establishing, if possible, its invalidity."[5] A. Bequest had been one of those representing Charleston County and was on the Association's special committee "to consult and employ counsel." However the dealers association subsequently pursued the dispensary matter, by the end of the year it was reported that the Charleston liquor dealers—Bequest among them—were to receive "the rebate on their liquor licenses as asked for."[6]

As for the bank, the charter for the German-American Trust and Savings Bank of Charleston was granted within two weeks of Bequest's election as cashier. It was capitalized with $40,000 paid in cash, and business commenced on February fifteenth:

> A number of invitations had previously been sent out to the effect that the bank would be open for business, and during the day scores of bank officials and employers and numbers of other

---

4. *News and Courier*, January 29, 1893.

5. *News and Courier*, January 25, 1893.

6. *News and Courier*, December 11, 1893.

CHAPTER 8: THE RISE AND DOWNFALL OF AUGUST

gentleman dropped in to say a pleasant word for the new bank, which starts out under such bright prospects. Notwithstanding the large number of pleasant calls that were made during the day, President J. Fred Lilienthal, Cashier A. Bequest and Outdoor Clerk W. D. Nelson were at their posts to attend to business. . . . The headquarters of the bank are fitted up in elegant style, and the friends of the institution predict for it a most successful career.

The bank immediately ran advertisements in the local papers delineating the range of its banking services: "Transacts a general banking business"; "Checks exchanged with all city banks"; "Exchange bought and sold"; "Money to loan on good security at low rates"; "Deposits in small or large sums received"; "Interest allowed on deposits in savings department at 5 per cent per annum semi-annually, or 4 per cent per annum quarterly"; "Interest mailed to non-resident Depositors on receipt of order or Pass Book."[7] The ads ran continuously for the next several years in acknowledgement of the competition for the city's monies: there was no lack of other banks, e.g., The First National Bank, People's National Bank, Bank of Charleston, South Carolina Loan and Trust Co, Carolina Savings Bank, Miners' and Merchants' Bank, Exchange Banking and Trust Co., Hibernia Savings Bank, State Savings Bank, Germania Saving Bank, Charleston Savings Institution, Nickel Savings Bank, American Savings bank, and the Columbian Banking and Trust Co. With the bank's ads and notices in the newspaper, the Bequest name was added to those of the officers serving those other institutions, all of whom were prominent in the community and who commanded the respect of their clientele.

The first quarterly statement issued in June showed undivided profits of $1,422.01, indicating that things were going

---

7. *News and Courier*, March 1, 1893.

well. The profit margin continued to increase with each quarterly statement all through the following year. Not until the tenth quarterly statement of January 1895 did the amount begin to decline, although by mid-year it was again on the increase. In January of 1894, the bank declared a dividend of 6 percent on the capital stock, and in February the stockholders met to vote on raising the capital stock from $40,000 "to an amount not exceeding the sum of $100,000." [8] At the anniversary meeting of the stockholders in February of 1895, August was elected to the board of directors, and at a subsequent meeting, he was elected president "to supersede Mr. J. Fred Lilienthal, who on account of his business affairs declined re-election."[9] At the annual meeting in February of the following year (1896), "the financial statement, which was read by President Bequest, showed the bank to be in a most flourishing condition," and August was again named as president.[10] It would not be until June that the bank's condition would come into question.

Back in 1893 when the first quarterly statement was issued, it might have been noticed that the newly formed institution was not rigorously checked and balanced: no one questioned whether the word of the founding group of trusted men who were in charge was sufficient to consider the operation objectively audited. The published quarterly statement included the following statement of assurance:

> Personally appeared before me August Bequest, Cashier of the German-American Trust and Savings Bank, who swears that the above statement is true to the best of his knowledge and belief. / A. Bequest, Cashier / Sworn to before me this 15th day of May, 1893. J. D. Cappelmann, /

---

8. *News and Courier*, January 20, 1894.

9. *News and Courier*, February 21, 1895.

10. *Evening Post*, February 20, 1896.

CHAPTER 8: THE RISE AND DOWNFALL OF AUGUST

Notary Public. / Attest: / J. Fred Lilienthal, Henry C. Wohlers, Henry Schachte, Directors.

At the time, apparently, the stockholders were not inclined to question whether this arrangement might not raise the risk of conflict of interest.

There was also no question but that August Bequest, in his capacity as cashier of a Broad Street bank, had gotten himself into the ranks of Charleston's successful businessmen. He was able to leverage that success so that now he could move his family for the summer over to Sullivan's Island along with the other families so fortunate—the "summer swallows" who "have taken a brief sea voyage across the Cooper River and the Cove, and are rejoicing in the exhilarating breezes of Moultrieville."[11] The summer island "society" comprised most of the city's important citizens, among others, George W. Williams, J. C. Blohme, George M. Trenholm, St. J. P. Kinloch, John Knobloch, W. M. Bird, etc. It was always the case that Charleston's residents would want to escape the summer heat by going to the mountains or to the shore. For the Bequests, it was surely a combination of financial success and the parents' upbringing near the North Sea that made this particular family's escape to the seashore a most desirable annual event. It was entirely to be expected that Geestendorf would want to go to Sullivan's Island to find the cooling breezes.

But while Augusta and the children were enjoying themselves in their cottage by the sea, August was in town incorporating yet another enterprise. The corporators A. Bequest, A. F. C. Cramer, E. C. Metz and John D. Cappelmann received a charter from the Secretary of State in July (1893) incorporating the Palmetto Soap Manufacturing Company "to manufacture and sell all kinds of soap." The capital stock was $25,000, with 500 shares

---

11. *News and Courier*, June 28, 1893.

at $50 each.[12] The organizing meeting of subscribers was held at the German Artillery Hall, with Bequest calling the meeting to order and requesting John Cappelmann to chair it. Bequest could report that of the $25,000 capital stock "three-fourths had been subscribed in cash and property, of which 251 shares were represented at the meeting." He, along with Cappelmann, Metz, Ignatius P. O'Neill, Charles F. Middleton, D. A. Amme, and C. D. Gartleman were elected as directors. The *News and Courier* announcement under the headline "The Civilizer of the Age / A New Soap Factory organized in Charleston by well-known and energetic citizens," explained:

> It is the purpose of the corporation to continue the soap factory conducted for some time by Capt. E. C. Metz at No. 355 Meeting street. Capt. Metz has recently secured the services of a most competent and experienced person in the manufacture of soap, Mr. D. H. Greene, formerly of Philadelphia, but now of Charleston. The energy and activity exercised and displayed by Mr. Greene since his connection with the Palmetto Soap Factory gives assurance of success. This is an undertaking which will not only bring money to the city, but will keep for circulation at home much which is now sent elsewhere for an article of necessity which can be as well manufactured here.[13]

By September, the factory was reported as "already doing a paying business."[14] In December, the newspaper was promoting

---

12. *Reports and Resolutions of the General Assembly of the State of South Carolina at the regular session commencing November 28, 1893.* Vol. 2 (Columbia: Charles A. Calvo, Jr. State Printer, 1893), 58.

13. *News and Courier*, July 12, 1893.

14. *News and Courier*, September 10, 1893.

CHAPTER 8: THE RISE AND DOWNFALL OF AUGUST

it enthusiastically as one of the new enterprises "which [give] promise of great results":

> Comparatively few people have any idea of the extent of the business of this new industry. The factory is equipped with all the newest machinery used in the manufacture of washing and toilet soap. And has a capacity of turning out 125,000 pounds of soap a month. This will be increased by the new and improved machinery now in process of construction to 400,000 pounds per month. This involves the construction of two new kettles of 60,000 and 40,000 pounds capacity respectively to reinforce the one now in use, and which has a capacity of 45,000 pounds.
> In a conversation with Mr. D. H. Green, the intelligent superintendent, it was learned that the factory now manufactures about $6,000 worth of soap every month. This is sold all through the South as well as to the wholesale grocer and provision dealers of Charleston. Only resin and tallow are used in the manufacture of the soap, the company purchasing its tallow and grease already rendered. . . . The factory employs about twenty hands and pays out about $900 a month in wages. . . . All in all the Palmetto Soap Factory is essentially a Charleston enterprise, and like many industries of the kind inaugurated here will doubtless become a financial success.[15]

This was indeed a case of some of Charleston's "energetic" businessmen putting the entrepreneurship of one of their associates into the public domain, both as an investment opportunity for local citizens and as a stimulus to help the city out

---

15. *News and Courier*, December 4, 1893.

of its economic doldrums. In a list of twenty "new enterprises undertaken in Charleston during the year,"[16] August Bequest was named in three: the German-American Trust and Savings Bank, the Palmetto Soap Manufacturing Co, and the Charleston Improvement Company.

Charleston suffered a severe hurricane in late August of 1893, and it was the Bequest couple's young son, Henry, who became something of a local hero. The hurricane had struck Sunday afternoon the twenty-seventh, and it took a while to assess the damage done to Sullivan's Island.[17] But the *News and Courier* of the twenty-ninth reported that "young Mr. H. Bequest went out to save lives and do heroic work, and he did it. From house to house he went, giving aid. At Mrs. Gadsden's he found his services most in demand and like a Trojan, he led the ladies to places of safety, having to carry the last one through the surging billows."[18] Like his uncle John, the sixteen-year-old was instrumental in saving lives on Sullivan's Island. He was another Bequest with the Geestendorf genetic heritage. The house where the Bequests were staying (the C. W. Drake cottage) was reported badly damaged and submerged.

For Henry's father, the year 1893 was one of considerable success. To cap it off, in December he was admitted as a member of the German Friendly Society, joining some of his best friends: J. C. Blohme had been a member since 1885, John D. Cappelmann, since 1883, and J. Fred Lilienthal, since 1880. As if to celebrate his acceptance into that austere society of Charleston

---

16. *News and Courier*, September 11, 1893.

17. Hurricane winds "reached a velocity of 120 miles per hour by midnight, terrifying the citizens and causing vast damages. Roofs were ripped off homes, wharves smashed, most of the Battery promenade demolished, and the new bridge across the Ashley River was destroyed. Four hurricane-related deaths occurred in Charleston and property damage reached $1,160,000, but south of the city a huge wave had swept over the islands from Hilton Head to John's Island, drowning about 2,000 blacks..." (Fraser, *Charleston! Charleston!*, 326-27.)

18. *News and Courier*, August 29, 1893.

CHAPTER 8: THE RISE AND DOWNFALL OF AUGUST 203

Germans, less than two weeks later the couple bought a Sullivan's Island cottage of their own for $300 dollars—in Augusta's name.

The real estate purchase was doubtless something of a status symbol, appropriate for someone on the move up, and the fact that it was put in Augusta's name suggests an attempt to keep it safe, "on the side" so to speak, should there be any threat to what was held in August's name. It may also have been August's attempt to sniff out an investment opportunity. In June he was signatory to a petition to the United States Secretary of War Daniel Lamont, requesting that federal troops be garrisoned at the island's Fort Moultrie. The fort had been all but abandoned after the Civil War: the last troops had left at the end of 1866. Congress' 1871 Fortifications Bill had resulted in sporadic work at rebuilding, but that had ceased in 1876. The arguments to the Secretary of War were rather specious—the climate was good, and the troops would be welcomed and treated well at relatively low cost to the government—and seemed to be based on the between-the-lines notion that a federal presence on the island would bring economic benefits. The request did not fall on deaf ears, and the growing tensions between the US and Spain that resulted in the brief Spanish American War of 1898 enabled work to resume on the fort in 1897 to significantly expand and improve the fortifications. The federal government's intentions were clear already by 1896, at which time the Bequest property was bought by the government, along with numerous other properties that were needed for the fort's expansion. Unfortunately for the Bequests, they lost their little "keeping place" on the island with no financial gain: the government paid the same $300 that Augusta had paid two years earlier.

The Moultrieville purchase in Augusta's name in early 1894 was only one of the couple's several real estate acquisitions: these were undoubtedly seen as further investment opportunities, or, equally important, the exercise of *ownership* appropriate to the couple's rising status. In July, Augusta purchased a property on West Street, in December, a residence on Society Street, and finally, in March of 1895, another house on the corner of Archdale and Queen Streets. Two of these were turned over, no doubt at a profit, between April 1895 and March 1897.

In his capacity as cashier at the German-American Trust and Savings Bank, August's duties and responsibilities were greater than that of a bank teller. In the archives of the South Carolina Historical Society there is a January 23, 1894, letter addressed to "Mr. A. Bequest, Cashier G.A.T. & S.B." from Paul Whipple in Riverdale, SC, in which Mr. Whipple requests a loan of $4,000, enclosing as collateral seven deeds and five insurance policies. He suggests how the note should run, and indicates that he wants the first $2,500 by February twentieth. The letter is in English, but the orthography of the word "expreß" is indicative of a German hand. The tone of the letter suggests that Whipple and Bequest had had a previous conversation about the matter, and it is only in a follow-up letter from Whipple that we learn that Bequest and his bank were capable of driving a hard bargain. Mr. Whipple writes on February 1, 1894:

> Dear Sir
> Yours of the 27th received tonight. I was shocked at the price your Atty made out. I can have the work done here for five dollars. And do not think it right—that I should pay street price. My titles are all good. And I do not propose to take advantage of you. If I did I should not have offered you security on twenty-five thousand worth of property—at least for the loan of four thousand. The track of land I bought from Charles Alston is ample as the buildings are all on that track, and the insurance on them are about seven thousand, and not all insured. If you think it just let the work go on. But I hope to God you don't think I am a Tillmanite. As for my integrity I will refer you to W. K. Ryan, Bollmann Bros., [illegible] of your city or other banks of Darlington. Enclosed I return your Atty letter.
> Yours respectfully, / Paul Whipple

CHAPTER 8: THE RISE AND DOWNFALL OF AUGUST

Lacking any follow-up evidence, it seems unlikely that Mr. Whipple got his mortgage with a reduction in the legal fees, and Bequest did not take the bait that the bank was charging exorbitant fees because it was dealing with a member of "Pitchfork" Ben Tillman's camp.[19] The high fees charged by the bank's solicitor Cappelmann were doubtless the going rate and part of the strategy to increase the balance sheet's "undivided profits," which in the fourth quarterly statement issued in February 1894 had grown to $6,873.95.

Before the family could leave Charleston that summer for the stay on the Island, two minor incidents broke the routine of the bank cashier and restaurant owner. A "crook" claiming to be a representative of a Grand Rapids, Michigan, furniture manufacturer tried to pass a bad check at the bank. "Cashier Bequest...was suspicious and notified the police." The man spent the night in the city jail and "declined to talk to reporters, and had very little to say to anyone after he found that he could not work any bluff game."[20] Two months later, there was a minor fire "in the rear of Bequest's, in King Street" that was "extinguished before any considerable damage was done, but came near being the occasion of one of the faithful employees of the fire department losing his life." Charlie Brown was not seriously injured, and "Engine No. 1 got to the scene of the fire in excellent time."[21] If August Bequest was keeping track, this fire "of little consequence" at his restaurant was at least the fourth time his property had been visited by flames. Both the incident at the bank and the fire at his restaurant would have required the Cashier/Restauranteur to juggle his attention between his two jobs: that it was difficult to keep his domains and their respective responsibilities separated is visible in the want ad he put in the

---

19. The "radical" farmer from Edgefield County had railed against bankers and aristocrats for their part in ruining the state.

20. *News and Courier*, March 31, 1894.

21. *News and Courier*, May 26, 1894.

News and Courier in June, "Wanted, a good milk cow. A. Bequest, 58 Broad street": he needed the cow at the restaurant he owned on King Street, not at the bank on Broad Street where he was the Cashier. No doubt he was running a little ragged trying to fulfill his duties at both operations.

In any case, he was more than occupied by having his fingers in so many pies. In July, he was elected vice president of the Palmetto Soap Factory: the newspaper reported that "the results of the first six months' work of this enterprise were better than was expected by the most sanguine."[22] Then, in October, the first issue of the newly established *The Evening Post* announced the formation of yet another new enterprise, the German American Mutual Life Association:

> The Post, today, introduces to its readers a new enterprise which is largely due to Charleston Capital for existence, and which comes to us now with the highest endorsement that such an enterprise could have, the practical cooperation of men whose name in the business would stand as high as the highest in the country.
> The public needs no introduction to James Redding, H. C. Wohlers, Geo. A Huguelot and A. Bequest, the Charleston directors of the German American Mutual Life Association.
> The association was organized among the capitalists and business men of Atlanta and Charleston a short time ago. The president and manager is James G. West, one of the best known insurance men of the South. He, with his co-laborers have prepared a beautiful system of

---

22. *News and Courier*, July12, 1894. The enthusiasm was almost palpable in September: "The . . . Company is now doing a fine business . . . and its rapid growth certainly reflects credit on the city for patronizing home industry. . . . [I]ts output averages $60,000 a year. . . . Fourteen hands are employed in the factory." (*News and Courier*, September 5, 1894).

insurance, that cannot fail to recommend itself to the public.[23]

The *Post* ran the Association's first full-column ad the next day, offering any and everything the reader could want in life insurance:

> Policies clear, simple, and free from technicalities; the largest possible amount of insurance that can be secured for the smallest outlay consistent with security; special features: annual cash dividends / cash surrender of policy / loans / nonforfeiture clause / no restrictions as to travel, residence or occupation / continuation of policy without further payment / women insured

The ad carried the names of the officers, including A. Bequest. Since the company's headquarters were in Atlanta, James F. Redding was listed as the "Assistant Local Representative" at 59 Broad Street; Jac. D. Lesemann was the "Gen'l Agent for South Carolina" at 56 Broad Street. If anyone was taking notice, these men and the company itself were business neighbors of the cashier of the German-American Trust and Savings at 58 Broad Street.

Later that month, in addition to the Soap Factory and the Insurance Association, Bequest's name as a director could be added to yet another star on Charleston's horizon:

> The Consumers' Coal Company of Charleston is the latest stock company that has been formed here. It will be under the control and management of progressive and enterprising business men.
>
> Recognizing the importance and volume of the coal business in Charleston a number of representative citizens have combined and put in existence a company which is expected to extend the coal trade and enlarge the commerce both with

---

23. *Evening Post*, October 1, 1894.

the interior of the state and with the numerous trading vessels which come to this port.

The officers are: A. F. C. Cramer, president, E. H. Jahnz, vice-president, Henry Schachte, secretary and treasurer. Directors, Aug. Bequest, H. A. Heiser, Henry C. Wohlers and Henry Sold.

Arrangements were completed this morning by which the company enters into immediate possession of Merchants' wharf, one of the most desirable localities in the city, affording facilities for shipping by rail and water.

The capital stock is $25,000 and has been subscribed up to a very small balance by the local investors. The property just purchased will be carefully overhauled, and all modern improvements for hauling coal will be added.[24]

Pausing a moment to take stock of August Bequest's ascendancy into the upper echelon of Charleston's business community comprising its elite company of officers and directors, it would be reasonable to suggest that he had leveraged himself into that company with his money and his mouth. His transitions from grocery/dry goods store proprietor in Abbeville, to grist mill operator, to owner of "Bequest's" on King Street, must have provided him with enough cash flow that, in combination with his extrovert personality, he could transform his numerous friends and acquaintances—the majority of them successful Germans—into business partners willing to acknowledge his financial participation with a position of rank. It was not that he had any particular knowledge, or ability, or training that made him valuable to any of these new ventures—not to the banking industry, not to the local soap manufacturer, not to the Atlanta-based insurance company, nor to the port city's commerce and trade in coal. August Bequest could be numbered among Charleston's "progressive and enterprising business men" because

---

24. *Evening Post*, October 22, 1894.

CHAPTER 8: THE RISE AND DOWNFALL OF AUGUST

he indeed had talents: he was not risk-averse, he knew in which circles he wanted to move, he aspired to succeed as others with the same German blood had done, and he recognized no limitations on what might be possible. With some—or all—of the balls he had in the air, he was determined to succeed. Each undertaking represented an opportunity for him to gain even more traction in getting to the top.

On his way there, he put yet another feather in his cap. Early in 1895, the *News and Courier* announced the opportunity to subscribe to the capital stock of the Equitable Fire Insurance Company at the office of James F. Redding at 59 Broad Street. August had joined him and two others as incorporators of the new insurance company. The charter had been granted the incorporators on January thirty-first. This would add another directorship as well as a vice-presidency. Everything had fallen into place by March:

> One of the largest and most enthusiastic meetings of business men held in this city in a long time was that at Hibernian Hall yesterday afternoon in the interest of organizing a fire insurance company. The Equitable Fire Insurance Company of Charleston, was regularly organized, one hundred and ninety stockholders being present. The authorized capital of the company is $500,000, and at the meeting yesterday three-fourths of the subscriptions were represented.
>
> Mr. Geo W. Williams, Jr. was called to the chair, and the charter from the State Legislature was read and accepted. The by-laws were then read and adopted, and the form of policy submitted and adopted.
>
> A committee of three was appointed to nominate a board of eleven directors, and the following gentlemen elected: W. H.[*sic*] Bird, Geo A. Wagener, A. Bequest, A. F. C. Cramer, F. Q. O'Neil, B. I. Simmons, Geo W. Williams, Jr., J. L.

David, John B. Adger, M. D. Maguire, James F. Redding.

Before the stockholders' meeting adjourned they were requested to give the new company all the business they could and thus make it one of the most successful home enterprises of Charleston. Several of the stockholders gave the Equitable a number of risks before leaving the hall.

The directors' meeting then convened and elected the following officers. Mr. Wm. M. Bird is the chair: James F. Redding, president; A. Bequest, vice president; Wm. G. Mazyck, secretary and treasurer; Smythe & Lee, solicitors.[25]

As usual, the new company immediately began advertising its existence and the services provided in the newspaper: the business was underway and August, in the company of some of Charleston's leaders, was one of those whose enterprising efforts promised to be another success story. A month before the Equitable Fire Insurance Company's organizing meeting, the German-American Trust and Savings Bank had held its anniversary meeting and, as was noted previously, elected August president to take the place of J. Fred Lilienthal who declined re-election. If he was keeping track—and no doubt he was—August had been one of the named corporators of four businesses, was now on the board of five enterprises, and was president or vice-president of three. As if there were not much left for him in Charleston proper, he sought and found a niche in another part of the state. Columbia's newspaper, *The State,* announced on March 5, 1895, that "the progressive people of the State seem to be going ahead with the building of new cotton mills with home capital."[26] The state issued a charter for the Central Cotton Mills Company in

---

25. *News and Courier*, March 20, 1895.

26. *The State,* March 5, 1895.

CHAPTER 8: THE RISE AND DOWNFALL OF AUGUST

Pickens County to the corporators D. K. Norris of Anderson, J. F. Lay of Central, J. F. Norris, A. Bequest and George Von Kolnitz, Jr. of Charleston. The capital stock was $100,000 divided into $100 shares, and the mill was to be located upstate in Pickens County. The German Charlestonian, among his other friends, foresaw the potential of monetary gain to be had from the burgeoning textile industry in up-state South Carolina.[27]

Compulsively busy, Bequest and his son Henry took a brief respite in Summerville in April. They were reported staying at Captain Frederick Wagener's much-favored Pine Forest Inn, along with a number of other distinguished guests. While re-charging, the father undoubtedly continued to plan and negotiate. By the end of July he had again aligned himself with colleagues to start a piano manufacturing company: *The State* recorded the commission to J. Fred Lilienthal, A. F. C. Cramer, A. Bequest, P. H. Gadsden and Theodore Wenzel to incorporate the Wenzel Piano Company of Charleston with a capital stock of $50,000 divided into 200 shares. "The company proposes to manufacture, sell and deal in pianos, and all kinds of musical instruments, print and sell sheet music, etc."[28]

All the while he was gathering additional plumage, August Bequest, naturally enough, was taking part in the Democratic machine that was by this time the only political game in town. As a member of the German Artillery, he would have been among those in adulation of the aged, but still venerated ex-US Senator Wade Hampton who came to Charleston in May 1895 to "deliver the Confederate oration before the 'young Confeds." The Artillery's Captain Frederick Wagener had begged to have the honor of being part of the reception planned for the General.

---

27. After construction that began the same year that the Central Cotton Mills Company was chartered, the Olympia Mill in Columbia became the world's largest textile mill under one roof. (George C. Rogers, Jr. and C. James Taylor, *A South Carolina Chronology 1497-1992*, 2nd ed. [1994], 114.)

28. *The State*, August 1, 1895. The *News and Courier* (August 7, 1895) followed with the notice of subscription opening at the office of Mordecai & Gadsden at 43-47 Broad Street.

Writing to the chairman of the event committee, Wagener pleaded that it would "afford the command, as well as myself, great pleasure to participate in the reception of Gen Wade Hampton on the occasion of his visit to our city to deliver the address before the Confederate Veterans, either by taking part in the escort or by firing a salute."[29] August had not been in the war, but he would not have missed the chance to mingle with the members of the post-Reconstruction Democratic party still aligned to the "old cause." The democratic fervor was celebrated again at the end of the year with "a great democratic rally":

> At the German Artillery Hall last night a scene was enacted that brought back to a majority of the great crowd present in the days of 1876. It was the sons of the unterrified Democracy of this grand old city in conference upon the eve of a great political contest. The assemblage represented every section of the city from the Battery walls to the city boundary, from the Ashley to the Cooper: every trade, art, profession and calling, every creed and nationality. On the stage were men who have stood at the front in battles fought for honest government, white supremacy and personal liberty.

"Mr. A. Bequest" was one of those named in attendance. The rally was in celebration of the passage of the Constitution of 1895—the legacy of Benjamin Tillman who, in his efforts to "transform white supremacy into something more than a slogan," had called for a new state constitution "carefully crafted to exclude most black men and safeguard 'Anglo-Saxon supremacy, good government, and . . . our civilization'."[30]

---

29. *News and Courier*, April 26, 1895.

30. Stephen Kantrowitz, *Ben Tillman & the Reconstruction of White Supremacy* (Chapel Hill and London: The University of North Carolina Press, 2000), 198.

CHAPTER 8: THE RISE AND DOWNFALL OF AUGUST

The post-Reconstruction era in which August Bequest and his two brothers were participants has been summarized as follows:

> When federal troops were withdrawn in 1877 South Carolinians were again allowed to govern themselves. Political power alternated uncertainly between representatives of the old gentry class on one hand, such as Wade Hampton, Duncan Clinch Heyward, and Richard I. Manning, who, moderate and reasonable as they were, could do little to revive the crippled economy, and flamboyant demagogues on the other hand, such as Ben Tillman and "Coley" Blease, who did incalculable harm by playing on the fears and resentments of the impoverished and demoralized whites. During the 1880s textile mills, which had been present in the western part of the state since before the Civil War, grew into a major industry. The plight of many blacks appeared worse at this time than it had been under slavery, for they now lived in a society that simply had no jobs for them. Many whites wished that the blacks would simply go away and they embodied their feelings in segregation laws and customs. Acceptance of the black citizens' rights and place in the society was retarded by laws that resulted in their disenfranchisement and segregation. The march toward this segregation of society culminated in the Constitution of 1895 which effectively permitted the blacks to be ruled out of the political life of the state.[31]

---

31. George C. Rogers, Jr. & C. James Taylor, *A South Carolina Chronology 1497-1992*, 2nd ed. (1994), 95.

Such was the social and political context in which Charleston's nineteenth-century German immigrants, whether they arrived before or after the Civil War, operated—willingly or otherwise. It was nearly impossible to swim upstream against the currents if one wanted to get ahead or even just manage to stay afloat. It was necessary to forfeit the beliefs and values of one's German past in order to function in Charleston's present. Some might have struggled mightily with this requirement. In the case of August Bequest, he appears to have embraced it.

The previously cited newspapers' positive commentaries accompanying their reporting of new enterprises—in many of which August Bequest participated—signaled the somewhat desperate need for the city to expand its economic horizons and to deal with its declining economic status: "In 1900 Charleston's economy was moribund."[32] Before the turn of the century, nonetheless, an effort was being made to improve the state of things in the city and to generate a kind of economic upswing:

> The song of the hammer to the accompaniment of trowel and saw has been echoing through this old "City by the Sea" during the past twelve months. The song has told of magnificent residences and comfortable homes, of splendid business houses, and of churches and school houses being erected and rebuilt for the good people of Charleston. There are but few streets that one can enter without seeing new houses or improved ones. . . . There have also been marked improvements on the waterfront, the most recent being by the Consumers' Coal Company, on Central wharf, and of all the points noted in the list of building permits the one most to be lauded and giving the greatest cause for gratification is that so large a number of people are building comfortable and

---

32. Fraser, *Charleston! Charleston!*, 339.

CHAPTER 8: THE RISE AND DOWNFALL OF AUGUST 215

> convenient houses for themselves, costing from $500 to $5,000 each. The books of City Assessor Kelly's office show that since last September . . . permits have been issued for 707 new buildings, estimated to cost $151,405, and for additions and improvements to 91 old buildings, estimated to cost $33,000.[33]

One of the building permits listed was to the Bequest property at No. 8 Horlbeck Alley, a two story frame stable. It seemed that the Bequests were doing their part to improve the neighborhood, but the permit to improve the stable was but a feeble attempt. Their house at No. 6 Horlbeck Alley, for whatever reason, was taken by the City Council and was to be auctioned in a Sheriff's Sale scheduled for early December.[34] It was apparently not lost to the Bequests at this point, but the foreclosure action nonetheless suggests some degree of financial stress and could have been interpreted as a forecast of clouds on the horizon.

Back in May, a week before the Hampton celebration at Artillery Hall, August's Aunt Adelheid had died at age eighty-six. Her funeral "was largely attended from St. Matthew's German Lutheran church at 10:30 o'clock this morning."[35] With her passing, the three Bequest brothers were the only Charleston residents who would carry the name through the last decade of the nineteenth century. It was at the end of the decade's midpoint that the *News and Courier* praised both Bernhard and August, with their respective European Fish Smokery and Equitable Fire Insurance Company, as "men who have done much to build up Charleston's credit at home and abroad."[36] However differently,

---

33. *News and Courier*, September 14, 1895.

34. *Evening Post*, November 11, 1895.

35. *Evening Post*, May 4, 1895.

36. *News and Courier*, December 21, 1895.

these two German brothers were firmly established as Charlestonian businessmen in the New South, each seemingly at the top of his game.

The new year of 1896, however, would bring change. Already by mid-January, August was in the public eye when he was appointed by a state court judge as receiver to manage the affairs of the local, but insolvent, Palmetto Brewery.[37] Almost immediately he would find himself one of the leading actors in a courtroom drama that would last for the better part of the year. The *Evening Post* broke the story on the fourteenth, first with a short statement in its "Little bits" column, saying that "Judge Benet in Orangeburg last night appointed August Bequest receiver of the Palmetto Brewery and required him to furnish a $25,000 bond," then, in another column, offered a fuller explanation:

> The Palmetto Brewery now has two receivers to manage its affairs. Last week Mr. A. F. C. Cramer was appointed receiver of the company in the United States court, and last night Judge Benet in the state court appointed Mr. August Bequest receiver.
>
> The Post understands that the way the question will be settled is that Mr. Bequest as receiver appointed by Judge Benet will make a demand upon Receiver Cramer to turn over to him the business of the company, and if receiver Cramer refuses then receiver Bequest will go before the United States court and set up his claim to the office of receiver by appointment of the state court and will ask the United States court to dismiss its receiver.[38]

---

37. Founded in the 1870s by J. C. H. Claussen. John Bequest had worked briefly as a driver for the Brewery in 1884.

38. *Evening Post*, January 14, 1896.

That action took place the following day. The *News and Courier* reported that Bequest and his attorney, Mr. Mordecai, made their formal demand before federal Judge Simonton who would then decide the question of jurisdiction "for or against the State Court," adding that "no actual conflict, it is said, will arise out of this matter."[39] That turned out not to be the case, with running commentary on the various proceedings keeping the public informed on the issue. It should be noted at this point that A. F. C. Cramer and August Bequest were at the time both co-directors of the Consumers' Coal Company, co-corporators of the Palmetto Soap Manufacturing Company, co-corporators of the Wenzel Piano Company, and close friends of J. C. Blohme. A. F. C. Cramer was a director of the Germania Saving Bank, August, the president of the German-American Trust and Savings.

On January eighteenth, it was clarified that Cramer had been appointed in the federal court on the petition of the De La Vergne Refrigerator Machine Company, and the state court judge, Benet, had appointed Bequest on the petition of the minority stockholders. The case was described as a "three-cornered fight." Bequest's attorneys, Mordecai and Gadsden, would argue that the U.S. Court had no jurisdiction in the matter: Cramer's attorneys, Nathans, James Simons, and Henry A. M. Smith, argued their opposition. By the end of the month, Judge Simonton decreed that each represented a different interest and that both must "hold until their claims . . . have been adjudicated by the court of last resort."[40]

Outside the courtroom, of course, life went on: A business property on King Street, corner of Mary Street, was put up for auction, and Bequest, along with his attorneys Gadsden and Mordecai constituted the Committee of Creditors. The stockholders of the German-American Trust and Savings Bank

---

39. *News and Courier*, January 15, 1896.

40. *News and Courier*, January 28, 1896.

met for their annual meeting. Bequest read the financial statement which "showed the bank to be in a most flourishing condition."[41] He was re-elected president.

Temperatures in the courts, meanwhile, were rising. Judge Benet "issued an order upon Cashier Edward E. Sparkman of the Security Savings Bank, A. F. C. Cramer, as president of the Coal Consumers' Company [sic], and John E. Doscher, as president of the Palmetto Brewery Co., each and all to show cause at 10 o'clock next Monday, March 2 . . . why they should not be attached to contempt of court." Bequest had filed a report with Judge Benet clarifying that Cramer had not yielded to him, and asked the judge to "release his bondsman or . . . instruct him how to proceed further."[42] The lawyers threatened with contempt filed their returns at the end of April, but it was not until early July that matters came to a head. On the second, Federal Judge Simonton "handed down an order for the sale of the Palmetto Brewery on the 13th day of September next."[43] On the fourth, Judge Benet fined Sparkman, Cramer and Doscher one hundred dollars each, disbarred Messrs Mitchell, Smith, Nathan and Sinkler, "pending the undoing of the action in the United States Court," and fined them five hundred dollars each. No action was taken against Attorney James Simons.

The heat of Charleston's August bore down both outside and inside the courthouse:

> No case that has come before the State supreme court in recent years has excited more widespread interest than the appeal of the leading Charleston attorneys who were a short time ago held in contempt by Judge Benet and disbarred by him in his sentence. It is to be a big fight. The State

---

41. *Evening Post*, February 20, 1896.

42. *Evening Post*, February 24, 1896.

43. *News and Courier*, July 2, 1896.

yesterday morning gave the names of the distinguished attorneys who are to appear before the court in behalf of the members of the fraternity who have been disbarred by Judge Benet.

The general opinion of the leading members of the bar of the State who have been approached upon the subject is that the court will not sustain Judge Benet. If this court does then the case will go to the supreme court of the United States as the case over which the trouble occurred was in both the State and the United States circuit court. The matter sifted down to its meat is simply a question as to whether the United States court had any jurisdiction in the case over which the trouble occurred. If the supreme court says that the State court did not have jurisdiction, it will say by implication that the United States court did have jurisdiction, and then Judge Benet's action cannot be sustained.

The suspense finally ended in April of 1897 when the State Supreme Court ruled on the contempt case—the subsidiary action that had overtaken the initial dispute as to the rightful receiver. The Court struck down Judge Benet "in one, two, three order" and Charleston's most distinguished lawyers were allowed to resume their practices. "Thus ends another historic case."[44]

By this time, August Bequest's name and function relative to the Palmetto Brewery case had been long forgotten. When in early summer the case seemed to move ever so slowly, he and A. F. C. Cramer could not afford to let the jurisdictional dispute come between them or to take the issues personally. Their cooperation was needed on several fronts, for example, on the board of the Equitable Fire Insurance Company. In mid-May 1896

---

44. *News and Courier*, April 20, 1897.

the company was reported to be flourishing, "with branches soon to be established in Georgia and Tennessee,"[45] and both were re-elected as directors. August was still vice-president.

However, just one month later, August Bequest's coat of many colors began to unravel. The headline in the *Evening Post* of June 18, 1896, was ominous: "Stockholders will meet. / The failure of the German-American bank. / Effort to reorganize / will be made on Saturday—President Pringle of the Charleston [Bank] to be co-receiver—bank's condition unknown. / The details followed:

> The doors of the German-American Trust and Savings bank at 58 Broad street are closed to-day.
>
> Business has been suspended and the affairs are in the hands of Capt. James F. Redding, who was appointed receiver by Judge Brawley last afternoon.
>
> The inability of the bank to meet maturing papers has caused the embarrassment or failure. The exact condition of affairs of the bank are unknown and cannot be ascertained for several days until a thorough examination, which has already been instituted by the receiver is completed.
>
> The defunct bank was organized three years ago, on the 19th of January in 1893, with an authorized capital of $1,000,000, but the capital stock paid up was $60,000.
>
> The bank has a very large deposit account and the depositors are on the anxious bench to know if they will get all or a part of their money back.
>
> There will be no answer to that question until the examination of the affairs is concluded.

---

45. *Evening Post*, May 15, 1896.

CHAPTER 8: THE RISE AND DOWNFALL OF AUGUST

Under the state law the stockholders of the bank are responsible for the amount of their stock and 5 per cent.

The alarm of the depositors was precipitated when it became known that several checks had been refused payment during yesterday.

To-day it was agreed that President Pringle of the Charleston Bank should be appointed co-receiver with Capt. Redding and a petition will be presented to Judge Brawley sometime this afternoon.

Bequest is president of the bank, B. I. Simmons, vice-president and J. A. Patjens, cashier.

The petition for a receiver was filed in the United States circuit court late yesterday afternoon, and in the absence of Judge Simonton District Judge Brawley granted the prayer and fixed the 23rd inst. as the date for the hearing on a question of permanent receivership.

The petition was filed by Attorneys Mordecai and Gadsden, representing Van Wych Horton, of . . . Massachusetts. He states that he has a deposit account of 6,000 in the bank and alleges that the institution is unable to meet its debts, that the bank has been mismanaged, has suspended payment and failed. He prays the court's protection by the appointment of a receiver to manage its affairs properly.

It will be seen from the advertising columns of The Post that a meeting of the stockholders of the bank will be held at noon on Saturday with a view to the reorganization of the bank. It goes without saying that there will be a large attendance. It is hoped and believed that a plan for the successful reorganization of the bank will be suggested and this financial institution which has done in many respects a prosperous business will not be lost to the city.

Saturday was the twenty-first, and the *News and Courier* found it more than newsworthy to report on the stockholders' meeting:

> A majority of the stockholders of the German-American Trust and Savings Bank held a meeting yesterday in the office of the Equitable Fire Insurance Company and discussed plans for reorganization. Although the reorganization will not be made until next week, yet the meeting yesterday was by no means a fruitless one. Mr. Henry Buist presided and Mr. J.A. Moreso [?] acted as secretary. Messrs E.[sic] N. Hesse, B. I. Simmons and J. F. Norris, the three directors not under obligation to the bank, made a report on the condition of affairs. The report is not the result of an actual and thorough examination such as the receiver could give, but nevertheless these three gentlemen had made themselves conversant with the condition of things and all of their figures are conservative estimates. The assets were shown to be about $217,600 and the liabilities $235,000. The directors think that these figures are rock bottom ones and that there is good reason to believe that a good deal of the assets at present doubtful will be realized on in a short time. The first step to reorganize was taken by Mr. H. A. M. Smith, who presented this resolution:
>
> 1. That the subscribing stockholders of the German-American Trust and Savings Bank will agree to pay 33 1/3 per cent on their stock in cash to enable the bank to proceed, or
> 2. That in case any stockholder subscribing is unable or unwilling to pay such 33 1/3 he will

CHAPTER 8: THE RISE AND DOWNFALL OF AUGUST

surrender his stock on payment to him of $2 per share.

3. That to make this agreement effective it must be signed within six days by at least 85 percent in value of the stockholders, and there must be agreed to be paid in cash not less than $15,000.

4. That in addition said committee shall procure the consent of at least 80 per cent of the depositors in the savings department to an extension of at least six months from the first day of July, 1896, and the consent of the same percentage of the holders of bills payable to the same extension.

5. That the present administration of the bank shall be succeeded by a new administration to be elected by the stockholders paying such cash assessments or 33 1/3 per cent, and that a meeting of the stockholders shall be called to be held on the 28th day of June, 1896, to carry the agreement into extension.

This resolution was unanimously adopted and before the meeting adjourned the majority of those present had already given their names in as being willing to accord with their money to the resolution. There seems to be but little doubt but that the stockholders will furnish the necessary amount to keep the bank going.

Mr. Hastie offered a resolution providing for a committee of three to investigate the prominent causes for the failure of the bank. This committee, composed of the Messrs Hastie, O. G. Marjenhoff and S. E. Welch, was nominated from the floor. It will make its report at the next meeting, which will be held Friday noon at the Chamber of Commerce building.

The extensive coverage in the *Evening Post* on the twenty-sixth let the newspaper's readers know that the additional money based on the 33 1/3 percentage had been subscribed and a plan for the future was in the works. The committee that had been formed presented its report, and a number of new details came to light. Recounting the bank's founding history, the committee acknowledged that a minute book had not been kept so that it had had to rely on "loose memoranda" in its investigation of what had gone wrong. The following "facts" had been ascertained:

--On the first of February, 1895, J. F. Lilienthal resigned as president and A. Bequest was elected a director in the place of Mr. Hunt who at some previous time had declined re-election. Subsequently Mr. Bequest was elected president of the bank....

--The bank ledger shows that on the 1st of March, 1896, Bequest's account was overdrawn $9,821.46 and that subsequently this was enhanced by his notes for $1,600, $1,400 and a memorandum check for $251.56, making $13,100.60, to this must be added an overdraft of $4,363.95, and a note of A. C. Bequest for $2500 and a note on which he is endorser and which is prorated for $2,730 making the Bequest indebtedness $22,956.xx[46]

--To secure the payment of this sum it is alleged that Bequest surrendered as collateral 25 shares of a "Guaranty and Investment Co.," 14 shares of German-American Trust and Savings bank stock, and three life insurance policies payable on death of the assured. That all of such collateral have not yet been found by the receivers. None of the life policies are in our opinion properly assigned, and

---

46. Some of the numbers are illegible, but in any case do not seem to add up exactly as reported; the inaccuracy is likely attributable to the newspaper reporter, not the stockholders' committee.

CHAPTER 8: THE RISE AND DOWNFALL OF AUGUST

in the case of two of them there is no evidence of any attempts to assign.

--It would appear from the books that J. F. Lilienthal has made call loans for (est. J. F. Lilienthal) $3,000 and for $2,500, and personal memorandum checks dated March 1896 for $1,500, $1,670.91, $363.37, $236.83 (aggregating $9,361.11), and he is an endorser on a note for $3,800 due next month. (The drawer of this note has recently died). Amount of this indebtedness is $12,743.96.

--The only attempt to secure this sum that we hear of is 60 shares of the Southern Prepared Flour and Grain Co. stock, 3 shares Palmetto Brewery stock and 6 shares of the German-American Trust and Savings bank stock.

--In addition to this Lilienthal also gave a mortgage on property in Thomas street for $7,000, dated May 2, 1895. This mortgage was not recorded until the 10th of June, 1896 when the receivers took possession of the bank and it was then found that a prior mortgage existed on the same property dated May 1st, for $3,000.

--Of the present board of directors it does not appear that Messrs Simmons, Norris or Hesse ever used the bank for their own advantage.

--We also note that loans have been made by the bank on stocks of merchandise, the goods remaining in the hands of borrowing firms, in one case for $15,000, and in another instance for $12,000.

--We have further to report the existence of notes discounted which were drawn by firms and endorsed by some young men in their employ apparently without means. One of these notes is for $3,000 and has been protected for non-payment.

--Another note for which $2,500 was paid is drawn for $2,500 in figures, but the amount is written in the body of the note is twenty-five dollars.

--We have had no funds to use in consulting a lawyer, but we find in the 'acts of 1893' an act to affirm, amend and extend the charter of the 'German-American Trust and Savings Bank,' which states 'that no director or other officers of said corporation shall borrow any money from said corporation. If any director or other officer shall be convicted on indictment of directly or indirectly violating this section, he shall be punished by fine or imprisonment at the discretion of the court.'[47]

Such evidence laid out before the public was utterly damning. Neither Bequest nor Lilienthal would ever recover the good reputation they had before June 18, 1896. And this was just the beginning.

The *News and Courier* repeated the *Post*'s story of the previous evening but tried to sound encouraging: "There is now no reason to believe otherwise than that the affairs of the German-American Trust and Savings Bank will within a few days be in the hands of a new set of directors, composed of Charleston's cleverest business men. The reorganization of the bank was decided on yesterday and as soon as the Court is heard from the stockholders will get together, shoulder to shoulder, and show the Charleston people what they can do."[48] Although it was never

---

47. *Evening Post.* June 26, 1896.

48. *News and Courier*, June 27, 1896. Not much had changed: the local press was still capable of paternalistic references to the ethnic community, suggesting that it would be "they" who would show the "Charleston people" what the former could do. That, in effect, was to say that Charlestonians/"We" should be encouraged that "They"/the predominantly **German** Americans—directors,

CHAPTER 8: THE RISE AND DOWNFALL OF AUGUST

stated in print, it was understood that the bank's doors about to be re-opened were to be forever closed to Messrs Bequest and Lilienthal.

Within a week, the "All around town" column in the *News and Courier* would gossip that Vice-president A. Bequest had resigned from the board of the Equitable Fire Insurance Company.[49] There was no further news until August. In the interim it was likely that the Bequests were skipping the summer trip to Sullivan's Island and keeping a very low profile, they and the Lilienthals waiting to see what would follow on the heels of their embarrassment and how their friends and associates would pursue them for the crimes they had committed. What was surely agonizing suspense ended on August seventh: "Mr. August Bequest former president and director of the German-American Trust and Savings Bank was arrested at one o'clock this afternoon under three warrants issued by Magistrate Rouse." Former friends and business colleagues were no longer amicable: "The warrants were taken out at noon by Messrs B. I. Simmons and Henry Buist and were sworn to by F. Jordan, A. F. Doscher, J. D. W. Claussen, Wm. Bargamann and W. A. Meyer."

> The first warrant charges Mr. Bequest that on the 22nd day of April, 1895, he fraudulently and feloniously obtained $1,400 from the German-American Trust and Savings Bank by falsely representing that he had deposited with the bank as collateral security fourteen shares of the stock of the German-American Trust and Savings Bank and that he knew his pretense and representation was false and untrue.
> The second warrant charges him with borrowing $9,797.15 from the bank for which he gave his

---

stockholders, depositors—associated with the bank's identified ethnicity would reorganize and rescue one of the business community's fledgling institutions.

49. *News and Courier*, July 2, 1896.

note, while his personal account with the bank was credited with the amount.

The third warrant accuses him of having on the 4th of May, 1895 taken a Northeastern Railroad coupon bond of the value of $500, the property of Edmund Ravenel, which had been deposited with the bank as collateral on a note for $165. Bequest is charged with committing a breach of trust in committing the bond to his own use and that he feloniously carried the bond away from the bank.

Constable Duke was given the warrant to execute and he went direct to Mr. Bequest's house on Society street and found him there.

The officer took charge of the ex-bank president and escorted him to Magistrate Rouse's office where he is now held.

Mr. Bequest took his arrest coolly and when he reached the magistrate's office he went to a private adjoining room and sat quietly by himself and commenced reading the New York World. He smiled as he read the warrants. He spoke about sending for his attorney, Mr. Bryan, but when the reporter left the court room at 2 o'clock no lawyer or friends had then called.

It is expected that Mr. Bequest will have to give a $5,000 bond in each case and unless he can raise the $15,000 surety before night he will be committed to jail.[50]

Reflecting on the account in the *Evening Post*, the reader might have thought that J. Fred Lilienthal fared a little better—at least that he appeared the lesser scoundrel:

At 2:15 o'clock this afternoon Alderman J. Fred Lilienthal was arrested by Constable Duke in

---

50. *Evening Post*, August 7, 1896.

CHAPTER 8: THE RISE AND DOWNFALL OF AUGUST

Mordecai & Gadsden's office in connection with the case against Bequest. The warrant was sworn out by the same parties.

Mr. Lilienthal is charged with borrowing from the German-American Trust and Savings Bank, of which he was a director, by overdraft $582.83, which is in violation of the state law, a bank officer borrowing from his own bank. It is classed as a misdemeanor.

Mr. Lilienthal was represented by Mr. P. H. Gadsden.

Judge Rouse fixed his bond at $300[51], and Mr. F. W. Wagener was offered as security, which was accepted.

Judge Rouse fixed the bond for Mr. Bequest in the three cases at $9,500. Mr. Buist asked Mr. J. P. K. Bryan[52], who represented Mr. Bequest, who he offered as bondsmen. Mr. Bryan was not at that hour, 3 o'clock, prepared to say who would become surety for his client.

Mr. Bequest is still in the custody of the magistrate.[53]

The reported attitude of August Bequest in his predicament would have done nothing to endear him to the colleagues who had sworn to the warrants for his arrest. Nor did his "coolness" add much to the character portrait that at this point has only been partially analyzed.

From details in the next day's *News and Courier* report, it was clear that the vultures were circling: "The arrests have been

---

51. Subsequent accounts indicate that this amount is erroneous: the bond was fixed at $3,000.

52. Bryan represented Bequest at a later point in the Palmetto Brewery dispute.

53. *Evening Post*, August 7, 1896.

looked forward to by all those knowing the circumstances surrounding the failure of the German-American Trust and Savings Bank. Last Saturday Messrs Bequest and Lilienthal were sent cards telling them to appear at the bank by noon Wednesday and settle their indebtedness. This was practically a notice from the directors of the bank that it was a case of pay up or be arrested."[54] No doubt was left to the seriousness of the charges: Affidavits were detailed, charging Bequest with breach of trust with fraudulent intent and grand larceny. When found at his home, the "cool" Mr. Bequest "remarked to the constable while getting ready that some remarkable things would happen after his arrest....several others connected with the bank would find themselves explaining things." Fred Lilienthal apparently heard that a deputy had been sent for him and more forthrightly appeared at the Magistrate's office on his own. The Magistrate set Lilienthal's bond at $3,000. Capt. Frederick Wagener (of the German Artillery) signed for him and Lilienthal was released from custody. For the three cases against Bequest, bond was set at $10,000 ($500 more than the *Evening Post* had reported). "During the afternoon Mr. A S. Emerson went on one bond for Mr. Bequest to the extent of $5,000 and upon this Mr. Bequest was released until today when he will be returned to give two more bonds, one of $2,000 and another of $3,000."[55]

August went home for the night and did indeed show up the following morning to post the $2,000 bond: his wife Augusta and his brother Bernhard each posted $1,000. The evening paper reported that Bequest expected the $3,000 bond to be paid by his brother-in-law, Christian Amme, a director of the Germania Bank married to Augusta's sister. The *News and Courier* of the ninth,

---

54. *News and Courier*, August 8, 1896.

55. *News and Courier*, August 8, 1896. A. S. Emerson owned the "Emerson Steam Laundry" but was one of Bernhard Bequest's competitors in the wood business. He typically advertised "Wood, Wood, Wood, Wholesale and retail. By the carload, cord, or cartload. Best yellow pine blocks. No rotten wood. No knots. Prompt delivery. Courteous drivers." Competitor notwithstanding, he must have been one of August Bequest's most loyal friends.

CHAPTER 8: THE RISE AND DOWNFALL OF AUGUST 231

relishing the melodrama, offered that Bequest's son, "a young man of 20, was with him at the Magistrate's office, and worked industriously for him."

> As the time came for closing up the office Magistrate Rouse took from his desk a little blue paper and commenced to fill it out. It was the commitment paper and was to put in jail the man who was once the president of the German-American Trust and Savings Bank. Mr. Bequest seemed a little gloomy, but was perfectly cool and collected. The magistrate informed him that he would take his release papers home with him, and if the bond was secured during the night he would send them to Capt. Kelly. There was nothing else to do. Mr. Bequest's buggy was outside and the constable rode with him to the jail.[56]

Amme and another friend, D. W. Gotjen, posted the bond the next morning, and August Bequest had his overnight in jail behind him. Not that he was entirely free: He was released under a $19,990 bond for trial at the Court of Sessions on the original three charges. That experience did not begin until almost three months later, when in November the grand jury found "true bills" against both Lilienthal and Bequest. The hearing date was set for November 25, but must have been continued, because on the seventeenth of December the *New York Tribune*, *The State*, the *Baton Rouge Daily Advocate*, the *Charlotte Observer*, and the *Columbus Daily Enquirer* all reported under a "Charleston December 16" dateline that

> Fred Lilienthal and August Bequest, former officials of the German American Trust and Savings Bank, were arrested here to-day and charged with a conspiracy to defraud that institution last May. Lilienthal was president and

---

56. *News and Courier*, August 9, 1896.

Bequest cashier of the bank at the time. It is alleged that Lilienthal as president, drew a check that had been given to him with fraudulent intent by Bequest. Both men waived the preliminary examination and gave bond in the sum of $10,000. The same men have been arrested before on similar charges and cases are now pending against them in the court of sessions.

This second arrest and prolongation of the agony had come about when a new cashier of the German-American Trust and Savings went over the books and discovered the alleged conspiracy. The *News and Courier* explained:

> August Bequest and J. Fred Lilienthal were arrested by Constable Dukes of Magistrate Rouse's court, yesterday afternoon at 7 o'clock on a warrant charging them with a conspiracy to defraud.
> The warrant was sworn out in the morning before Magistrate Rouse by Mr. W. Richmond Pinckney, cashier of the German-American Trust and Savings Bank.
> The discovery of the alleged conspiracy was made about a month ago by Mr. Pinckney, while going over the books and passes of the bank.
> The officers and directors of the bank are determined to push this last case as vigorously as the others. Mr. Pinckney said yesterday that there were some of the bank's patrons who did not believe that Messrs Bequest and Lilienthal would have the charge pressed against them as they should, and that there were others who were dissatisfied on account of the continuances at the last term of court of the cases first made against them. As soon as this last transaction was discovered the officers of the bank decided to

carry it into the courts, and the warrant yesterday was the result.

Mr. Bequest was found at home by the constable. He expressed a desire that he be allowed to wait until the next morning, but the constable could not grant such a request. Mr. Lilienthal showed some agitation when the warrant was shown him at his home and wanted to go to see his lawyer, but this request had also to be refused.

Pinckney claimed that Bequest had drawn a check on the bank in the amount of $793.14 and gave it to Lilienthal, who cashed it: "August Bequest, not being authorized to give said check, and he, the said Lilienthal, not being entitled to receive the same. But said transaction was done by them unlawfully and fraudulently and without the knowledge or consent of the board of directors and with intent to defraud the said bank."[57] Augusta came to her husband's rescue and posted the $1,000 bond. Fred Lilienthal's mother, Mrs. Lucy Lilienthal, did the same for her son.

Three days later the State Supreme Court heard and disposed of the case of the Charleston lawyers appealing their disbarments by Judge Benet in the dispute over the Palmetto Brewery's dually-appointed receivers. Judge Benet's actions were summarily struck down by the higher court. He would nonetheless retain his seat on the bench and not suffer terribly from the reversal. August Bequest and Fred Lilienthal, on the other hand, had been dealt their twice-earned, near-fatal blows. Christmas 1896 would not have been a festive occasion for either man or for their respective families—immediate and extended. Whether or not quiet John Bequest on Mt. Pleasant suffered any embarrassment because of his brother's infamy, for certain August's fall from grace surely would have left a bad taste in his elder brother's mouth. There was no doubt that August's scandal had brought the Bequest name into question just when Bernhard

---

57. *News and Courier*, December 17, 1896.

Heinrich was trying to get his new European Fish Smokery established. It is not unreasonable to think that the arrest and humiliation of August took years off the life of Bernhard.

It was not until February 1897 that the cases reached the Court of Sessions, by which time they had lost any aura of hubris that they might have started with. The defendants were treated like any other criminal. The *Evening Post* reported on the Court's convening on the twenty-second and objectively commented that "in addition to these, besides quite a number of minor cases, there are two murder cases which have not been passed upon by the grand jury as yet; five cases against Mr. August Bequest for breach of trust, one similar case against Mr. J. Fred Lilienthal, a rape case against Henry Simmons, colored, and rape cases against Wm Campbell as principal, and John Brooks as accessory."[58]

There must have been some not-unexpected negotiations and plea bargaining between the accused and their former associates as the days and months of 1897 dragged on. It was an awkward affair among friends, relatives, acquaintances, partners and associates of the ethnic community trying to save face while meting out appropriate punishment to some of their own. The "sentences" of Bequest and Lilienthal seemed to fade into the recent past with the hope by everyone concerned that the whole thing could be forgotten. *The State* reported in early July that "the grand jury demurs against the not processing and compromising against J. F. Lilienthal and August Bequest, against whom were found true bills."[59] Nothing more revealing found its way into the Charleston newspapers. Whatever the final disposition,[60] August Bequest, for one, would have to start a new life, cast down as he

---

58. *Evening Post*, February 22, 1897.

59. *The State*, July 2, 1897.

60. While the grand jury demurred against the "not processing and compromising" against the two, the lack of any further reporting of legal action against them suggests that they were never sentenced, but also never formally declared "not guilty."

CHAPTER 8: THE RISE AND DOWNFALL OF AUGUST

was from the peak on which he had enjoyed a brief existence, undone by the crimes he had intentionally or unwittingly committed.

It is doubtful that he could have lingered unemployed for long if he was to keep his family together. The 1897 City Directory shows the family still at their residence on Society Street, although no occupation is listed for August. Augusta is not listed at all, but their son John L. is shown as being employed as a "helper" at the Palmetto Soap Mfg. Co. The eldest son, Heinrich Christian, had gone[61] to Bedford, Virginia, the previous year to attend college: which institution he attended and for how long is not known, but he ended up in New York and is accounted for there as a lodger in a hotel in the 1900 Federal census. In 1899 on a visit to Charleston, he was reportedly "engaged in business in New York."[62] The youngest, August Blohme, is not accounted for until 1901 when he enrolled as a freshman in South Carolina's new Clemson University.[63] It is likely that August, Sr. and his son John took off for California sometime in 1897—both to escape the embarrassment of life in Charleston and to find work. The San Francisco City Directory for 1898 lists "Bequest August, bartender, B. N. Rohde, r 24 Metcalf Pl" and "Bequest John L., clerk Henry A. Wuhrmann, r 400 6th." The former, tending bar for B. N. Rohde, signals an offer of assistance from one of Augusta's relatives (she was Augusta Catherine Rohde), possibly August's brother-in-law. John had apparently found a position with the relative of one of Charleston's German merchants. August Sr. stayed in San Francisco only for a year: the 1899 Directory indicates that John L. stayed on longer, taking over his father's bartending position at Bernard Rohde's San Francisco establishment. By 1900, the nineteen-year-old was still in

---

61. According to the *Evening Post* of January 9, 1896.

62. *Evening Post*, July 15, 1899.

63. He attended for only one term, 1901-02. He nonetheless attended the Clemson reunion/homecoming in August of 1914. (*News and Courier*, July 19, 1914.)

California working as a "rubberworker," probably glad to be on his own and not living at home in disgrace.

There is no documentary evidence to relate how his elder brother's unexpected death in October of 1899 affected August Sr. upon his return from California. To suggest how close he felt toward the brother who had posted bond for him, or for his brother John living in Mt. Pleasant, would be purely conjectural. In any case, August was determined to get something of his life back, and to that end finally managed to find employment as an agent with the Mutual Life Insurance Company of New York. In an ad for the company in the *Charlotte Observer* of November 11, 1900, A. Bequest is listed as "Special agent, Charlotte, N.C." A month later, the Charlotte paper reported that the *Wilmington Star* on the fifteenth had noted that:

> Mr. A. Bequest, the popular and energetic special agent of the Mutual Life Insurance Company of New York, who has been here on business, left yesterday for Monroe. Mr. Bequest will spend the holidays at his home in Charleston. After which he will go to Charlotte and open a permanent office for his company. His many friends in Wilmington will regret to learn that he will not locate here.

Apparently, August had found himself a place in the insurance business and been fairly successful in shaking off the scandal that had all but finished him in South Carolina four years earlier. He seemed to be back on his feet, able to charm the folks in Wilmington with his energy and salesmanship abilities. The *Wilmington Star* column suggests that Augusta and the children were on their own in Charleston while the former bank officer was re-locating elsewhere. The 1901 Charleston City Directory confirmed that the household comprised Augusta married to August, an insurance agent, with August B[lohme] working as a clerk for F. Von Oven, and John L., back from San Francisco, also working as a clerk, with the family living at 4 Cumberland Street. To be noted here are the repercussions occasioned by the bank scandal: The couple had bought—in Augusta's name—a residence at 56 Society Street in 1894; in 1897 the house was conveyed to "D. Rohde," obviously a relative of Augusta's, either under financial duress or as a means of keeping the property in the family until things improved. Not until 1905 were they able to re-occupy 56 Society Street: it remained the family residence, ultimately to become the long-standing address of bachelor August Blohme Bequest

It appears that selling insurance was either not sufficiently profitable or was not sufficiently satisfying for the fifty-year-old August. By October of 1901 he was advertising in the *Charlotte Observer* to sell typewriters: prospective buyers should apply to the manager of the Mutual Life Insurance office. Although the *Observer* seemed to be keeping its eye on him, noting in its society column in March of 1902 that "Mr. A. Bequest will leave in a few days to visit his family in Charleston, S.C.," there was no indication that he was, in fact, settled. In July, he was in partnership with "Smith" in Columbia, S.C. selling Fay-Sho typewriters—"the leading typewriter now in the market."[64] He was still selling insurance while he advertised: "Wanted—Agents in every county in North and South Carolina for the Fay-Sho Typewriter: monthly payments. Apply Bequest & Smith over Abbott's Cigar Store. P.O. Box 384, Columbia, S.C."[65] Once again, there was little grass growing under the feet of August Bequest. By April of 1903 he had become an agent for the Piedmont Fire Insurance Company of Charlotte, again in a partnership—this time with "Dudley and Mann." That arrangement, however, lasted only briefly. Only a month later, the *Charlotte Observer* carried a "Dissolution Notice" stating that "The partnership heretofore existing between August Bequest of Columbia, S.C. and Charles H. Dudley of Charlotte, N.C., under the firm name of Bequest, Dudley and Mann, is hereby dissolved

---

64. *The State*, August 2, 1902.

65. Ibid.

by mutual consent and the said Charles H. Dudley is hereby authorized to collect all debts due said firm and to pay all debts against said firm."[66] The partnership/firm of "Bequest & Smith" in new and rebuilt typewriters continued nonetheless in Columbia.

His dual life in Charlotte and Columbia would have put him back in the mode in which he had operated earlier, juggling more than a few balls in the air and working in several spheres at once. He appears to have always had the talents of a salesman who could talk fast and convincingly. That he seemed always to be moving quickly and not infrequently a little out of breath is in evidence in a letter to Attorney John Cappelmann[67] that he wrote hurriedly in October 1904. The letter displays his fluency in English—not surprising by this time—as well as the quick pace of his thoughts. It is written in a fairly legible hand on letterhead of the National Life Insurance Company, Montpelier, VT, with "A. Bequest" as "General Agent" and "C. A. Smith" as "Cashier," in Columbia, S.C.:

> (Verbatim!) Dear Sir / Please make the effort to have Bond transferred from C. Bart & Co as indicated in your letter ascertain from Mordecai the principle and int, I have been delayed in Columbia on account of the chief medical director of our Co making a trip through the territory the cost of services of $50.00 I will bring for you when I come down next week or as soon he leaves I fear M_ may take steps for another fee you know what I mean you can phone me tomorrow over the long distance phone #722 at Columbia reverse charges, when the will charge our offices for the call after you ascertain the amt you can prepare proper paper for Mrs. Bequest to sign acknowledge the amt to be due under the Bond

---

66. *Charlotte Observer*, May 19, 1903.

67. The attorney for the German-American Trust and Savings Bank and other businesses with whom Bequest had earlier been involved.

CHAPTER 8: THE RISE AND DOWNFALL OF AUGUST

the rest such as the title from D. Rohde we will get in proper form when I come down / with kind regards / Verry truly / A. Bequest[68]

We can deduce that Cappelmann in Charleston is still acting on behalf of Bequest in Columbia in a transaction that almost certainly involves getting the house on Society Street transferred back from "D. Rohde" to Augusta. In that case, the inference mentioned earlier—that the 1897 conveyance by Augusta to her relative, D. Rohde, was a temporary maneuver when her husband was being accused of a felony—is confirmed. It would turn out that Cappelmann would keep Mordecai at bay for a lot longer than a few days: the arrangements Bequest promised to make when he got back to Charleston, as well as others made in connection with the matter, were postponed for years. Nonetheless, the couple was "at home" on Society Street by the time the 1905 City Directory was published.

August's peripatetic activity on several fronts in an effort to achieve a semblance of financial stability was a struggle, and if one thing got fixed, another did not. The property at 6-8 Horlbeck Alley still plagued him, and delinquent tax notices appeared in the *Evening Post* in December 1904 and February 1905. By July, it went up again for auction in a Master's sale. Another personal blow had come in February when the couple's daughter Agnes died, five months short of her eighteenth birthday. Augusta was left in Charleston with the couple's two sons, August B, working as a collector for the Consumers' Coal Company that his father had helped incorporate, and his older brother John L., still working as a clerk. August Sr., of course, is not resident at the Society Street address, but in 1907 is still identified as an insurance agent. In the 1908 Directory, he is listed as a traveling salesman. To all appearances, August Bequest had worked for at least a decade to put his past mistakes behind him. He effectively had been sent on the rails out of town, but after a time it looked as though he had

---

68. One of the few Bequest documents in the South Carolina Historical Society's archives (Simons, Siegling and Cappelmann Collection).

been able to restore his name by staying clear of Charleston and accepting a less vaulted role in the business world.

It must have been hard, then, for his wife and sons to find out that he was once again the subject of scandalous accusations and in trouble with the authorities. The *Charlotte Observer* broke the story on May 6, 1908, with the headline "Alleged accomplice of Mills arrested in Athens, Ga":

> Insurance Commissioner Young is notified by Deputy Commissioner Scott of the arrest by the latter, at Athens, Ga., after a hot pursuit, of A. Bequest, an insurance agent who jointly with W. J. Mills, perpetrated upon a lady at Laurinburg five years ago the biggest insurance fraud ever known in North Carolina. Mills was arrested at Philadelphia a few days ago after a year's chase, and is in jail at Laurinburg, where his accomplice was taken to-night. They five years ago represented the Mutual Life at Charlotte, and as its agents perpetrated most of the fraud. The company made good its part.[69]

By May tenth, the word had spread to Winston-Salem, where the *Winston-Salem Journal*'s Raleigh bureau reported:

> Deputy Insurance Commissioner Scott is back at his desk after having taken the insurance swindlers, Mills and Bequest, to jail at Laurinburg. He says that Mills and Bequest make no confession but that each charges the other with being a rascal of the first order, using oaths to accentuate this charge.

---

69. *Charlotte Observer*, May 6, 1908.

CHAPTER 8: THE RISE AND DOWNFALL OF AUGUST

Deputy Scott says that both men have plenty of nerve, cheek and everything else except money. He says it is rumored that Mills has two wives.[70]

Poor Augusta! Once again her husband has been accused of fraud and this time has been jailed in North Carolina No doubt the details of the scandal and the circumstances of August's arrest reached Charleston quickly, so that it is not surprising that on the first of June Augusta would write to John Cappelmann—in German—to register her dismay that attorney Mordecai was acting unmercifully (*unbarmherzig*) in demanding interest payments on the mortgage for the home on Society Street. She encloses the receipts for the interest payments and hopes he (Cappelmann) appreciates how difficult it is for her to be paying this obligation. She refers to Cappelmann as "old friend," and signs her letter "Relying on your good graces, I remain, Your friend, Augusta C. Rohde."[71] In the context of her husband's second offense, she might reasonably be thought of as a victim—the wife who all along remained "by her man." Yet her affront at their legal obligations—complicated as they were by her husband's felonious activities—just as reasonably makes her appear as a reluctant, but nonetheless somewhat defiant partner. By signing her letter with her maiden name she rather obviously was trying to separate herself from the Bequest scandals while doing her best to hold up her head in the Charleston community. A June 27, 1908 letter from Attorney Mordecai to Attorney Cappelmann offers an explanation for why Mordecai was acting so *unbarmherzig*:

> Dear Sir: in the matter of Bart & Co. v. Bequest
> I have received your message, through our Mr. Pearlstein, that this matter will be settled immediately after the first of July.

---

70. *Winston-Salem Journal*, May 10, 1908.

71. "Mich ganz auf Ihren Güte verlassen verbleibe ich in aller Freundschaft, Augusta C. Rohde."

> If it is proposed to settle this on July 2nd,—which is next Thursday,—and I have your guarantee to that effect, I of course will proceed no further; but as we have had so many promises from your clients which have been ruthlessly broken, I cannot accept anything in this matter except your guarantee to me, which of course is all I ask. Mr. Bequest has been promising me for four years to close this matter up, and I have learned to take these promises at their true value.
> Yours very truly,
> T. Moultrie Mordecai

It would have been difficult for Attorney Cappelmann to promise that anything connected with August Bequest would happen on a date certain when the latter was being charged with embezzlement in Laurinburg, North Carolina. What had started in May, 1908, with Bequest's arrest went through two courtroom trials in the course of the following year. It would turn out that the insurance salesman would escape once again with only his name having been dragged through the mud. The *Charlotte Observer* followed the case closely, starting June 3, 1908:

> Laurinburg, June 2.—Just a little over seven years after the time of the commission of the alleged crime W. J. Mills and A. Bequest were placed on trial here to-day charged with having embezzled about $1,400 belonging to the Mutual Life Insurance Company, of New York. The crime is alleged to have been committed about November 11th, 1901, while they were its agents in this territory. The alleged embezzlements were discovered during the last of November, 1906, some five years after their perpetration. At that time complaint was made to Insurance Commissioner Young and as a result of such both Mills and Bequest were indicted, finally

CHAPTER 8: THE RISE AND DOWNFALL OF AUGUST

apprehended about the first of May and brought here for trial.

They also stand indicted jointly on a charge of conspiracy to cheat and defraud Mrs. Hattie McLaughlin in the same insurance transaction. Mills stands further indicted on a charge of having embezzled $1,400 on December 5th, 1901, belonging to Mrs. McLaughlin.

After the usual motions for a continuance had been made in behalf of Defendant Bequest and overruled on the ground of no good cause shown by Judge Jones, the matter of selecting a jury was gone into about 11 o'clock this morning and when court adjourned for dinner the jury had been selected. The afternoon was mostly taken up with the evidence of Mrs. McLaughlin, who identified several papers and testified that at the time of the issuance of the insurance she was a widow by the name of Bryant and that Mills took her application for two policies of insurance, one for $2,000 and the other for $5,000, both to be paid-up after her marriage. Bequest came and delivered those policies, telling her they were just such policies. She stated that she had never seen either Mills or Bequest since then until now, but that just five years after receiving her policies she received notices from the company stating that premiums were due on them and that then she learned for the first time what a trick had been played on her. She said she paid Mills $9,209 for this insurance.

Mr. P. H. Hyatt, of Columbia, S.C., general agent of the company for North and South Carolina, was put up to prove the agency of Mills and Bequest and to show that all money collected by the agents under him was remitted through his office.

> Court adjourned with Mr. Hyatt on the stand. Much documentary evidence was introduced to-day, and to-morrow the case is expected to be fully developed and prove interesting.
>
> Mr. Adams, of Monroe, with the solicitor are leading counsel in conducting the case for the State, while Colonel McLean and Mr. Stephen McIntyre are leading in the defense of Mills and Bequest. Bequest is a man of some 50 years, very plain and simple in his manners and dress, sits quietly by and shows not the greatest interest in what is going on, while Mills is the type of college athlete, well dressed, spry as a cricket, ever on the alert and never lets anything funny pass without a good laugh. He is as handsome as a picture, with captivating eyes.
>
> The case is on and by the time the week ends these gentlemen will know their fate.

The next day, further details followed which made Bequest seem the more culpable of the two:

> Laurinburg, June 3.—After a day of tedious examination of witnesses, the most of whom testified from records as made in books and letters, the State closed its case just before adjournment and Defendant Bequest put up some character witnesses, who testified that his character was good during the years 1901 and 1902, while he resided in the City of Charlotte.
>
> Taking things as they happened, however, Mr. Hyatt's examination was continued this morning. He states that both Bequest and Mills were agents of his insurance company and that in so far as his knowledge and belief were concerned there had been collected from Mrs. Bryant $1,473.44, for which receipts had been given, but no remittance made to his office as should have been. This was

done after there had been quite a great amount of quibbling over the introduction of certain books and papers in evidence. He also stated that inasmuch as she had paid cash for several premiums she ought to have had discounts to the amount of $460.45 and for this amount Mrs. McLaughlin holds no receipts, although the company ordered Bequest to remit the discounts to her. He said "If you will take the $1,473.44 and the $460.45 and add them together you will have the sum of $1,933.89, which was collected from Mrs. Mclaughlin and never accounted for."

It is but just to say right here that the evidence all showed that Defendant Mills turned all the money collected from her over to Bequest and that the evidence is strongest against him.

W. D. Love, book-keeper for the Hyatt offices, was next put up and testified that they had not received at their offices the sum of $1,473.44 for which Bequest had given receipts and that that amount was still short and unaccounted for.

Insurance Commissioner Young then testified that his department was prosecuting these cases and that witnesses were here at his request. At this point the State rested its case with the result above set out. During the day a letter was introduced, purporting to have been written by Mr. Bequest during the latter part of 1906, saying he was arranging to pay the McLaughlin claim of $1,173.44 but Bequest claims to have written this letter under duress, all of which is denied.

The defendant Bequest, will disclose his hand to-morrow and the case is expected to develop some interesting facts. Somebody got Mrs. McLaughlin's money and the question is "Who got the thimble." Over this question both Colonel McLean and Stephen McIntyre are fighting and that to show their particular clients innocent. It is probable that we will see the end of the case by Thursday night.

On the fifth, as the evidence was concluded, the judge ordered a verdict of "not guilty" for Mills: "The evidence all showed that the moneys collected by him from Mrs. McLaughlin were turned over by him to Bequest—in fact, Bequest himself so testified. Only one material witness was introduced by Bequest and that was himself." That went as follows:

> Upon the convening of court this morning he took the stand in his own behalf and testified to having received the moneys in dispute from Mills, and then stated that he had put it in Mr. Twitty's bank in Charlotte, from which he had checked it out to the Mutual Life Insurance Company of New York. He denied most emphatically that he had retained in his possession a single cent that belonged to the company or that he or anyone else had collected for the company and put the money into his hands. He also testified to having signed the letter dated December 24th, 1906, stating that he was arranging to pay the McLaughlin claim and would do so by the end of the year, but stated that he did it under protest and only after Mr. Hyatt had told him that he could have him arrested in twenty minutes. All this was later denied by Hyatt and his assistant, Hendley. The direct examination of Bequest was short, but the cross-examination of him by Solicitor Robinson was long and tedious and cleared up many heretofore unexplained circumstances, besides bringing to light a very peculiarly worded telegram from Mills to Bequest. On November 13th, 1901, Mills took Mrs. McLaughlin's application for insurance and received her check in the sum of $4,604.50 and that night sent to his superior in Charlotte the

CHAPTER 8: THE RISE AND DOWNFALL OF AUGUST

247

following telegram: "Meet me to-night, rain or shine, late or ahead of time," he himself following it to Charlotte.

By this point, it was a confusing alternation of who did what and when, and who was telling the truth or making up excuses. The jury was sufficiently confused that it could not agree in "the case against Bequest," and Judge Jones on the seventh ordered a mistrial. The Insurance Commissioner had brought "other" (read *additional*) cases against the two agents, however, and those had been postponed earlier on the sixth until the court could take them up in November. Bond had been fixed at $2,500 and $2,000 for Mills and Bequest, respectively, so that neither man was in the clear after the case against Bequest ended in a mistrial. For five more months the axe would hang over their heads

While out on bail, August would have had a hard time functioning as a salesman if his reputation at this point was preceding him wherever he went. To add to his travail, his son, John L., aged twenty-seven, died of a chronic heart condition in July, 1908. With her son Henry still in New York, Augusta was left with her youngest son, August Blohme, her only support during these troubled times.

Her husband's second appearance in court loomed toward the end of April, 1909. The *Charlotte Observer* reported on April twenty-seventh that Insurance Commissioner Young had gone to Laurinburg "to appear for the State in the notable case against Mills and Bequest, charged with swindling Mrs. McLaughlin out of some $3,000, representing that they were agents of a noted insurance company."[72] The report in the *Observer* of May fourth replayed the courtroom melodrama:

> Laurinburg, May 4.—The case of State against A. Bequest, charging the embezzlement of certain funds from the Mutual Life Insurance Company of New York, was not called last week but was

---

72. *Charlotte Observer*, April 27, 1909.

continued by consent until the June term. The case against W. J. Mills, charging the embezzlement of $1,400 from Mrs. Hattie W. Bryant, now Mrs. Hattie W. McLaughlin, in December, 1901, was called for trial on Thursday morning. By 3 o'clock in the afternoon a jury had been selected and the taking of testimony began. Mrs. McLaughlin was the first witness for the State. She stated, among other things, that she turned over to Mills the $1,400 in question to be placed on interest to her credit in the Commercial National Bank of Charlotte, and the deposit slip to be brought to her on Christmas Day. She stated that it was in 1906 before she again saw Mills and that she had never received the deposit slip, nor any of the money back. Captain Breniger, of Charlotte, cashier of the Commercial National Bank, was next called to the stand and testified that no money had ever been placed in the bank to the credit of Mrs. McLaughlin. The State rested its case.

The defendant went upon the stand and testified to having received the money from Mrs. McLaughlin to be placed where he could get the best interest on it, as he had done with $10,000 for her in November, 1901. He further testified that upon representation from A. Bequest that he (Bequest) could get a better rate of interest from the Charlotte National Bank with which he was doing business, he turned the money over to Bequest on the square in Charlotte and that Bequest went at once to the bank and deposited it and afterwards reported that he had done so at a good rate of interest.. Mr. W. H. Twitty, of the Charlotte National Bank, was then introduced by the defendant showing that a deposit was made in the bank in the name of A. Bequest on the 4th day of December, 1901, for $1,800. But he further testified that the writing on the deposit slip was the same as was contained in a letter which Mills admitted that he wrote to Bequest from Elizabeth City, in 1901, and was the same handwriting as the name, A. Bequest, written [on] one of Mills' personal cards. Bequest went upon the stand for the State and testified that Mills made the deposit in his absence from the city and to his credit. That he did not know whose money it was until in March when he received a letter from Mrs. McLaughlin, and at that time, he says, Mills had drawn all the money in checks and drafts on him. Mr. Bequest produced his accounts to corroborate his statement. The defense made a fierce attack upon the books and the character of Mr. Bequest.

Judge Biggs made his charge to the jury Saturday night, concluding at 10 o'clock. The jury deliberated all Saturday night and until 5 o'clock yesterday afternoon when they reported that it was impossible for them to reach a verdict. Thereupon the court ordered a mistrial and dismissed the jury. The defendant was ordered in jail until his bond could be renewed.[73]

What happened after that is unclear. The carry-over until the June session is corroborated by the *Observer*'s notice on the first of June that Commissioner Young had again left for Laurinburg to testify "in the case against two former insurance agents, Mills and Bequest, on a charge of swindling...," but that is the last mention by the newspapers in either North or South Carolina of the case that had held the public's attention for more than a year. It is doubtful that Bequest spent any more time in jail, and likely that the final disposition of the case was a mistrial. By summer of 1910, he appears to have become more famous than

---

73. *Charlotte Observer*, May 5, 1909.

infamous, with the name of "Mr. A. Bequest" frequently mentioned in the Charleston *News and Courier*'s "Among the travelling Men" column. He was purportedly "one of the most popular men on the road.

That was, in fact, August Bequest's final claim to fame. The *News and Courier* columnist who regularly reported on the whereabouts and activities of the "travelling men" during the early decades of the twentieth century—when newfangled consumer goods were peddled door-to-door to the rising middle class—seems to have taken special notice of the former bank president who had fallen several notches down the ladder. Possibly it was because Bequest had a past that still dogged him that "news" about him had an appeal for the local readers. Perhaps it was genuine empathy for a man who demonstrated an ability to pick himself up, dust himself off, and continue to run the race. There was nonetheless a hint of sarcasm—a little schadenfreude—when the columnist repeatedly paired the German Bequest, "who sells scales, refrigerators and things"[74] with the Irish "'Little Willie' Keenan, the crockery and chinaware man, from Charleston":

> Mr. Keenan displays his wares at one of the hotels in Florence, and then has his customers to come here and make their stock selection. During the week patrons from all over the section came here and made large purchases to the delight of "Little Willie" and his house. Little Willie pulled in his sails Friday night and will "tie up" on the "Bartery" till Monday eve, for a deserved rest.
> Mr. A. Bequest, the Southern Scales Company representative in this section, was in and out of the city this week. Mr. Bequest is one of the most popular men on the road, but, oh my, he does get so hot when he is trying to catch a train, or when

---

74. *News and Courier*, August 1, 1910.

CHAPTER 8: THE RISE AND DOWNFALL OF AUGUST

he is after a baggage hand for "laying his traveling case flat." [75]

Having survived the Laurinburg scandal, Bequest had managed to talk himself into a new sales position so that by 1910 he had become "the Scale man." The columnist would continue to have fun with August Bequest and Willie Keenan as subjects for his column for the next several years:

> Mr. A. Bequest, the Scale man, suffered rather a severe but short illness on Thursday night of last week and had to "run in home" for a week. It practically "done him up," and he is able to be out on the road again, but he "slipped up" on getting to Conway yesterday, No. 54, the Wilmington train having "skidooed" out just as he reached the station. Ask him now about "Little Willie Keenan" and the "Fish" if you want to get up a scrap. [76]

A couple of weeks later:

> Mr. A. Bequest, who has about recovered from his recent illness from having eaten too much fish and from keeping company with "Little Willie Keenan," was in town to-day. Mr. Bequest said that he had been carried out to Magnolia Cemetery and the keeper was clearing away a place to make an excavation for "A. Request" and that "A Bequest" made a "Request" of the keeper that he wait with time and patience until a later day. The "Request" was granted and "A. Bequest" was the happier when he awoke and found that he

---

75. *News and Courier*, July 4, 1910.

76. *News and Courier*, August 8, 1910.

was really alive and could continue to sell scales.[77]

If the columnist seemed frequently to be lightheartedly joking with his travelling men, he was also capable of lecturing them on how they should stop contributing to the "tale of woe" that was depressing the business atmosphere in South Carolina. In a November 1910 column, he questioned what "a long-faced drummer" could sell to a "merchant inclined to be blue":

> Travelling men on the trains, in hotels and in the stores are talking hard times. There seems to be a depression among the merchants and business people, generally surprising when the prices of all farm products are considered. This cry of hard times in South Carolina is imaginary to a great extent, but it is a fact that must be faced by the men on the road, and faced with a smile and a boost instead of a long face...
> A stiff upper-lip and a cheerful face go a long ways on the road, and if the travelling man will begin to boost the business conditions instead of pulling the other way, business will begin to look brighter and the merchant will begin to get busy and everything will pick up.[78]

It is doubtful that August Bequest was one of the long-faced drummers on the move throughout the state, although he would have had ample reason to display a frown rather than the called-for smile. But given his personality and his modus operandi, he would likely have been one of those putting a happy face on the job he had to do.

---

77. *News and Courier*, August 22, 1910.

78. *News and Courier*, November 21, 1910.

CHAPTER 8: THE RISE AND DOWNFALL OF AUGUST

Although he was still not able to reside full-time in Charleston, the *News and Courier* columnist let everyone know that for Christmas 1910, "A. Bequest and Willie Keenan are enjoying the sights down on 'de Bartery,' and incidentally eating Christmas turkey at home to-day."[79] As a travelling salesman, he was not entirely sidelined. He likely attended the meeting of Post E of Charleston Travellers' Protective Association in February, 1911, at which time the chapter reorganized in an effort to "upbuild" the city, and to make the organization "a force in itself beneficial to its membership and forming another agency for boosting Charleston." Linked to the report about the Association's meeting, the chatter continued: "Mr. A. Bequest, the Southern Scale Company's representative in this section, who spent Sunday with his family in Charleston, was out for business this week, and he got it. Mr. Bequest says that when the Irish and Dutch, 'Little Willie Keenan' and 'A. Bequest,' go after 'biz' there's going to be 'something doing.'" Making "biz" happen could not have been easy: August and Willie were two of some four hundred travelling salesmen operating out of Charleston.[80] This particular report was not the first in which Bequest had been identified as a "Dutchman," a term, not necessarily of endearment, that had come into the local vernacular to accommodate the transition of the *Deutsche* into Charlestonians of a particular heritage. It was the lazy tongue of the Southerner who found it easier to use that label even if it had nothing to do with the inhabitants of the "other" Low Countries.

If he was the Dutchman one week, the next week he might be referred to as "Major A. Bequest," or "Lieut. A. Bequest," or "Capt. A. Bequest," or a combination of such "honorary" labels:

> "Lieut." A. Bequest, the scale, furniture and fixture man, who sells refrigerators and all kinds of nice looking things, was in Florence last week,

---

79. *News and Courier*, December 26, 1910.

80. *News and Courier*, February 6, 1911.

> but he left "Little Willie" behind him. The "Lieutenant" says that it won't do for the Dutch and the Irish to hit Florence together too often for fear the "fish" won't bite.[81]
>
> Capt. A. Bequest, the genial Charleston "Dutchman," was here this week, doing business for the Southern Scales and Fixtures people. Capt. Bequest is greatly attached to Florence and his friend, Jim Muldrow, and he's thinking of moving up to the "Little Gate City" from Charleston, so that he will not have to lose time to "run in" on Saturday nights.[82]
>
> There was a reunion of the Dutch and Irish in Florence during the past week. "Uncle" A. Bequest and "Little Willie" Keenan met here and enjoyed one of their 'fish dinners' at a certain local hotel. Their friends were with them and enjoyed the evening as much as the two gentlemen alluded to above did.[83]

This constant reporting on the activity of her husband, more often than not incorporating a little snideness between the lines, might have understandably gotten the best of Augusta, even though her husband's out-of-town movements were the lifeline of financial support for her in Charleston. In any case, she left for New York at the beginning of June, 1911, to sail four days later on the North German Lloyd steamship *Kronprinz Wilhelm* for Bremen: "Mrs. August Bequest has gone abroad to spend three months in Germany."[84] The fifty-three year old who had kept things together in Charleston, suffered much indignity, and lost

---

81. *News and Courier*, March 20, 1911.

82. *News and Courier*, May 8, 1911.

83. *News and Courier*, May 22, 1911.

84. *Evening Post*, June 9, 1911.

CHAPTER 8: THE RISE AND DOWNFALL OF AUGUST

two adult children to their early deaths, doubtless deserved a much-needed rest. While she was gone, her husband settled "officially" in Florence, SC:

> Mr. A. Bequest, of Charleston, that "staid old gentleman," who sells scales, typewriters, refrigerators and the like for the Southern Scale and Fixture Company, of Columbia, was one of the eleven drummers who made Florence headquarters this week. He now travels in his own "private carriage" when he calls on the trade in the city.[85]

Whether before or after his mother's return from her summer in Germany, August Jr. visited his father in Florence for a few days. "Mr. August B. Bequest, of Charleston, is spending a few days with his father at the Hotel Florence in this city. He, too, likes Florence, for he has gained seven pounds in avoirdupois since he arrived here last Sunday." The columnist responsible for the state's "travelling men" did not hesitate to include details of a personal nature when he "played" with his subjects. August, Jr.'s visit in Florence was apparently an initial step toward forming a business partnership with his father. The following January, the column reported that "A. Bequest, the former representative of the Southern Scales and Fixture Company of Columbia, has recently resigned his position with that company, and has opened a business for himself in Florence. He will represent a number of manufacturers and will 'have the goods.' The temptation was too great for the Colonel, and he just had to locate in Florence, the coming city of South Carolina."[86]

Another "temptation" for the "Colonel" might have raised a red flag for his friends and relatives, although it seems that the senior Bequest was just responding to the evidence that the central location of Florence in the state was making it a growing center

---

85. *News and Courier*, July 24, 1911.

86. *News and Courier*, January 22, 1912.

from which salesmen could easily reach their surrounding territories. After all, it would have been unreasonable to expect him at this point to willingly lose out being part of the "action."

He was apparently working so hard that he suffered something of a physical breakdown in March:

> The many friends of Mr. August Bequest will be pleased to learn that he has about entirely recovered from the recent illness which confined him to a local infirmary, and later to his home in Charleston, for several weeks. He is hustling around again selling scales, furniture and fixtures to beat the band. "Uncle August" says that you can't keep a "working man down," even if the Good Lord does stop him occasionally.
>
> Willie Keenan is the happiest man in the State—but it's not what you think it is this time—it's because his "old friend," Uncle "Gus" Bequest, is on his feet again.[87]

It took a month for the "working man" to recover so that it could be reported in early April that he was again "on the road." The partnership with his son was formalized to the degree that in October of 1912 the "travelling men" columnist—"at considerable effort"—"secured an authentic list of all travelling men who either reside in Florence or make their headquarters at Florence." The list included "A. Bequest, scales and store fixtures, for A. Bequest & Son, Florence, S.C."[88] In November, August Bequest, Sr. was "the happiest man in town—what you think it was though—he has moved into new quarters in the Buchheit block at No 53 East Evans street, where A. Bequest & Son will carry a full line of fixtures, refrigerators and scales on display."[89]

---

87. *News and Courier*, March 11, 1912.

88. *News and Courier*, October 21, 1912.

89. *News and Courier*, November 4, 1912.

CHAPTER 8: THE RISE AND DOWNFALL OF AUGUST
257

Down in Charleston, the city was still having its "Fair Week" each fall, and ever since August had operated the restaurant on King Street, he had been a contributing "merchant" and the Bequests had listed their home as being able to accommodate visitors coming to town for the fair. Since his dismissal from the bank in 1896 he had obviously not been a participant, and it is doubtful that the Bequest home was subsequently offered for accommodations once it had come under the cloud of that scandal. In November of 1912, nonetheless, the *Evening Post* listed "Mrs. A. Bequest, 56 Society street" as being able to accommodate six visitors to the Fair. The ads for the fair made the event sound quite impressive:

> Greatest county fair ever pulled off in South Carolina, Nov 18th to 23rd. . . . No other city in the South Atlantic States and but very few in the country can ever have an armada of battle ships and their ancillaries as will be in Charleston Nov 18th to 23rd. . . . No other city in the South ever attempted such a display of dazzling illuminations and gorgeous decorations as the merchants of Charleston will show in Nov 18-23.[90]

This annual affair that brought business to the city was an opportunity for Augusta to have supplemented the family finances, at least after they had regained the property on Society Street as the family residence in 1905. There is no evidence, however, that she had been forced to turn 56 Society Street into a boarding house while her husband was selling his wares in the state's other cities.

Regardless of whether Augusta had had to concern herself with guests during the Fair Week, two days later she would have had some concern for her husband who "met with a very bad accident" on November twenty-fifth.

---

90. *Evening Post*, November 16, 1912.

He was well enough known that the mishap was reported by the *News and Courier*:

> Florence, November 25.—Special: Mr. August Bequest, the well-known scale and fixtures travelling salesman, of Charleston, now of this city, met with a very bad accident yesterday, in which he was painfully injured about the face, and for a time was knocked unconscious.
>
> Mr. Bequest had joined Deputy Sheriff Coin's party in J. C. Williamson's automobile to go to the scene of the highway robbery of Mr. J. C. McLendon at High Hill Creek.
>
> They were returning in the city with Dr. Williamson at the wheel, and as they approached the crossing at Mr. Mumford G. Scott's ginnery a man driving a horse attached to a buggy turned directly across the road in front of the car. Quick as a flash Dr. Williamson saw that it was kill the horse or go into the field, and he did the latter, but instead of going into the field the car plunged over and across a three-foot ditch. In the lunge and jar Mr. Bequest's face struck the back of Mr. James R. McBride's head and knocked out his teeth and otherwise bruised him up about the face and head. Mr. Bequest, for a time, was knocked unconscious, but by the prompt attention of Dr. Williamson and others he was soon brought to, and with blood streaming from his nose, mouth and face, he was rushed to the city in a passing car and given medical treatment. To-day he is confined to his bed but is getting along nicely.
>
> The car, a Franklin, was uninjured, except the steering gear.[91]

---

91. *News and Courier*, November 26, 1912.

CHAPTER 8: THE RISE AND DOWNFALL OF AUGUST

He would continue to "do nicely" and not long afterward would again have had reason to be the "happiest man in town" and feel a great sense of accomplishment in the face of significant odds. In December his Florence Scale and Fixture Company was commissioned as one of the State's new enterprises. He was once again an incorporator, this time with his son, August Blohme, and E. D. Lide of Hartsville, SC. The new business was capitalized at $6,000.[92]

With father and son working in Florence, the decision was made at some point to put the Society Street property in the senior son's name, even though Henry was still living in New York. The "City Council proceedings" announced in the *Evening Post* of June 13, 1913, shows an assessment to Henry C. Bequest in the amount of $113.53 for 37.2 square yards of asphalt for road repair. Whether Augusta was relieved of this legal responsibility by a helpful son or whether the property was transferred out of her name by a calculating husband is of little consequence to the story that is about to end. There is no doubt that the new Florence Scale and Fixture Company was very much a family matter: The Florence City Directory for 1913 shows A. Blohme Bequest as "v-pres-treas" of the Florence Scale and Fixture Co," but "res Charleston, S.C."; Augusta is listed as "pres" of the company, boarding at the Central Hotel. The listing for A. Bequest & Son is a simple cross reference to the Florence Scale and Fixture Co. It would seem now that Augusta was the one travelling back and forth between Charleston and Florence in her capacity as president of the firm. That she would lodge at the Central Hotel suggests that August's accommodations were inadequate or, for whatever reason, undesirable. August Blohme, while he was "in business" with his father, chose to remain a Charleston resident in the house on Society Street. The house was at that point still the responsibility of his older brother, who in early 1914—perhaps true to his parentage—was delinquent on the property taxes for the

---

92. *News and Courier*, December 15, 1912.

year.[93] The house remained in Henry's name until it was sold in 1925 after his parents' deaths.

By the middle of the second decade of the twentieth century, August Sr. was sufficiently removed from his past embarrassments that he could resurrect something of his political self and participate in local Democratic party activities. The Columbia newspaper, *The State* quoted A. Bequest as the "Florence man" reporting to the editor that "Richard I. Manning is gaining strength in every section throughout the Pee Dee and Florence county."[94] Manning was running for the governorship and was elected. Although not in any official capacity, as he travelled throughout his region Bequest kept his political ear to the ground, and his assessment of the political temperature was sufficiently well regarded that the newspaper editor found it worth mentioning. August Sr.'s democratic leanings flowed naturally enough to his son August Blohme. The younger Bequest's name—along with that of his first cousin, John Frederick Bequest—had consistently appeared in the *News and Courier's* listings of those enrolled in the Democratic Club. The junior August advanced to be a "manager" for his Ward 5, Precinct 1 in the November election of 1918. That "membership" in the Democratic Party was in no way surprising. In these years, Charleston was a one-party town.

After the cursory mention of the "Florence man" in *The State* in 1914, August Bequest, Sr. disappeared from the media's radar screen. Whatever his activities or involvements or those of the Florence Scale and Fixture Company, they were apparently of no interest to South Carolina newspaper reporters or editors. In these years, August— like his brother John—lived in the shadow of the increasingly hostile anti-German sentiment that developed during and after WWI. If he had entered the salesmen's race as a middle-aged man handicapped by a history of bad decisions, there was little he could do to make up for his German heritage as the

---

93., *Evening Post*, March 25, 1914.

94. *The State*, August 24, 1914.

"Dutchman" with a past. He died in March of 1923 of "chronic nephritis and arterial hypertension," his condition exacerbated by an enlarged heart. There was a single funeral notice in the *News and Courier* of Sunday, March 4, 1923: "The relatives and friends of Mr. and Mrs. August Bequest are invited to attend the funeral services of the former at his late residence, No. 56 Society street, this afternoon, 3:30 o'clock. Interment Bethany Cemetery."

Augusta died the following year. Their son Henry had been a regular visitor to Charleston ever since he had moved to New York in the late 1890s. On his visit in 1914, he was described by the *News and Courier* as "a Charlestonian who has made good in New York . . . making a visit to friends and relatives in Charleston, his birth place. He is now employed by the great American Locomotive Works as supervising inspector of automobile parts and accessories, a very respectable position."[95] He never returned to Charleston to live there permanently. There was no issue from his marriage, and when he registered for the draft in 1918, he was forty years old. Despite his "very respectable position," the childless couple was renting a house on Payson Avenue, according to the 1940 Federal census. Having left the place of his birth, he apparently had forgotten his birth year and reported his age to the census taker as fifty-eight: born in 1877, he was actually sixty-three and clearly not a Charlestonian.

The bachelor August Blohme and his first cousin John Frederick are the two native, Charleston-born, scions whose headstones bear the name *Bequest* in Charleston's Bethany Cemetery, the resting place of most of Charleston's Lutheran Germans. Their immigrant fathers, one of whom brought shame and embarrassment to the German-French name of Geestendorf origin, both lie in unmarked graves in the cemetery's Lowcountry sandy soil.

---

95. *News and Courier*, August 14, 1914.

AFTERWORD

The final chapters about Bernhard Heinrich, Johann Ludwig, and Carsten August Bequest end somewhat anticlimactically in the realization that the efforts of the Brothers Bequest to achieve any degree of notable success in Charleston were largely in vain. Not that any one of them came to establish a new-world dynasty or to make such a mark on the host society as to ensure that his legacy would be remembered for generations to come. The brothers' immigration to Charleston was a means to an end, a chance they took to find a better life than what they could expect in their native homeland. North Germany came to South Carolina because it promised opportunity—however it might materialize. That their stories should fail to develop into impressive "success stories" is not out of the ordinary for such ordinary men as they.

It was suggested earlier that the North Germans who immigrated to Charleston in great numbers during the nineteenth-century brought with them their European roots and values, moreover, that that European heritage was instrumental in modifying to some degree the unique culture that the Lowcountry city embodied during those years when the newcomers and the host society were forced to interact. It was also argued that by the time South Carolina led its companion southern slave states into secession and ultimately to defeat in the resultant Civil War, the post-colonial "culture" that was Charleston's had forced the immigrants who had come before 1861 to accommodate themselves to the peculiarities of their sectionalist host society. In their efforts to align themselves with the culture they were adopting, they themselves had been modified as much as they had effected any change in the attitudes of their paternalistic native befrienders whom they sought to please. When the war was over, those who followed their pre-war predecessors along the established chain of immigration—the Bequest brothers, as examples—faced the different context of a culture that was transitioning to the new realities presented by the reconstruction of the Union. And although the post-war cultural shifts within the host society were radical in nature, the same process of modification would be realized from the interplay between the post-war immigrant and the native-born hosts accommodating themselves to new game rules.

Within the broad framework of the role nineteenth-century German immigrants played in contributing to the evolution of nineteenth-century Charleston, the stories of the Bequest brothers' experiences in becoming Charlestonians in the years following the war give measure to three versions of that interplay between the immigrant and the society he infiltrated. The Brothers Bequest were but three ordinary German immigrants who, for their own reasons, came to a down-and-out Charleston looking for a chance to gain a foothold on existence in another city by the sea, albeit in one that could not have been more different than the one they came from. They were members of an unusually homogeneous ethnic group who came to a unique city in the American South, late-comers into a community that produced exemplars both of outstanding financial, political, and social success as well as specimens of disappointing, heart-wrenching personal failure. The stories of the Bequest brothers occupy a place somewhere in the middle: although they arrived late on the Charleston stage, their stories articulate the experiences of so many of the city's nineteenth-century German immigrants who did not rise to such heights as to warrant fame and fortune, or at the opposite extreme, who sank into total anonymity as derelicts of Charleston's pressurized urban context.

If each of the brothers approached life in Charleston as a distinct personality, they had in common the fact that Charleston presented a unique civic environment—not quite like any other southern city in its history or its composite social makeup—during an historical time that was likewise unique. The courses of the

Bequest brothers' lives ran in tandem to the course of Charleston's passage from the nineteenth to the twentieth century, from a rebellious, militant, paternalistic, defensive "hotbed" of antipathy to a semi-reconstructed, redeemed but effectively un-emancipated, southern backwater. It was not entirely unforeseen that their respective trajectories would each form an arc that would trail off into a less than climactic ending. As for every immigrant, opportunity frequently proved difficult to assess, often lured the uninformed or inadequately prepared into inappropriate actions, and sometimes disappeared elusively by virtue of factors beyond purposeful control.

That there are so few headstones bearing the name *Bequest* in the Charleston cemetery that embodies the history of the German immigrants to the city is a reminder that the Bequest brothers' legacy in Charleston is slight. August's lineage did not pass beyond his two sons who survived him, the one a Charlestonian bachelor, the other a married New Yorker without issue. John's children had left Charleston for Florida's more culturally open Jacksonville: he was survived only by his married, but childless daughter. Only Bernhard Heinrich's lineage extended into future generations—through the daughters of his son John Frederick, and through his Gieschen granddaughters. All of these female descendants' marriages would provide only a maternal link to the name that had been invented in North German environs early in the nineteenth century. That was likely the case for the numerous families descended from immigrant Germans who dedicated themselves to becoming citizens of Charleston. Even if the German heritage was carried forward through male descendants, the significance of the ancestors' contribution to the civic cultural heritage was fated to be lost to all but the most dedicated preservationists. The history of Charleston the city overtook the history of its German immigrants as they molded themselves according to its demands and became Charlestonians. Even if anniversaries of historic events are celebrated in the present, it is unlikely that they can ever tell the whole story of those who lived those times past, making the history recounted here.

WORKS CITED

A History of the Lutheran Church in South Carolina. Columbia: South Carolina Synod of the Lutheran Church in America, 1971.

Acts of Assembly relating to, and Ordinances in force of the Town of Mount Pleasant from the Act of Incorporation to the Present Time, also Rules for the Government of Council. Printed by Order of Council. Mount Pleasant, 1883.

Anonymous. "An Eye Witness Account of the Occupation of Mt. Pleasant: February 1865." *The South Carolina Historical Magazine* 66, no. 1 (January 1965): 8-14.

Barnwell, John. *Love of Order: South Carolina's First Secession Crisis.* Chapel Hill: University of North Carolina Press, 1982.

Bell, Michael Everette. "Hurrah für 'dies süsse, dies sonnige Leben': The Anomaly of Charleston, South Carolina's Antebellum German-America." PhD diss., University of South Carolina,, 1996.

Bell, Michael Everette. "Regional Identity in the Antebellum South: How German Immigrants became 'Good' Charlestonians." *The South Carolina Historical Magazine* 100, no. 1 (January 1999): 9-28.

Berlin, Ira and Herbert Gutman. "Natives and Immigrants, Free Men and Slaves: Urban Workingmen in the Antebellum South." *American Historical Review* 88, no. 5 (December 1983): 1175-1200.

Bernheim, G.D. *History of the German Settlements and of the Lutheran Church in North and South Carolina.* Philadelphia: The Lutheran Book Store, 1872.

Berthoff, Rowland T. "Southern Attitudes toward Immigration." *The Journal of Southern History* 17, no. 3 (August 1951): 328-360.

Bullerdiek, Jörg and Daniel Tilgner. *'Was fernen vorkömmt werde ich prompt berichten':* Der *Auswanderer-Kapitän Heinrich Wieting Briefe 1847 bis 1856.* Bremen: Temmen, 2008.

Capers, Ellison. *Confederate Military History: a Library of Confederate States History: South Carolina.* Edited by Clement A. Evans. Vol. 5. Atlanta: Confederate Publishing Co., 1899.

Clark, Thomas D. *Pills, Petticoats and Plows. The Southern Country Store.* New York: Bobbs-Merrill, 1944.

Clark, Thomas D. "The Furnishing and Supply System in Southern Agriculture since 1865." *The Journal of Southern History* 12, no. 1 (February 1946): 24-44.

Cooper, Jr., William J. *The Conservative Regime: South Carolina, 1877-1890.* Baltimore: The Johns Hopkins Press, 1968.

Declaration of the Immediate Causes which Induce and Justify the Secession of South Carolina from the Federal Union; and the Ordinance of Secession. Charleston: Evans and Cogswell, 1860.

Doyle, Don. *New Men, New Cities, New South: Atlanta, Nashville, Charleston, Mobile, 1860-1910.* Chapel Hill: University of North Carolina Press, 1990.

Foner, Eric. *A Short History of Reconstruction. 1863-1877.* New York: Harper & Row, 1990.

Fraser, Walter. *Charleston! Charleston! The History of a Southern City.* Columbia: University of South Carolina Press, 1991.

Friedrichs, Erika and Klaus. *Das Familienbuch des Kirchspiels Geestendorf (heute Bremerhaven-Geestemünde) 1689 bis 1874.* Bremerhaven, 2003.

Gongaware, George J. *The History of the German Friendly Society of Charleston, South Carolina, 1766-1916. Compiled from original sources.* Richmond: Garrett & Massie, 1935.

Goodheart, Adam. *1861. The Civil War Awakening.* New York: Alfred A. Knopf, 2011.

Graham, Jr., Cole Blease. *South Carolina Politics and Government.* Lincoln: University of Nebraska Press, 1994.

Gregorie, Anne King. *Christ Church, 1706-1959: A Plantation Parish of the South Carolina Establishment.* Charleston: Dalcho Historical Society, 1961.

Grob, Alexander. *Napoleon and the Transformation of Europe.* New York: Macmillan, 2003.

Holden, Charles J. *In the Great Maelstrom : Conservatives in Post-Civil War South Carolina.* Columbia: University of South Carolina Press, 2002.

Jenkins, Wilbert L. *Seizing the New Day: African Americans in Post-Civil War Charleston.* Bloomington: Indiana University Press, 1998.

Johnson, Michael. "Planters and Patriarchy: Charleston, 1800-1860." *The Journal of Southern History* 46, no. 1 (February 1980): 45-72.

Jones, Mark R. *Wicked Charleston, Volume 2: Prostitutes, Politics, and Prohibition.* Charleston: The History Press, 2006.

Kantrowitz, Stephen. *Ben Tillman & the Reconstruction of White Supremacy.* Chapel Hill and London: University of North Carolina Press, 2000.

Klenck, Willy. *Das Dorfbuch von Mulsum im Lande Wursten, Kreis Wesermünde in Niedersachsen.* Frankfurt am Main, 1959.

Konstam, Angus. *Confederate Blockade Runner 1861-65.* Oxford: Osprey, 2004.

LeMay, Michael C. *From Open Door to Dutch Door: An Analysis of U.S. Immigration Policy Since 1820.* New York: Praeger, 1987.

McCandless, Amy, ed. "The Historic Landscape of Mount Pleasant: Proceedings of the First Forum on the History of Mount Pleasant." Mt. Pleasant, 1993.

Mehrländer, Andrea. *The Germans of Charleston, Richmond, and New Orleans.* Berlin/New York: DeGruyter, 2011.

Mehrländer, Andrea. "'With more freedom and Independence than the Yankees': The Germans of Richmond, Charleston, and New Orleans during the American Civil War." In *Civil War Citizens: Race, Ethnicity, and Identity in America's*

Bloodiest Conflict, edited by Suzannah J. Ural, 57-97. New York: New York University Press, 2010.

Miles, Suzannah Smith. *East Cooper Gazetteer.* Charleston: The History Press, 2004.

Münch, F. *Das fünfzigjährige Hochzeits-Jubiläum des Gold-Jubelpaares J.C.H. Claussen und seiner Gattin Dorothea, geb. Fincken: feierlich begangen als Familienfest, Sonntag, den 25. April 1897, als Volksfest, Montag, den 26. April 1897, als Nachfest Montag, den 3. Mai 1897.* Charleston, 1898.

Orvin, Maxwell Clayton. *In South Carolina Waters.* Charleston, 1961.

Pech, August F. "Bevölkerungsentwicklung und Sozialstruktur eines nordniedersächsischen Geestdorfes im 18. Jahrhundert, aufgezeigt an dem Dorf Flögeln im Landkreis Cuxhaven." *Jahrbuch der Männer vom Morgenstern,* 1981: 49-75.

Phelps, W. Chris. *The Bombardment of Charleston 1863-1865.* Gretna, LA: Pelican, 2002.

Powers, Jr., Bernard E. "Community Evolution and Race Relations in Reconstruction Charleston, South Carolina." *The South Carolina Historical Magazine* 101, no. 3 (July 2000): 214-233.

Radford, John P. "Race, Residence and Ideology: Charleston, South Carolina in the Mid-Nineteenth Century." *Journal of Historical Geography* 2, no. 4 (1976): 329-346.

Reinert, Gertha. "'Turning my Joy into Bitterness': A Letter from John A. Wagener." *The South Carolina Historical Magazine* 100, no. 1 (January 1999): 49-70.

Reports and Resolutions of the General Assembly of the State of South Carolina at the regular session commencing November 28, 1893. Vol. 2. Columbia: Charles A. Calvo, State Printer, 1893.

Rogers, Jr., George C. and C. James Taylor. *A South Carolina Chronology 1498-1992.* 2nd ed. Columbia: University of South Carolina Press, 1994.

Rogers, Jr., George C. *Charleston in the Age of the Pinckneys.* Norman: University of Oklahoma Press, 1969.
Rosengarten, Dale and Ted. *Portion of the People.* Columbia: University of South Carolina Press, 2002.
Rubin, Louis. *My Father's People: a Family of Southern Jews.* Baton Rouge: Louisiana State University Press, 2002.
Sheehan, James J. *German History 1770-1866.* Oxford: Clarendon, 1989.
Silver, Christopher. "Immigration and the Antebellum Southern City." Master's thesis, University of North Carolina, 1975.
Simkins, Francis Butler. *Pitchfork Ben Tillman, South Carolinian.* Baton Rouge: Louisiana State University Press, 1944.
Strickland, Jeffery G. "How the Germans became White Southerners: German Immigrants and African Americans in Charleston, South Carolina, 1860-1880." *Journal of American Ethnic History* 28, no. 1 (2008): 52-69.
Verfassung der Deutsche Schützen-Gesellschaft in Charleston, Süd Carolina. Gegründet am 21. Mai 1855. Gesetze revidiert Mai 1868 und Januar 1872. Charleston, 1872.
Walker, Mack. *Germany and the Emigration 1816-1885.* Cambridge, MA: Harvard University Press, 1964.
Williams, George W. *Jacob Eckhard's Choirmaster's Book of 1809.* Columbia: University of South Carolina Press, 1971.
Wilson, A.N. *Victoria. A Life.* New York: Penguin, 2014.
Wise, Stephen R. *Lifeline of the Confederacy: Blockade Running During the Civil War.* Columbia: University of South Carolina Press, 1988.
Zuczek, Richard, ed. *Encyclopedia of the Reconstruction Era. Vol 1: A-L.* Westport, CN: Greenwood Press, 2006.
—. *State of Rebellion: Reconstruction in South Carolina.* Columbia: University of South Carolina Press, 1996.

INDEX

A

Aichel, Oskar, 137
American Civil War, ix, 7, 22
Amme, D.A., 200, 230, 231

B

Bachman, Rev. John, 93, 94, 95–97, 99
Barden, I.V., 194
Bargamann, Wm., 227
Bennett, H.M., 194, 195
Bequest, Adelheid, née Rosenbohm, 17, 18, 30, 45, 50, 58, 111, 144, 215
Bequest, Annie Agnes, 125, 130; death in 1905, 239
Bequest, August, 18, 45; 1893 naturalization, 131; and Central Cotton Mills Company, 211; and Charleston Improvement Company, 193; and Consumers' Coal Company, 208; and Democratic Party, 122, 260; and dispensary law, 196; and Equitable Fire Insurance Company, 171, 209, 215, 219, 227; and Florence Scale and Fixture Company, 259, 260; and grand jury demurral, 234; and insurance fraud, 247–50; and liquor laws, 130; and Little Willie Keenan, 250–56; and Mutual Life Insurance Company of New York, 236, 242, 247; and Palmetto Soap Manufacturing Company, 199; and Southern Scales and Fixture Company, 255; and summers on Sullivan's Island, 130, 199; and Wenzel Piano Company of Charleston, 211; arrest, 227; arrival in Charleston, 59; as cashier of German-American Trust and Savings Bank, 183, 195; as clerk for Bernhard Heinrich, 81; as corporator of German-American Mutual Life Association, 206; as corporator of German-American Trust and Savings Bank, 194; as director of German-American Mutual Life Association, 206; as merchant in Abbeville, 62, 117; as receiver of Palmetto Brewery, 216; as restaurant owner, 127; as treasurer of Democratic Club, 131; as typewriter salesman, 237–38; death in 1923, 261; elected president of German-American Trust and Savings Bank, 198; elected to German Friendly Society, 202; elected VP of Palmetto Soap Manufacturing Company, 206; loss of Horlbeck Alley property, 215; purchase of pine land from Platt, 123; settles in Florence, SC, 255–56
Bequest, August Blohme, 119, 235, 236, 255, 259, 261; and Democratic Party, 260; and Florence Scale and Fixture Company, 259; as collector for Consumers' Coal Company, 239
Bequest, Augusta, née Rohde, 118, 119, 125, 130, 199, 235–37, 230, 235–37, 239, 247, 257; and John Cappelmann, 241; as President of Florence Scale and Fixture Company, 259; death in 1924, 261; posts bail for August,

230, 233; sails to Bremen
(1911), 254
Bequest, Bernhard Heinrich, 18,
45, 46, 137; 1868 Mt. Pleasant
election, 86; 1873 Mt. Pleasant
real estate sale, 104; 1881
purchase of Clayfield acreage,
143; admitted into German Rifle
Club, 78; and European Fish
Smokery, 215; and German
Artillery, 156; and schooner
Lenore, 160; as baseball player,
162; as blockade runner, 48–50;
as grocer, 61, 64, 81; as Mt.
Pleasant town councilman, 63;
as planter in Mt. Pleasant, 63; as
Schützenfest King, 101, 103; as
sharpshooter, 90; as wood
merchant, 105, 142, 145;
business in Nassau, 55; election
as Mt. Pleasant mayor, 108;
funeral, 174; Mt. Pleasant real
estate purchases, 79;
naturalization, 61; posts bond
for August, 230
Bequest, Catherine Margarethe, née
Rigbers, 62, 111, 116
Bequest, Catherine, née Mehrtens,
63, 67, 81, 116, 175
Bequest, Gesine, née Rigbers, 59,
62, 63, 66, 81, 91
Bequest, Heinrich Christian, 118,
202, 235, 259, 261
Bequest, John, 18, 45; 1875
naturalization, 110; and Morris
Island boating accident, 180–86;
and Sullivan Island's life-saving
crew, 180; arrival in Baltimore,
59, 62; as mate on the steamer
Sappho, 183, 189; in Baltimore,
109; rescue of Ned Schachte,
186–88
Bequest, John Frederick, 54, 64,
69, 116, 145, 146, 162, 176; and
Democratic Party, 260

Bequest, John L. (son of August),
190, 235, 236, 239; death, 247
Bequest, Ludwig, 45, 49
Bequest, Mary Emma, née Condon,
116, 179, 184; and "white
school", 190; death in 1919, 191
Bequest, Tette, née Hencken, 45,
49
Bethany Cemetery, 1, 23, 25, 30,
175, 261
Bird, W.M., 199, 209, 210
Black Codes, 56, 64, 65
blockade runners: *Margaret and
Jessie*, 51, 52, 81; *Rothersay
Castle*, 47, 49; *Ruby*, 48, 50;
Stonewall Jackson, 49; *Syren*,
49; *Watson*, 49, 55
blockade-running, 41, 47, 48, 49,
50, 51, 52, 173
Blohme, J.C., 125, 128, 199, 217;
and Charleston Improvement
Company, 193
blue laws, 128
Bremen, 1, 2, 20, 23, 24, 43, 254
Bremerhaven, 4, 20, 22, 23, 24, 46,
49
Bryan, J.P.K., 228, 229
Buist, Henry, 222, 227, 229
Bulwinkle, H. & Co, 128

C

Calhoun, John C., 16
Capers, Ellison, 48, 50, 53, 173
Cappelmann, John, 193, 195, 198,
202, 205, 238, 239, 241, 242;
and Charleston Improvement
Company, 193; as corporator of
Palmetto Soap Manufacturing
Company, 199; as solicitor of
German-American Trust and
Savings Bank, 194–96
Central Cotton Mills Company,
210, 211
chain migration, xii, 1, 10, 14, 17,
20, 23, 56, 58, 264

INDEX

Chamberlain, Daniel H., 68, 110, 136
Charleston Improvement Company, 193, 202
Charleston Telephone Exchange, 123
Claussen, J.C.H., 26, 111, 137
Claussen, J.D.W., 227
Confederacy, x, 22, 33, 41, 43, 46, 48, 50, 53, 54; and Anaconda Plan, 56
Congress of Vienna, 5
Consumers' Coal Company, 127, 128, 207, 214, 217, 218, 239
Coste, Charles M., 186
Cramer, A.F.C., 128, 199, 208, 209, 211, 216–20

D

De La Vergne Refrigerator Machine Company, 217
Democratic Party, 122, 137–38, 212, 260
Der Teutone, 22, 24
Deutsche Schützen-Gesellschaft / German Rifle Club, 78–79, 137, 146, 173
Deutsche Zeitung, 23, 37
Dispensary law, 159, 196
Doscher, A.F., 227
Doscher, John E., 218

E

Eight Box Voting law, 158
Emerson, A.S., 230
emigration, x, 5, 7, 10, 19, 23, 49
Equitable Fire Insurance Company, 171, 209, 210, 215, 219, 222, 227

F

Fehrenbach, Anna Maria, née Rosenbohm, 18
Fehrenbach, Nicholas, 18
Fehrenbach, Nicholas, Jr., 18, 30, 51–53
Fischer, August H., 195
Florence Scale and Fixture Company, 259, 260
Fort Fisher, 47, 49, 56
Fort Sumter, 22, 25, 29, 43, 46, 50, 56
Fraternal Order of Knights of Pythias, 151, 153, 173, 174, 183, 185

G

Gadsden, P.H., 211, 217, 221, 229
Gala Week, 125, 130
Gartleman, C.D., 200
Geestemünde, 4, 14, 19, 23, 49, 98
Geestendorf, 1, 4–6, 3–6, 14, 17, 18, 19, 43, 44, 46, 49, 58, 59, 63, 98, 110, 117, 147, 180, 186, 199, 202
German Artillery, 25, 54, 120, 124, 128, 142, 155, 173, 194, 200, 211, 212, 230
German Fire Company, 24
German Friendly Society, viii, 9, 35, 202
German Fusiliers, 36, 104, 113
German Ladies' Society, 90, 100
German Rifle Club / Deutsche Schützen-Gesellschaft, 78–79, 137, 146, 173; constitution, 78
German-American Mutual Life Association, 206
German-American Trust and Savings Bank, 183, 194, 196, 198, 202, 207, 210, 217, 225, 220–33, 238
Gieschen, John Henry, 63, 176

Gieschen, Theresa Louise, née Bequest, 54, 63, 67, 81, 146, 176
Gotjen, D.W., 231
Grant, President Ulysses S., 67, 110

H

Hampton, Wade, 68, 136, 137, 211
Hayes, President Rutherford B., 68, 136
Heiser, H.A., 128, 208
Hesse, J.N., 195, 222, 225
Horstkamp-Delmenhorst/Oldenburg, 59
Huguelot, George A., 206
Hunt, N.A., 195, 224

J

Johnson, President Andrew, 56, 64, 70
Jordan, F, 227

K

Kalteisen, Michael, 35
Kinloch, St. J.P., 199
Knee, Catharina, née Rosenbohm, 14, 18
Knee, Hermann, 18, 79, 117
Knobloch, John, 199
Ku Klux Klan, 119

L

Land Wursten, 1, 3, 4, 5, 19, 24, 191
Lehe (Geestendorf), 1, 18
Lilienthal, J. Fred, 193, 195, 197, 198, 199, 202, 210, 211, 223–34, 234; and Charleston Improvement Company, 193; and Germania Bank, 193

Lincoln, President Abraham, 40, 43, 56, 64, 84
Lower Saxony, 1
Lutheranism in South Carolina, 94–100

M

Marjenhoff, O.J., 223
Melchers, Alexander, 23, 87, 156
Melchers, Franz Adolph, 23, 36; and German Rifle Club, 78
Meyer, W.A., 227
Middleton, Charles F., 200
Mordecai, T. Moultrie, 148, 211, 217, 221, 229, 238, 239, 241, 242
Morris Island, 111, 180, 182, 184
Mt. Pleasant, SC, 61, 63, 64, 65, 68, 86, 112, 135, 136, 138, 140, 143, 148, 180, 189, 190
Mutual Life Insurance Company of New York, 236, 237, 242, 246, 247

N

Nassau, 47, 49, 52, 53, 55, 56, 58
Nelson, W.D., 195
Nohrden, Johann, 45
Nohrden, Meina, 44
Norris, J.F., 211, 222, 225
nullification, 16, 31, 35, 40

O

O'Neill, Ignatius, 200
Olivier, Bequet Benoit, 44

P

Palmetto Brewery, 111, 216, 218, 219, 225, 229, 233

Palmetto Soap Manufacturing Company, 199, 200, 202, 206, 217
Patjens, J.A., 221
Perry, Benjamin, 56

R

Ransier, Alonzo, 137
Redding, James F., 171, 206, 207, 209, 210, 220, 221
Rigbers, Frederick H., 179
Rosenbohm, Caroline, née Huhn, 14
Rosenbohm, Caspar, 14, 45
Rosenbohm, Johann Heinrich, 13, 15, 31, 56

S

Sahl, H., 128
Sass, Jacob, 35
Scarborough, C. Adeline Therese, née Bequest, 111, 116, 189
Schachte, Henry, 128, 149, 188, 195, 199, 208
Schachte, Ned, 186–88
Schroeder, Adeline, née Bequest, 17, 27, 29, 30, 45, 50, 58, 63, 111
Schroeder, Frederick Eduard, 17, 27, 45, 51, 58, 111
Schützenfest, 87, 90, 101, 102, 103, 104, 108, 146, 150, 151, 152, 153, 174
secession, 22, 33, 36, 39–40, 46, 84, 263
sectionalism, 17, 71
Siegling, John, 35
Sievern, 24
Simmons, B.I., 195, 209, 221, 222, 225, 227
Simons, James, 217, 218, 239
Sold, Henry, 208
Southern Scales and Fixture Company, 255

St. Andrew's Lutheran Church, 189
St. Benoit des Ondes, 44
St. John's Lutheran Church, 9, 27, 93
St. Matthew's Lutheran Church, viii, 17, 22, 24, 27, 30, 59, 63, 91, 93, 99, 100, 101, 107, 111, 117, 155, 174, 189, 215
St. Michael's Episcopal Church, 60
Sunday Law, 128

T

Tew, Henry Slade, 82, 86
Tillman, Benjamin, 157–59, 205, 212
Trenholm, George M., 152, 199

V

Vesey, Denmark, 12, 28
Von Kolnitz, Jr: George, 211

W

Wagener, Capt. Frederick, 137, 155, 156, 157, 174, 211, 212, 229, 230
Wagener, George A., 209
Wagener, John Andreas, 24, 25, 36, 41, 74, 78, 92, 93, 99, 117, 137, 155; and German Rifle Club, 78; as mayor of Charleston, 137
Walhalla, SC, 18, 25, 100, 117
Wenzel Piano Company of Charleston, 211
Wenzel, Theodore, 211
Wieters, Otto F., 63, 137, 143, 148, 160
Wieting, Captain Heinrich, viii, 20–25, 26, 29, 36, 46, 50, 117, 174
William Bee Importing and Exporting Company, 42

Williams, George W., 60, 94, 126, 199, 209
Wohlers, Henry C., 128, 195, 199, 206, 208

www.ingramcontent.com/pod-product-compliance
Lightning Source LLC
Chambersburg PA
CBHW062004220426
43662CB00010B/1227